Challenges for Nonprofits and Philanthropy

CIVIL SOCIETY: HISTORICAL AND
CONTEMPORARY PERSPECTIVES

Series Editors:

Virginia Hodgkinson
Public Policy Institute
Georgetown University

Kent E. Portney
Department of Political Science
Tufts University

John C. Schneider
Department of History
Tufts University

Challenges for Nonprofits and Philanthropy

The Courage to Change

Three Decades of Reflections
by Pablo Eisenberg

~

EDITED BY STACY PALMER

Tufts University Press
Medford, Massachusetts

Published by University Press of New England
Hanover and London

Tufts University Press
Published by University Press of New England,
One Court Street, Lebanon, NH 03766
www.upne.com
© 2005 by the Trustees of Tufts University
Printed in the United States of America
5 4 3 2 1

This book was published with the generous support
of the Nathan Cummings Foundation

Library of Congress Cataloging-in-Publication Data

Eisenberg, Pablo.
Challenges for nonprofits and philanthropy : the courage to change : three decades of reflections / by Pablo Eisenberg ; edited by Stacy Palmer.
p.   cm. — (Civil society)
Includes bibliographical references and index.
ISBN 1-58465-421-x (cloth : alk. paper)
1. Charities—United States.   2. Endowments—United States.
3. Nonprofit organizations—United States—Endowments.
I. Palmer, Stacy.   II. Title.   III. Series.
HV91.E383   2004
361.7'63'0973—dc22
2004016156

Dedicated to Helen and Marina

Contents

Editor's Note

Pablo Eisenberg has been one of the most influential and outspoken voices in philanthropy for nearly three decades. His speeches and articles have done much to provoke debate—and lead to change—throughout the nonprofit world. As leader of the Center for Community Change, one of the nation's most highly regarded poverty-fighting organizations, Mr. Eisenberg has helped thousands of low-income people learn advocacy skills and become successful advocates for policy changes that would benefit the most vulnerable people in our society. As a founder of the National Committee for Responsive Philanthropy and as its chairman emeritus, he has helped to shine a light on the ways that foundations, United Ways, and others in philanthropy have strayed from their missions to serve the needy. As a regular columnist for *The Chronicle of Philanthropy* for more than a decade, he is one of the nation's most prominent observers of the nonprofit world.

Because Mr. Eisenberg takes strong views and never pulls punches when he is disappointed in an organization or public figure, he has outraged many in philanthropy—but he has always commanded respect. His analysis always demonstrates a keen intellectual vigor, so his crusades are not those of a gadfly but of an honest critic; even those who disagree with him—and many people do—often say they are impressed by his courage and determination to speak his mind.

Mr. Eisenberg's articles and speeches from the past 30 years show that the questions and challenges facing philanthropy today are hardly new; many had their seeds in the events of the past three decades. What's more, his articles show much about how the nonprofit world really works—not necessarily how it is supposed to work in academic or legal theory.

Sadly, Mr. Eisenberg is one of the few with the courage to speak candidly and not worry about the consequences of speaking out. He has never allowed himself to be silenced by grant makers who have threatened to pull their support out of pique with his public views, and he has not mellowed his blunt assessments of the nonprofit world's failings even though he retired as head of the Center for Community Change in 1998. Today, as a senior fellow at the Georgetown University Public Policy Institute, he continues to be actively involved in conducting research and teaching graduate students to become effective nonprofit leaders, and he continues to write and lecture about what he sees as the failures of philanthropy and government to adequately serve the disenfranchised.

As an advocate for change, Mr. Eisenberg has primarily sought in his speeches and articles to provoke serious thinking and action. But this volume offers more than his trenchant insights. It offers a first-hand account of many pivotal moments in the nonprofit world at some of the most crucial times in recent history. Mr. Eisenberg entered the field at a time when nonprofit organizations were growing rapidly in the wake of the War on Poverty, and he has witnessed a doubling of the number of nonprofit groups in operation and a stunning increase in the wealth of the nation's foundations. In addition, he played a key role in shifting the focus of a national blue-ribbon commission studying the responsibility of private foundations to society. Mr. Eisenberg's 1975 article for *Grantsmanship News* (included in this volume) helped to guarantee that the commission, and later the nation, focused on whether foundations were doing enough to help the poor. He also pushed the commission to be sure to include the views of those who receive financial support from foundations— and to not just consider the opinions of grant makers themselves.

Throughout the years, Mr. Eisenberg has been an astute observer of philanthropy's shortcomings as it grew rapidly in wealth and in number. He has written extensively about the potential problems facing philanthropy in the years ahead, as trillions of dollars are expected to flow to nonprofit groups in the greatest intergenerational transfer of wealth in U.S. history. He points out in speeches and articles that neither donors nor nonprofits seem to be prepared to handle such a significant influx of funds, and he suggests steps that can be taken to better prepare for the future.

Mr. Eisenberg's commentaries often focus on how public policy should be reshaped to ensure that charities and foundations are accountable to the public. For example, he looks at how the Internal Revenue Service can be given better financing and stronger tools to fight abuse. In his articles and speeches, Mr. Eisenberg shows how changes in government policy—such as the devolution of power from the federal government to the states begun in the Reagan era—affect nonprofit groups and their ability to serve the needy. Drawing on his experience at the U.S. Office of Economic Opportunity, in addition to his years of advocacy work, Mr. Eisenberg in his writings points out how some of the most promising ideas of the Great Society years became disappointments. For instance, he highlights how community development corporations, which were supposed to serve as advocates for the poor, instead have often promoted policies that end up hurting the people they were supposed to serve. He also examines how philanthropy could do much to ensure that government operates better.

In his writings Mr. Eisenberg has chronicled how nonprofit groups and foundations themselves have changed over recent decades, becoming more professional and often emulating businesses. In this area, as in so many of the topics he takes on, Mr. Eisenberg often goes against conventional wisdom. While many in the nonprofit world spent much of the 1980s and 1990s borrowing the language, techniques, and approaches of business, Mr. Eisenberg worries that the embrace of corporate values has undermined the effectiveness and integrity of many charitable organizations.

For instance, his articles on the United Way of America scandal, which erupted in the early 1990s, show how one of the most prominent nonprofit organizations in America suffered a devastating blow when its top executive, William Aramony, was found to be embezzling from the charity. Mr. Eisenberg argued that the scandal at United Way came about not simply because of one corrupt man, but was emblematic of the problems caused by the corporatization of nonprofit groups. Throughout the 1990s, Mr. Eisenberg regularly pointed out how United Way of America, and all of America's nonprofits, failed to learn the lessons of Mr. Aramony's downfall and kept repeating many of the same mistakes—causing many Americans to lose faith in charities they had long respected.

Although Mr. Eisenberg has spent most of his professional life working in the United States, he began his career in Africa as a foreign-service officer with the United States Information Agency. In his writings, he often puts to use the expertise he developed overseas, such as in an article he wrote suggesting ways that foundations could help improve foreign policy making.

Perhaps Mr. Eisenberg's most illuminating articles are his tributes to the lives of the key figures in American philanthropy in the late twentieth century, moving and personal accounts of the lives of John Gardner, Paul Ylvisaker, John Filer, and David Hunter—all men he knew well.

Many people have contributed their ideas to the works in this volume. In particular, I want to thank Phil Semas, the founder of *The Chronicle of Philanthropy,* who recruited Mr. Eisenberg to become the first regular opinion columnist for the newspaper. While we don't necessarily share all of Mr. Eisenberg's views, we—and many others—respect his unwavering passion and vigorous efforts to ensure that the nonprofit world lives up to its promise.

Stacy Palmer, editor of *The Chronicle of
Philanthropy,* Washington, D.C.

Preface

I have been asked by many people to write a book about the nonprofit sector, based on my experiences and observations as an active participant in charitable organizations, both as a staff executive and board member, for more than thirty-five years. This is the product of these entreaties.

Rather than produce a book from scratch, I have chosen instead to compile many of the articles and speeches I have written over the past three decades. The reason for this approach is that the fundamental issues and problems of the nonprofit sector have remained constant since I first ventured into this exciting, challenging, yet often frustrating world.

True, the environment in which nonprofit organizations operate today is somewhat different from what it was thirty years ago. The size and complexity of the sector have grown enormously in recent times—and the importance of civil society institutions to American democracy may be even greater today than at any other time in our history.

Yet the vision, problems, and challenges that drove charitable efforts when I began my involvement in the sector are remarkably similar today: the passion for public service, the commitment to social and economic justice, problems of public accountability; issues of access, fairness, and equity; maintaining the "nonprofitness" of charitable groups; the relationship of nonprofits to government, media, and the business community; questions of leadership, integrity, and courage; effectiveness of nonprofit activities and programs; and the role of nonprofit advocacy and activism in public life.

When I reviewed the articles and speeches I wrote in the past three decades, I found that most, if not all, had relevance today. They addressed the same topics, issues, and dilemmas that I would have raised in authoring new material. So why, I asked myself, repeat what I had already written?

This book is not intended as a definitive exploration of our vast nonprofit universe. I have neglected significant parts of the nonprofit world, not because they are unimportant but, rather, because I did not have the time or resources to focus on them. The health field and public education are two such areas.

I have approached the challenge of commenting on nonprofit activity not as an academic researcher but as both a practitioner and an observer and critic. Too many scholars lack deep roots in the reality of nonprofit activities; their studies, while important, often miss the flesh and blood of the actual nonprofit world. On the other hand, few practitioners have had the time, resources, or inclination to document their experiences and observations for the benefit of their colleagues and future generations of nonprofit practitioners.

The life of most nonprofit staff members is difficult and demanding. Underpaid, overworked, and frequently unrecognized, they are the lifeblood of our civil society. They have been overshadowed by some of the stars of the field—both high-paid foundation and large nonprofit CEOs—some of whom deserve neither the salaries nor the accolades they receive. While I frequently have been critical of foundations and nonprofits, I retain a profound admiration and respect for the millions of nonprofit workers and their board members who over the years have made our nonprofit organizations the most vital and successful civil society in the world. This book is dedicated to them.

Stacy Palmer, the editor of *The Chronicle of Philanthropy*, has been a friend and my best critic for many years. Without her assistance, this book would never have come to fruition. Her editing and commentary have been invaluable; for this support, I am deeply grateful.

My thanks also go to the Charles Stewart Mott and Public Welfare Foundations and the Open Society Institute for the financial support they have given me over the past six years. I am most grateful to them for encouraging me to be a free ranger, a gadfly, observer, and critic in a sector so often defined by caution, fear, and cowardice.

The nonprofit community is facing enormous challenges and opportunities in the next couple of decades that may well determine the health and strength of American democracy: helping restore the integrity and vitality of government; curbing the excesses of corporate power; building strong leadership for public service; promoting social capital and civic engagement; and making social- and economic- justice issues a national priority. It has the capacity to achieve these objectives, but does it have the will and support to do so?

Optimism is the trait that enables a person to pursue a mission and goals with determination and high spirits. Cynicism is that quality which leads one to question, and sometimes distrust, the actions and motivations of others in an effort to ascertain the truth. I consider myself a cynical optimist. In looking at the future of the nonprofit world after many years of observation, I share the view and enthusiasm of British Admiral Horatio Nelson who, at the Battle of Trafalgar, looked at the enemy through his telescope with his blind eye and proclaimed, "I see victory in sight."

Pablo Eisenberg

Challenges for Nonprofits
and Philanthropy

1

The Challenges for Today's Nonprofit World—and a Look at the Past

Introduction: The Key Issues Facing Nonprofit Groups in the Twenty-first Century

January 2004

Nonprofit organizations are the cornerstone of our civil society, that network of voluntary associations, individual volunteers, institutional relationships, and social contacts that makes our democracy viable, vibrant, and accountable.

These organizations are perhaps more important today than ever before. They not only supplement the activities of government and business but also provide the balance that keeps these sectors transparent and in check. Their work and influence will help determine whether our governmental institutions are strengthened and made more effective, our civil rights and liberties are preserved, our corporate institutions are reformed and held accountable, our environment and health are protected, and the poorest among us are given the opportunity to become first-class citizens.

The challenges that nonprofit organizations need to deal with today are stunning in breadth and depth. American society is being torn apart by internal and external tensions that threaten our well-being, our sense of community, our idealism, and our relationship with the rest of the world. The growing conservatism that has suffused our political system, our two major political parties, and our economy, as well as undercut our commitment to social and economic justice, is making it difficult to stem the growing inequality of income and wealth in the country. Federal domestic programs that aid the needy have been sacrificed at the altar of massive tax cuts for the wealthiest Americans.

According to the latest Census Bureau report, more than 33 million Americans, or 12.1 percent of the population, are mired in poverty, an increase of 1.7 million just in the past two years. Yet the official poverty index does not tell the real story. By any reasonable definition of poverty, twice the number of the "official" poor have incomes that are below the level required to overcome poverty. Almost one quarter of our population, then, is deprived of the resources needed to become productive members of our society at a time when the United States is struggling to compete economically and politically with the rest of the world.

Other social indicators are no more encouraging. Fully 18 percent of our children are growing up poor according to the official poverty index. More than 43 million Americans, almost all of them workers, do not have health insurance. Approximately 6 percent of our population is unemployed, but this figure does not include those who are part-time workers looking for full-time jobs or who have simply dropped out of the job market. On many social indicators, such as child poverty, infant mortality, and life expectancy, we are lagging way behind many of the world's modern industrial societies.

We have permitted the nation's physical infrastructure to deteriorate to the point that thousands of bridges, drinking water systems, schools, roads and other public facilities are in drastic need of repair. At least $1.6 trillion will be required over the next five years to address this problem, according to the American Society of Civil Engineers.

Our free-enterprise system, which historically has driven our enormous economic expansion, has in recent years been undermined and corrupted by corporate greed, excessive executive compensation, poor governance practices, and relaxed federal regulations and oversight. Corporate excesses, reflected in the recent scandals at Enron, WorldCom, Tyco, and other major companies, have adversely affected the pension funds of hundreds of thousands of workers, weakened the stock market, reduced corporate taxes, and shaken the confidence of millions of individual small investors.

While the past two administrations and the Congress ended the traditional welfare entitlement program for poor mothers with children and shred the social safety net, they have left in place a massive system of welfare for corporate America and wealthy farmers. Subsidies and tax breaks for farmers alone cost $23 billion in 2000. These unnecessary handouts, combined with the huge tax cuts for wealthy Americans and the increase in spending on defense, has resulted in a massive increase in our annual budget deficit and a severe shortage of money for domestic social programs, including sharp reductions in programs by state governments.

To make matters worse, our electoral and political systems have become corrupted by big money. Campaign-finance reforms are still in their infancy, yet, so far, not really adequate to provide serious corrections. Our elected representatives spend an inordinate amount of time fund raising for their campaigns. Few demonstrate any leadership qualities, integrity, or courage. They are the best members of Congress money can buy. They seem unwilling or unable to restore the health of our economy or support programs that can provide more jobs, greater skills, and a better life for all our citizens. As they fail to uphold our national interests, the values and priorities that have been at the roots of our democracy are being undermined.

Americans seem to be losing their sense of community and collective decency. Money, marketing, and self-interest are dominating our lives and, in doing so, are costing us the admiration and respect of our friends overseas. Only the raw strength of our military power preserves the leadership role we have played in world affairs.

How can our trusted values and priorities be restored and strengthened? How do we balance all the special interests, especially those of our large institutions like business and labor, to re-establish a functional society that works for all of us? Can we achieve a more equitable tax system that generates sufficient funds to pay for modernizing our infrastructure and supporting vital health and welfare programs? Can we reform corporate America through more effective regulations and demands for public accountability?

While the answers are by no means clear, what is certain is that the nonprofit sector has a major role to play in determining the country's future direction and priorities. Over the course of the nation's history, nonprofit institutions have had such an influence and impact. Can they continue this tradition, one that distinguishes our civil society from all others? Do they have the capacity to do so? More important, do they collectively have the vision, will, and courage to fulfill their historic mission? Will we be able to build a more effective system of government oversight and enforcement that can make the nonprofit sector more transparent, honest, and publicly accountable? Can we develop the public and nonprofit leadership that will be required in the twenty-first century?

These questions are the primary focus of this book.

Larger yet Weaker?

Over the past twenty-five years the nonprofit sector has grown enormously, largely as a result of the many new social movements and the demand from the federal government for many more social-service providers. It now numbers well over two million organizations when small, unstaffed organizations like neighborhood-watch groups, block clubs, volunteer social-service entities, mentoring associations, and other informal groups are included.

Today, more than 800,000 charities are registered with the IRS under Section 501(c)(3) of the Internal Revenue Code—meaning they can accept tax-deductible contributions. That's twice as many as existed in 1977.

Another 137,000 groups have qualified for tax-exempt status under Section 501(c)(4)—a category of organizations that have more freedom to lobby than those that offer tax-deductible contributions. In 2002 more than 80,000 nonprofit groups applied to the IRS to obtain tax-exempt status under Section (501)(c)(3).

The growth of grant-making foundations has been equally robust. In 1975, the United States had 21,877 foundations with assets of $30.13 billion. Today, the nation has some 65,000 to 70,000 grant-making foundations with a combined asset base of almost $500 billion. And the staggering intergenerational transfer of wealth that is scheduled to take place over the next thirty years is widely expected by scholars to create a substantial number of new, large foundations and add generously to the coffers of many existing institutions. Despite the vicissitudes of the stock market, philanthropy promises vast riches that were unanticipated ten years ago.

Yet, despite the sector's phenomenal growth—it now employs over 11 million people and comprises about 7 percent of our GNP—and expanding wealth, can we say that it is more powerful and influential than it was three decades ago?

In one sense it is. Its expansion gave rise to many new social movements that have improved the status and lives of many Americans: women, the poor, minorities, gays and lesbians, the disabled, and people with AIDS. The emergence of environmental organizations has, if not halted, at least stemmed what was a methodical despoliation of our natural resources by our corporations and greedy consumers. An enormous increase in the number of social-service organizations, especially at the local level, have enabled the sector to deal more effectively with the homeless and hungry, victims of rape and domestic abuse, troubled youths, job seekers, drug addicts, and others in need of assistance.

The flowering of community organizing groups and community development corporations has revitalized and strengthened low-income communities in both urban and rural areas. And the impressive increase in performing arts institutions, museums, universities, colleges, research institutes, think tanks, and public-interest law firms has enriched our lives and generated the intellectual foundation and skills necessary in a modern, industrialized democracy.

In another sense, however, our civil society may be weaker, less influential than it was years ago.

The extraordinary proliferation of issues, causes, social needs, and specialized interest groups has diffused the focus of the nonprofit sector, scattering its priorities and activities over a wide range of issues and concerns. Our nonprofit organizations are more fragmented than ever before, making it difficult for them to unite for collective action on serious matters of national significance. The vast number of one-issue or special interest organizations, whether they are involved in health, education, or gay-lesbian issues, have boards of directors that are passionate about the institution's one or two priorities, not about a broader agenda. Not surprisingly, they hold their staff directors accountable for their performance in these one or two priority areas. It is little wonder, then, that organizational vision is often supplanted by organizational mission. Narrow agendas increasingly govern nonprofit practice.

The one notable exception to these developments has been the success of a relatively small number of conservative nonprofit organizations such as the Heritage Foundation and the American Enterprise Institute that, with the focused, strong support of a few conservative foundations, have influenced the nature of our political debate and direction of our country during the past twenty-five years. United and committed to such principles as smaller government, fewer taxes, unfettered free enterprise, and less regulation, these groups are largely responsible for the growing conservatism of the country and the advent of the Bush administration. Their example reflects the potential influence nonprofits can exert if they possess vision, unity, and leadership.

Nonprofit staff members today are given little incentive to participate in broad coalitions to attack major issues, or to support efforts of organizations that are fighting on other matters outside their own subject area. In recent years, for example, it has been commonplace for affordable-housing groups to advocate for additional housing units without much assistance from child welfare, educational, or health groups, even though all these organizations are concerned about the welfare of low-income people. The extensive fragmentation of the nonprofit community is perhaps the principal reason the sector is not exercising its potential power and influence.

In the last quarter of the nineteenth century the grange movement, with more than 20,000 chapters, was responsible for major reforms in rural policies and the creation of the rural extension service. Similarly, in the 1930s, several million members of the Townsend Clubs succeeded in persuading Congress to establish the Social Security system. And right after World War II the American Legion almost singlehandedly secured the passage of the GI Bill, which made higher education available to all military veterans. Those days are gone. No longer can a single nonprofit organization, even with a huge membership, win a major policy battle by itself. Coalitions are now the essential ingredient for nonprofit policy victories.

The need to build, finance, and sustain coalitions will be a major challenge to the sector's effectiveness and influence, especially in confronting the power of major special interests and overcoming narrow constituency concerns in favor of broader national priorities. Only broad-based coalitions will enable us to establish some form of national health insurance, substantial eradication of air and water pollution, and the creation of adequate affordable housing, as well as to put in place other major efforts to meet urgent public needs.

Common Cause recently showed what can be accomplished by a broad coalition. Through skillful organization, the coalition persuaded Congress to pass an important campaign-finance reform bill.

Much of the nonprofit world's ability to promote social change hinges on the extent to which our nonprofit leadership is willing to put aside individual and organizational egos to work together for the public good, and on whether our foundations will abandon their historic reluctance to underwrite public policy, advocacy, and coalition activities.

Whether nonprofits can overcome their fragmentation and unite for collective action will be essential to determining whether the sector can reclaim its advocacy role.

Reclaiming the Nonprofit Sector's Advocacy Mission

The tradition of activism that has characterized American civil society from its very beginning is the envy of most countries throughout the world. Though it is responsible for many, if not most, of the significant social and institutional changes that have anchored and strengthened our democracy, this facet of our nonprofit sector, paradoxically, is not currently held in such high esteem domestically.

In fact, during the past thirty years, public advocacy, whether through efforts to influence public policy or organize Americans to press for change, appears to have lost much of its cachet and appeal. It has been under continual attack from a wide range of sources: conservatives, mea culpa liberals seeking atonement for their former support of advocacy, mainstream foundation executives afraid of risk-taking, and nonprofit leaders scared to leave their comfort zone of delivering social services. On the political front, right-wing members of Congress are still continuing their efforts to limit lobbying by nonprofit groups that receive federal funds, after their attempt to do so failed in the 1990s.

That the role of activism has become so muted after the stunning achievements of the social movements of the 1960s through the mid–1980s may come as a surprise. Constituency organizing, working with policy makers, and lobbying were the cornerstones of the civil rights, women's, environmental, gay-lesbian, peace, disabled, and antipoverty movements, as well as the reasons for their success. Their leaders gained national prominence, and politicians translated their efforts into widely accepted legislation and regulations. What happened, then, to turn the tide that had swept advocacy into the mainstream of nonprofit activity?

The causes for this change are many and varied. The conservative revolution in American politics that gained steam in the 1980s was a contributing factor that helped dampen the ardor of activists. So was the decline in the membership and power of labor unions, which had been the backbone of many advocacy and lobbying campaigns. The slackening of antipoverty efforts, long a rallying point for progressive and minority organizations, removed one of the major targets for advocacy activities. By the late 1980s poverty was off our political screen, abandoned by political leaders of both major parties. Wanting to move Democrats more to the center, the Clinton administration virtually eliminated the word "poverty" from its political rhetoric and platform.

Another major cause was the colossal growth of social service organizations over the past four decades, largely financed by federal, state, and local governments, a development that Lester Salamon, director of the Center for Civil Society Studies at the Johns Hopkins University, has called third-party government. The increasing dependence on public funds—which cannot be used for lobbying purposes—for a substantial portion of their budgets has tamed the enthusiasm of these social service groups for either policy advocacy or lobbying. Their staff directors, who have grown comfortable in delivering services, have also found it difficult to change their leadership styles to accommodate more activist initiatives.

Structural changes among nonprofits since the 1960s may have been another reason for diminished nonprofit advocacy. As Theda Skocpol, a sociologist at Harvard University, has observed, the transformation of large organizations with active members in local and state chapters into smaller, more centralized groups with highly professional staff members and lobbyists has tended to reduce the number of formerly active participants in civic life, especially at the local level. For many nonprofit groups, membership is currently more about contributing money than being actively involved in the operation of the organization.

Foundations and corporate donors are also responsible for helping put a lid on nonprofit advocacy. Not only have they been unwilling for the most part to underwrite any nonprofit activism themselves, but they also have continually warned grant recipients and grant seekers not to get involved in advocacy and lobbying, although such activities are legally permissible. It is not uncommon to hear nonprofit leaders say that "we were told by the foundation not to engage in advocacy if we wanted to receive or continue to receive a grant."

Nonprofits themselves must share the responsibility for undermining advocacy in this country. They have repeatedly failed to exercise their enormous potential for policy work and legal activities to influence legislation. Their leaders for the most part have placed a higher priority on timidity than courage, thereby ignoring the needs of their clients and constituents. Only a fraction of those nonprofit groups reporting to the Internal Revenue Service each year—

about 3,500 out of approximately 238,000 in 1999, for example—claim to have engaged in any lobbying efforts.

The country has paid dearly for this diffidence. Particularly at the local and state levels, the silence of nonprofits on matters of paramount policy and financial interest to their constituents has been deafening. Severe budget cuts in domestic social programs, the repeal of the estate tax, the erosion of environmental regulations, the corporate scandals and loss of pensions—these measures and events passed without a peep from local and state nonprofits or, for that matter, from many national nonprofit groups.

Recent studies by Jeffrey M. Berry, professor at Tufts University, and David Arons, former co-director of Charity Lobbying in the Public Interest, seem to suggest that more nonprofits have recently become involved in public-policy and advocacy work. And a small number of progressive, national lobbying groups have scored some notable lobbying successes over the past few years. The latter, however, are focused for the most part on middle-class issues, such as the environment, government reform, and Medicare, not on questions of poverty.

What will it take to restore the advocacy role of the nonprofit sector? Much will depend on the emergence and development of young nonprofit leaders willing to place a high priority on advocacy activities, including lobbying. Graduate academic centers for nonprofit management and public policy can assist this process by beginning to stress not only the requirements for sound management but also the qualities needed for nonprofit leadership: vision, risk-taking, advocacy and coalition-building skills, and courage. Efforts by organizations like Charity Lobbying in the Public Interest and the Alliance for Justice to inform nonprofit groups about their legal rights to advocate and lobby will help eliminate the enormous anxieties that these organizations still have.

For better or for worse, foundations will remain a major source of support for nonprofit advocacy. Can grant makers overcome their resistance to supporting activist programs and organizations? Will they learn the lessons of American history about the crucial role of nonprofit advocacy? Will they begin to realize what their grantees are now discovering: that social services by themselves are no longer sufficient to meet the needs of their constituents?

Will it dawn on them that investments in advocacy carry more bang for their bucks? And will mainstream philanthropy finally recognize and adopt the exemplary grant-making practices of the major conservative foundations that stress the importance of policy work, advocacy, and general operating support? Several big institutions like the Ford Foundation maintain in all their arrogance that they have nothing to learn from their conservative counterparts. They are dead wrong.

In fairness to foundations and other donor institutions, it should be noted that one reason that foundations behave the way they do, ignore the needs of their grantees, and operate with little sunshine and public accountability is that nonprofits have permitted them to do so.

Grantees continue to act like abject beggars, grateful for the philanthropic morsels tossed their way. They are afraid to forcefully state their real needs, or to insist on fair treatment by their potential supporters. They have rarely organized or been willing to support campaigns to increase the minimal amount of money foundations are legally required to "pay out" each year, to persuade Congress to appropriate more funds for IRS and state attorneys general offices to oversee and police foundation performance, or to work with journalists to encourage them to expose and change foundation practices. With few exceptions, nonprofit executives are scared to death to criticize foundations publicly. Only a handful of them are willing at any time to be quoted in the press about philanthropic matters that aren't lavish paeans to foundation excellence. Even the largest nonprofits with power and great influence are not willing to risk a negative word about the donor world.

The National Committee for Responsive Philanthropy, established in 1976 as a watchdog organization to monitor and challenge philanthropic institutions, has done a surprisingly good job in fulfilling its mission and maintaining a $1 million-plus–budget, raised chiefly from those whose hands it bites. But it is often a lonely voice in the philanthropic wilderness. As a founder and a current board member of the organization, I find it distressing that it still lacks the strong support of its natural constituency, nonprofits that are sympathetic to its mission and activities but are, nonetheless, afraid to follow.

An increasing number of organizations have signaled that they are becoming so fed up with foundations that they are beginning to be openly critical and ready to act in concert with others to push grant makers to change their ways. Serious changes in foundation performance won't happen without growing nonprofit pressure, as well as continuing media coverage and public dissatisfaction with the lack of foundation accountability. Only time will tell us the extent to which our nonprofit community will finally be willing to show some courage in forcing philanthropy to be more responsive to public and grantee needs.

The Challenge of Foundation Reform

Foundations have made enormous contributions to the health and success of our civil society and our democratic institutions. They have seeded many of the breakthrough initiatives in science and agriculture, established many of our foremost educational, health, and research institutions, supplemented government resources for important social and other services, and served as mechanisms by which Americans could channel their charitable impulses. A relatively small number of them initiated and supported the country's social movements—movements that have resulted in greater social and economic justice.

If any major criticism of philanthropy can be made, it is that foundations have not moved with the times. In many ways, they remain essentially the same as they were thirty to forty years ago. While their number and assets have grown exponentially, they continue to be a bastion of elitism, governed by boards of directors composed almost entirely of wealthy people and highly paid professionals, individuals who do not reflect the great diversity, values, and perspectives of our country. Though more women and people of color are now foundation trustees, they tend to resemble their wealthy white male counterparts, both in class and temperament. Teachers, social workers, community representatives, blue-collar workers, labor union officials, small business owners, creative artists, and nonprofit executives are unlikely candidates for these prestigious positions.

The arrogance of foundations, though more muted than several decades ago, is still a key factor that impairs the quality of grant making and inhibits more positive relationships between grant makers and grantees. To this day, many foundations, especially those small and medium-sized funds controlled by family members, regard their assets as "our money," not quasi-public and publicly accountable funds. That perception explains why the foundation community is plagued by problems of widespread—often large—trustee fees, excessive compensation, self-dealing, conflicts of interest, and the absence of transparency. And it is such arrogance that causes foundations to operate in ways that do more to benefit trustees and staff members than the grantees they are supposed to serve.

The most egregious example of the selfish concerns of foundations is their continued reluctance to provide general operating support, the kind of money that all nonprofit organizations, regardless of mission, nature, size, and age, claim is their most important priority. Currently, only about 13 percent to 15 percent of all foundation funds are distributed as general operating support. Nonprofits have been urging foundations for years to provide this type of support; foundations have refused to hear or act on this message.

Foundation priorities have changed little over time. Only a very small portion of foundation money goes to social movements, social and institutional change, and the neediest in our society. According to assessments by Craig Jenkins, an Ohio State University sociologist, as well as the National Network of Grantmakers, and the National Committee for Responsive Philanthropy, not more than approximately 3 percent of the $30 billion expended by foundations each year is allocated for these purposes. Of this small amount, much less is devoted to policy and advocacy activities. The established, mostly large, institutions of higher education, health, culture, and the arts still receive the overwhelming bulk of foundation munificence.

The technology boom of the 1990s stimulated the creation of new foundations by entrepreneurs who had become mega-rich as a result of their venture companies and the stock market. Their creations, dubbed "venture philanthropy," were at first hyped as a new form of giving that would capitalize on the donors' hands-on business expertise and would assure solid returns on their investments.

While these foundations may have gotten donors more involved in the philanthropic process, in general they have quickly become institutionalized like their more traditional foundation counterparts. If anything, their priorities resemble those of "old line" institutions, even more safe and unwilling to take risks because of their donors' primary interest supporting charities that will improve their children's education, as well as their own alma maters and organizations that promote environmental conservation. While some spokesmen for these social venture networks believe that their donors will evolve into more socially active givers interested in policy and advocacy, the record thus far doesn't give much credence to this view.

A lack of creativity and fear of risk-taking continue to mar the performance of most foundations. Regional inequities in grant making are a major impediment to rural development, at-risk constituencies, and potentially innovative programs. The South, Southwest, Northwest, and the Plains states have fewer foundations and corporate headquarters than other sections of the country. Because so few national foundations provide funds to local groups, these areas are not receiving a fair share of philanthropic money and are unlikely to do so in the future, as new sources of philanthropy will continue to flow into already rich philanthropy areas.

Major national foundations could take steps to rectify this situation, such as establishing new regional and rural foundations, giving money to respected umbrella groups to create small-grant programs for local groups, and opening satellite offices in parts of the country that don't get sufficient grant support. Thus far, with few exceptions, foundations are not responding to this urgent need.

Foundations have ignored many other important areas. State and local governments, especially in an age when more power is being shifted from the federal government to the states, are in desperate need of greater accountability, more effective staff members, and structural and procedural reforms. And, in keeping with civil society's mission of holding governments accountable, nonprofit organizations must be given the resources to monitor and evaluate the performance of government and quasi-governmental institutions. Foundations have proved unwilling to devote much of their money to such efforts.

Not a few foundation executives cite anxieties raised by the the the Tax Reform Act of 1969 as the reason for avoiding this type of grant making, a rationale often used by foundations reluctant to sponsor advocacy and risk-taking initiatives. Congress passed sweeping changes in 1969 to rein in private foundations, imposing strict rules to prevent donors from using foundations for private gain, requiring foundations to distribute a minimum percentage of their assets each year for charitable purposes, and forcing them to submit annual reports to the Internal Revenue Service about their activities. To this day, the notion of government intervention and regulation is resented and feared by many philanthropists.

The recent crisis in corporate America, characterized by financial scandals, excessive executive compensation, lack of public accountability, loss of pension assets, and criminal behavior by auditors and CEOs alike, has also called into question foundations' willingness to fund citizen organizations and other activities to reform corporate practices, the backbone of our free-enterprise economy. And why have large foundations invested so little money in building the capacity of low-income grassroots organizations and immigrant groups throughout the country, not to mention institutions that register voters, push for election-campaign reforms, provide legal services for the poor, advocate better health insurance systems, and promote youth involvement in civic engagement?

The Commission on Private Philanthropy and Public Needs, a prestigious study group sponsored by John D. Rockefeller and named after its chairman, John Filer, CEO of the Aetna Insurance Company, stated in 1976 that the primary mission of philanthropy is to meet the nation's most urgent public needs. Twenty-eight years later, it can be said that foundations are not meeting many of the country's most urgent public needs.

The foundation community, led by its major trade association, the Council on Foundations, has tolerated and implicitly condoned the abuses, arrogance, and secrecy of its members. Not even the growing profusion of newspaper stories detailing scandals and abuses in foundation operations has prompted little more than a yawn by foundation executives and the Council. Other than Emmett Carson, president of the Minneapolis Foundation, no chief executive officer of a major foundation has forcefully denounced these practices and demanded changes in foundation behavior.

Dorothy Ridings, president of the Council on Foundations, did write an editorial in the November–December 2003 issue of her organization's magazine, *Foundation News and Commentary*, expressing her dismay with the scandals and asking for corrective action. The editorial, however, was called "The Sins of a Few," an understated title to describe the widespread abuses in the foundation world. By the beginning of 2004, the Council itself had not yet issued a statement denouncing the abuses of some of its members as well as non-member foundations.

In the cozy collegial world of institutional philanthropy, few seem willing to champion reform or be critical of colleagues or foundation practices. When asked about the need for more government regulation, the insiders' cry is for more and better self-reform, a development that we have yet to see.

What does pique and mobilize the big foundations' energy is the threat of increasing the legal minimum payout that foundations must pay every year from their net assets. Since the payout is pegged at 5 percent—and can include in that figure all of a foundation's staffing and operating costs, the large foundations have been distributing only 3 percent to 4.2 percent of their assets in actual grants to nonprofit organizations. They tend to view the payout as a ceiling, not a floor. Despite the phenomenal 376 percent growth in foundation assets from 1985 to 2000, foundations actually reduced the percentage of their assets they distributed in grants during that same period.

For a long time, foundations have not given nonprofits a fair share of the charitable funds accumulated with generous tax benefits going to their donors. They have argued strenuously that anything above the 5 percent–level will force them to spend down their assets and eventually go out of business. Despite the predominance of research that undermines their position and affirms that the aggregate asset base of foundations can be sustained with 6.5 percent, 7 percent, and even higher payout rates, the large foundations continue to defend the mythology they have created with the fierceness of institutional Scrooges protecting their own wealth at the expense of the public interest.

When Congress last fall proposed to increase the amount of money foundations grant to nonprofits by prohibiting them from including administrative costs to meet their payout requirements, the Council and big foundation leaders organized a massive lobbying campaign, hired a high-powered lobbyist, intimidated nonprofits from supporting a measure that would have added at least $3 billion annually to their coffers, and lied to some members of Congress by stating that support for increasing the payout was a right-wing conspiracy. Sparing no effort or costs, the Council and its member allies made the payout issue its major priority and focus, spending hundreds of thousands of dollars in the process. Their effort succeeded in persuading Congress to drop the payout provision from a major piece of charitable-giving legislation.

The health of foundations, their performance, the effect of scandals and abuses on the public trust, the lack of oversight of their activities, the fragile relationship between grantees and donors, and all matters of substance were lost in the battle to keep the federal payout rules unchanged. What a reflection on foundation priorities. What a negative tribute to foundation leadership. Self-serving institutional greediness trumped the interest of the nonprofit community, the taxpayer, and the American public.

So what is required to reform American foundations? One answer is clear. Self-reform will not work. It never has and never will. Congress, with the assistance of the Internal Revenue Service and the state attorneys general, must pass legislation that tightens public-accountability requirements, eliminates trustee abuses, removes the loopholes in self-dealing regulations, and abolishes conflicts of interest between trustees, foundation CEOs, the foundations' lawyers and other service contractors, and grantees. In addition, Congress should make clear to the IRS that oversight of the nonprofit sector, including foundations, is a high priority that can't be given short shrift as in the past.

Yet if federal and state regulators are to oversee and police the charitable sector more effectively, they will need far greater resources than they have had to date. The money in theory is available for this purpose. The 1969 Tax Reform Act added an excise tax on the assets of private foundations and said that it should be used to oversee both foundations and nonprofits. Instead, for some reason, the money has gone into the Treasury's general funds. It is time for Congress to redress this oversight and target all or a substantial portion of the excise tax—in 1999 the tax raised approximately $500 million—for oversight and enforcement activities. Not only should the budgets for both the IRS and the state attorneys general be significantly increased, but additional funds should be used to finance research about philanthropy that is in the public interest, as well as efforts to post IRS information on the Internet for public use.

Lawmakers should also consider adding requirements that foundations have sufficiently large boards to ensure accountability. Too many small foundations have boards of one or two persons, too few to assure adequate perspectives, intelligent grant making, and public accountability. Foundation boards should be required to have at least five members. Congress should also give serious attention to requiring new foundations to have a minimal asset base for two reasons: to assure the creation of institutions that are serious and capable of sustaining themselves, and to generate the resources that would permit greater oversight of the foundation sector by regulators.

Eliott Spitzer, the attorney general of the state of New York, has suggested that all foundations be required to have at least $20 million at the start. But this requirement would deter potential philanthropists with good intentions but much less money. A more appropriate minimum would be $2 million, thereby affording opportunities to serious but moderate donors.

As long as foundations remain an elitist body of grant makers, they are not likely to change with the times, or become more publicly accountable. How to democratize these institutions without jeopardizing their independence and donor interests, however, poses a difficult challenge.

The growth of mega-foundations like the Bill and Melinda Gates Foundation makes the problem more urgent. With current assets amounting to $23 billion, the foundation will probably become our first $50-billion or $100-billion charitable institution. As other giant foundations emerge far richer than the Ford Foundation or the Lilly Endowment, our society will begin to have huge concentrations of quasi-public money, governed by a few family members and retainers. And in cases like the Gates Foundation, the big foundations sometimes oversee funds that are far greater than the budgets of most countries in the world.

Such a development would be a danger to our democracy, enabling a few super wealthy individuals to determine our public policies and priorities. How can we prevent this occurrence? One way would be for the Congress to enact a version of antitrust legislation, limiting the size of private foundations to $10 billion, $12 billion, or $15 billion. Another measure might require all private foundations of a certain size—say over $500 million to $1 billion—to have at least half of their boards composed of people specifically chosen to represent the public interest and selected by special advisory boards. While neither of these solutions would assure more democracy or better grant making, they would forestall the philanthropic march to even greater "bigness."

How to achieve greater diversity on foundation boards, a prerequisite for more thoughtful and effective grant making, is an even tougher challenge, especially for medium- and small-sized family foundations. Several possibilities exist, although none of these alternatives is totally satisfying.

Prohibiting all trustee fees above a very moderate level as well as all trustee compensation for services to the foundation could discourage the recruitment of some board members from the ranks of the wealthy, family members, and highly paid professionals, people who often seem to require payment for their charitable work on foundation boards. At the same time the Council on Foundations and other philanthropic leadership groups should aggressively encourage their members to diversify their boards.

Family foundations that appoint public trustees as a majority of their boards might be excused from paying the excise tax. Family-dominated foundations could be required to appoint public members as a majority of their boards after their first twenty years. Or family-dominated foundations that don't appoint public trustees as a majority of their boards after a certain number of years—say thirty—could be required to distribute all their assets and go out of business.

Opening foundations to sunshine is another key to democratization. At the time of the Filer Commission, a little more than six hundred foundations issued annual reports to the public. Today, almost thirty years later, about 2,200 out of more than 62,000 foundations publish annual or biennial public reports. This doesn't amount to much progress. To rectify this problem, all foundations large enough to be included in the Foundation Directory compiled by the Foundation Center—some 16,000—should be required to issue an annual or biennial report with programmatic information not found in the IRS reports.

Notwithstanding these suggested changes in the governance and accountability of foundations, the transformation of American foundations will not take place without the exercise of leadership by major foundation directors and the pressure exerted by nonprofits and the public. The Council on Foundations, the Philanthropy Roundtable, the regional associations of grant makers, and other philanthropic associations will have to rise above their current level of irresponsibility to demand higher standards of accountability and governance from their members. News media pressure can also make a huge difference: In Colorado, press coverage of a scandal over spending at the Daniels Fund, a $1-billion philanthropy, has caused many foundations to rethink how they reward their trustees and deal with other spending issues. Nonprofit leaders in Colorado have helped the major news outlets cover the issue, and have spoken out about the ways foundation behavior harm the neediest people in the state.

The potential for philanthropic reform is enormous. Only time will tell whether the nonprofit sector has the courage and determination to bring about these changes.

The Crisis of Leadership

Democracy depends on leadership, people with the values, vision, courage, and skills to shape and maintain strong institutions, as well as to lead efforts to bring about necessary social, economic, and political change. The strengthening of our nonprofit community and the transformation of philanthropy will require strong leadership. Unfortunately, we currently lack the leadership to accomplish these tasks. That is why the nonprofit sector is in serious trouble.

Observers of civil society believe that the ranks of nonprofit leadership are extremely thin. Nonprofit boards of directors and search firms continually complain about how difficult it is to find suitable candidates to fill positions vacated by executive directors and senior staff. A high rate of staff turnover in many organizations reflects a dissatisfaction with the way these institutions are run. Young people in particular decry the lack of collegial approaches to nonprofit governance. The growing emphasis on narrow management issues to the exclusion of broader vision and program goals has undermined the development of outstanding leadership.

The nonprofit world has tried to act more like business, but in so doing it has taken on some of the worst features of corporate America: unsavory ethics, conflicts of interest, worship of the bottom line, and the cult of the CEO. And the emergence of our celebrity or "star" culture is producing nonprofit executives more concerned about their personal recognition than the achievements of their organizations. Many are building egos, not institutions.

During the past two decades we have lost many of our most outstanding nonprofit leaders for a variety of reasons: retirement, burnout, inadequate salaries and benefits, disappointment with both their careers and the field, and the growing burden of fund raising. A large number do not appear to have been replaced with successors of commensurate quality. With their departure, there seems to have been a loss of idealism, passion, zeal, and commitment to public service, possibly the result of more conservative and passive times. For many, nonprofit work has become just another job in an increasingly large and more accepted sector, more open to technological skills and better paid than in the past. While the aggregate competence level of nonprofits may have increased, their dynamism has probably waned and, with it, that energy and devotion that sparks leadership.

Nowhere is this more visible than in the foundation world, where there are some good directors but no genuine leaders among all the CEOs of major foundations. Their hyper-collegiality and lack of introspection have muted any criticism they might have made about philanthropic priorities, foundation performance, or the relationship between donors and grantees. They have failed to speak out on the major public issues of the day, except when their own organizational interests were at stake. Few foundation executives point to one or more of their colleagues as leaders in the field whom they admire and follow. Their combined written contribution to the analysis and critique of philanthropy amounts to no more than a short story.

In thinking about past foundation leadership, I am reminded of John Gardner and Alan Pifer of the Carnegie Corporation, William Bondurant of the Mary Reynolds Babcock Foundation, Margaret Mahoney of the Commonwealth Fund, McGeorge Bundy, Paul Ylvisaker, and Harold "Doc" Howe of the Ford Foundation, Michael Joyce of the Lynde and Harry Bradley Foundation, David Hunter of the Stern Fund, and James Shannon of the Minneapolis Foundation. These were outstanding leaders who exercised enormous influence on philanthropy and nonprofit organizations. They launched bold initiatives and projects, took risks, hired outstanding program officers, and enjoyed, close ties with their grantees. And they were respected by their colleagues. There were others, too, who did a fine job in leading their institutions. The current crop of successors pales in comparison.

One of the possible reasons for today's shortage of leadership in the nonprofit sector, among both foundations and nonprofits, is the absence of any intellectual foundation that either shapes or drives the work of these institutions and their employees. There is virtually no introspection or critical thinking about the current or future operations of the sector. That is left to researchers and academics who, too often, don't have the practical experience to provide much guidance or even write meaningfully about nonprofit performance.

Few nonprofit executives reflect and write about their experiences, because they either don't have the time, find writing burdensome, or have not received any encouragement to do so. Surprisingly, very few nonprofits offer their staff members sabbaticals and other incentives that could provide opportunities for reflection, research, and publication. Nor have foundations had the foresight to provide funds for this purpose, not even for their own staff members. The lessons of nonprofit experience and history are being ignored and lost.

Most nonprofits are in a continual battle for survival and program stability. The staff members always face the pressing internal needs of their organizations, including fund raising, as well as the urgent demands of their clients or constituencies. That is at least a plausible reason for their lack of intellectual vigor; it is not a reasonable rationale in the foundation world. Foundations take their time awarding grants a few times a year; they do not rush to shift their priorities to meet new public needs; they are essentially unaccountable for their performance; and they have the luxury of sitting calmly while nonprofit organizations struggle in their battle for stability and survival.

Foundation executives have plenty of time for reflection and writing, yet they produce virtually nothing of significance to the critical analysis of their own field. What is particularly galling is that many of the CEOs of the major foundations have actually come from academe, an environment that one assumes provides training and stimuli for intellectual activity. Perhaps they have been captured by the comfort zone of collegiality, the tradition of foundation intellectual sterility, or the lack of pressure for improving the field. Whatever the reason, they are doing a disservice to a field that desperately needs introspection and brainstorming.

Leadership development is being increasingly impaired by the manner in which nonprofit organizations and foundations prepare for leadership changes and select new leadership. Among foundations, bright, talented, and energetic program officers are rarely given the opportunity to become the CEOs of large or even middle-sized organizations. What this practice does for the notion of career ladders and for staff morale is simply devastating. It also is probably responsible for lowering the quality of incoming leadership. For it has now become almost axiomatic that the large and middle-sized foundations turn to search firms to recruit an outside "hotshot" who is usually well known, credentialed, and safe, many of them ex-presidents and deans of colleges and universities. The result thus far has been, to put it mildly, disappointing.

Nonprofit organizations are afflicted by the same anti-leadership virus. Very few organizations have a succession plan or have recruited and trained future potential leaders for their staff. This was most recently confirmed by a study of New York City nonprofits, released in October 2003 by Baruch College's School of Public Affairs. Nonprofit executive directors seem either to believe they are immortal, are afraid to recruit strong, potentially challenging successors, or just don't care about the future of their organizations once they leave.

Their boards have done little or nothing to remedy the situation. In fact, they are abetting the problem of transition by increasingly insisting on outside searches by search firms, often unsuitable for the task, frequently bypassing qualified candidates inside their own organizations. Too many boards, like their foundation counterparts, appear to be looking for charismatic stars, often nationally known, who they hope will provide immediate success and financial support. Some of the search firms seem to be complicit in this unproductive strategy. A few of their principals have actually written articles arguing that it is advisable for nonprofits to recruit executive directors from outside the organization. This approach is certainly better for their bottom line, but is it better for the nonprofits themselves? Hardly. Millions of dollars are being squandered each year by formal searches, while excellent candidates from within the organizations remain unrecognized and passed over.

The most difficult question to answer about leadership is why such a critical shortage of leaders exists today. Why aren't we nurturing people with vision, integrity, courage, and other leadership skills? Is it our socialization process? Have the changes in our nonprofit sector—for example, its corporatization, the cult of celebrity, or the increased societal emphasis on money—undermined the values and commitment to the public interest that are the essential ingredients of leadership? Have our school systems and universities done a poor job of inculcating notions of leadership among our young people? Have narrow management skills been stressed at the expense of broader, more expansive leadership qualities? Can our middle-aged nonprofit executives rise above their undistinguished levels of performance with the proper training and inspiration?

We simply don't know the answers to these questions. But we do know that developing new leadership will be the key to a robust nonprofit sector ten to twenty years from now.

We also know that we need to change the way we go about creating and nurturing leadership. The sector has not had a carefully crafted strategy to do so; it has just assumed that leadership will evolve from the mass of organizations, programs, and activities that are part of the nonprofit world. It has invested very little money in efforts to build strong leaders and leadership teams. Young people in their twenties are the linchpin on which the sector will have to build its leadership development strategies; the older generations in their forties and fifties are probably too set in their ways and jaded to provide the dynamism, courage, and skills that will be required by the sector in the next couple of decades.

For the past thirty to forty years, federally supported volunteer programs such as VISTA, AmeriCorps, and the Peace Corps have provided an important core of our nonprofit leadership. They must be continued, strengthened, and expanded.

Congressional conservatives succeeded in reducing the budget of AmeriCorps last fall. Fortunately, by the end of 2003 congressional supporters appear to have succeeded in restoring the agency's budget. While the recipients of AmeriCorps funds mounted a strong lobbying campaign against the budget reductions, the rest of the nonprofit world did little or nothing to support its embattled colleagues. As long as the major nonprofit organizations and coalitions of nonprofits and foundations, such as Independent Sector, fail to recognize their importance to future leadership needs, these programs will be at risk and, possibly, marginalized.

Academic centers of nonprofit policy and management, mostly at the graduate level, could be another source of new leadership. They have not been thus far, though many claim that they currently are major producers of nonprofit leadership. These institutions have multiplied rapidly over the past ten years, driven by their moneymaking potential and the hunger of nonprofits for more skilled employees. More than one hundred such centers are in operation and many more are likely to be established in the near future. But can they be effective builders of leadership? Not unless they make major changes.

Academic centers are now the training grounds for technicians and budget analysts, not well-rounded and inspired leaders. Their curricula stress heavily those skills that make competent, if narrowly gauged, managers. Is it really important for nonprofit directors to be able to do regression analysis yet not develop those skills that build leadership? What the centers' curricula currently lack are such qualities as vision, a sense of ethics and integrity, courage, and an ability to lead. They minimize the significance of public policy, advocacy, coalition building, politics, and the role of government.

The great majority of courses are taught by academics, many of whom have not worked in nonprofits, government, or the private for-profit sector. They tend to approach nonprofits from theory and textbooks, not practice and experience. Since very few practitioners are part of the academic centers' faculties, and most of them are very part-time adjuncts with little influence, the balance that practitioners could bring to the study of nonprofits is sadly missing. Unfortunately, it is the students who are being deprived of a sound educational experience.

Can and will the academic centers change to become more relevant to the needs of nonprofit organizations? Will they begin to hire more practitioners not only as adjuncts but also as permanent faculty members? Faculty pressure to maintain their disciplines, undiluted by practitioners who lack Ph.D.s, will be difficult to overcome, yet a few universities have begun to make greater use of practitioners both as teachers and special program directors. Some are also discovering that people with nonprofit and government experience are well suited to serve as an important link between students' academic training and the world of work, a task for which academics are singularly unsuitable.

Not until academic curricula are modified, practitioners are added to university faculties, and students are more effectively matched with nonprofit or government jobs will the academic centers assume a major role in creating nonprofit leadership. Until then, the burden will continue to fall on government and nonprofit-sponsored volunteer and internship programs.

One other leadership development strategy could make a significant difference. University and college undergraduates and graduates, not to mention many out-of-school young people, are finding it difficult, if not impossible, to enter the nonprofit field. Opening level jobs paying decent salaries and benefits are at a premium. The reasons for their scarcity are many and varied: budget cutbacks; preference for older, experienced workers; limited staff time for supervision; no organizational interest in young staff; and little priority given to future leadership. Growing budget constraints are likely to make these jobs even more scarce.

The only way to create such jobs, and thereby provide greater opportunities for young people interested in nonprofit careers, would be to subsidize them for at least two years. Even a thousand of these internships a year could turn out to be one of the most effective leadership development programs in our history. While it could cost $40 million to $50 million annually—assuming salaries of $35,000 to $40,000 a year—the price would be a bargain, a pittance for our foundations, which give over $30 billion a year to charities, much of it pedestrian grant making. Building its leadership for the next twenty-five years is a challenge our nonprofit sector cannot afford to ignore.

A major impediment to the nonprofit sector's ability to meet future challenges is the lack of courage among its institutions and leadership. This is reflected in the unwillingness of nonprofit executives to speak out on potentially controversial issues or go on the record with their views. It is mirrored in the reluctance of grantees to criticize foundations or other donors. It is manifested in the fear of many nonprofits to engage in legal lobbying on tough public policy issues, or to reach beyond their narrow organizational priorities to embrace broader agenda. And it is demonstrated in the avoidance of risk-taking by philanthropy in general.

Nowhere was the gutlessness of nonprofits more in evidence than in the debate about the congressional proposal to increase the payout to grantees by requiring foundations to exclude administrative costs from the calculation of their minimum payout requirements. Only a handful of nonprofit organizations were willing to publicly support the measure. Many nonprofits admitted they were scared to offend some of their donors, even though they knew that the proposed change would add more than $3 billion annually to nonprofit groups.

As Peter Frumkin, an associate professor at the Hauser Center for Nonprofit Organizations at Harvard University, noted, "The spectacle of nonprofit leaders either backing the foundation world's arguments or simply sitting on the sidelines out of fear was remarkable . . . most of the sector's leaders were simply trying to stay clear of the controversy or were cowering at the thought of offending their funders by speaking out . . . there is no reason why the issue should have elicited such thundering silence within the sector."

Without a change in spirit and will, the sector is unlikely to renew and revitalize itself. Nonprofits will need to inject a large dose of courage into its individual and collective spines. It will require a growing number of organizations and leaders who can demonstrate that candor and courage, as well as intelligence, are the avenues to reform. Guts and brains: we need them both.

$\sim$

The Voluntary Sector in the 1970s:
Problems and Challenges

This paper was prepared at the request of the National Center for Voluntary Action for submission to the Commission on Private Philanthropy and Public Needs. It was originally published in 1977.

There is widespread belief that the voluntary sector is in a state of acute and prolonged crisis. Some attribute this situation to a serious shortage of money and the inability of private groups to finance their growing needs. Others point to the octopodan spread of government, a development that threatens the traditional balance between the public and private sectors. Yet others perceive the voluntary sector as a complex system of organizations often irrelevant to the pressing issues of social and economic survival in the 1970s and 1980s.

An element of insight and truth underlies each of these observations. Each focuses on an important part of the problem and directs our attention to a fundamental dilemma that clouds the future of the voluntary sector. Simply stated, the question is whether the voluntary sector—philanthropy, volunteerism, and private organizations—can meet the changing needs of society with its traditional assumptions, strategies, and operations.

There is a tendency among many observers to cite the proliferation of voluntary organizations, the amount of money spent by private groups, and the vast number of hours contributed by volunteers as tangible evidence that all is well with the voluntary sector. There is an Adam Smith quality in this view, reflecting the hope, if not the conviction, that all the parts of the voluntary mechanism are working effectively through a hidden hand on behalf of the public's good.

But statistics are only one indicator of the health of institutions. The quality of performance, the timing and politics of action, the significance of the activity, and the nature of the process are all elements that must be included in any overall judgment of an institution or the private sector in general. These tend to be much more difficult to assess. Little wonder, then, that so little attention has been paid to their evaluation.

The voluntary sector, its goals and functions, can be divided into two major facets. While they overlap, one is essentially private, the other primarily public.

The former refers to those not-for-profit activities of individuals and organizations that promote self-betterment, individual professionalism, personal services, and self-fulfillment through participation with others. This side is basically focused on individual wants, needs, and gratifications. The latter, the public side, is chiefly concerned with societal problems and the preservation of our democratic value system, the American ideals of justice, liberty, and opportunity. It is based on a traditional American view of society that has recognized the inherent dangers of big government and assigned to the private sector the responsibility for keeping government open, responsible, and in check.

It is in dealing with its public function that the voluntary sector is particularly derelict in fulfilling its mission and responsibilities.

The past few decades have witnessed revolutionary changes in our institutional arrangements, both domestic and international; in the growth of government and its bureaucracies; in the nation's economic condition, patterns, and problems; in the evolution of minority and disadvantaged communities; and in the emergence of unforeseen urban, rural, consumer, and ecological issues.

Not only have vast changes swept the country, but there is ample evidence that our society itself will have to undergo radical surgery if our democratic way of life is to survive. The market mechanism, long the mainstay of economic life, is breaking down and will have to be modified. Poverty has not been eliminated. Social injustice continues. Economic opportunity is undermined by racial discrimination. If the poor aren't getting poorer, they aren't getting much richer. An inequitable tax system perpetuates an inequitable economic social system. Essentially public decisions affecting not only Americans but other countries as well are still being made by private institutions and small groups of individuals. The pressure for distributing power and resources more fairly within our society is building as a result of both internal and external influences.

How to anticipate these changes and where to initiate preventive medicine should and must be the business of the voluntary sector, particularly its innovative components, the foundations and educational institutions. Few philanthropic organizations and private groups, however, appear to have a significantly altered their priorities and practices to adjust to recent developments. They remain cautious and conservative, preferring to avoid or ignore these new trends and issues. While the world has moved, they have tended to stand still. Their traditional purpose and current conceptual base have been undermined by the march of events.

The fossilization of traditional practices is everywhere in evidence. Over the past twenty years, hundreds if not thousands of new local organizations have been created to deal with issues such as ecology, consumer problems, economic and social self-determination, public interest, law, poverty, and neighborhood revitalization; yet philanthropy has made little or no provision for those new vital groups. Many social agencies and volunteer groups continue to serve their clients, old and new, as they have for years, irrespective of changing circumstances and the need for modern strategies and special skills. Nor have philanthropy and many private organizations demonstrated much interest in and concern for the New Federalism, with its dangerous implications for responsible democracy at the local level and for the continued vitality of the voluntary sector.

Special attention must be focused, therefore, on the public side of the voluntary sector, on the neglected public social and economic issues that must increasingly become a responsibility of local and national voluntary organizations.

The Expanding World of Private Organizations

During the last two decades the number of private organizations engaged in traditional philanthropy, community service, professional betterment, and social activities has multiplied significantly. Paralleling this growth has been the emergence of a new large group of local and national organizations with different purposes and structures and, in some cases, constituencies. While vocal, active, and productive, these volunteer groups are still struggling to gain acceptability, credibility, and recognition from the voluntary sector in general and the philanthropic organizations in particular.

Although all are concerned with major economic and social problems, they may be divided into two major groups. Many organizations combine the characteristics of both types.

The first is primarily involved in the identification, analysis, and resolution of public issues, local, regional, and national. In contrast to the largely middle-class better government and taxpayer groups of the past, the new groups comprise a wide and growing range of concerns and a rich diversity of class and ethnic backgrounds. Civil rights and antipoverty organizations emerged in the 1950s and 1960s, encouraged by increasing citizen responsiveness to social problems and governmental action. During the past ten years ecology and consumer groups have mushroomed as the threat to our natural resources was perceived and business malpractices became more clearly understood. Major areas of public needs and services have received attention with the creation of special citizen organizations to deal with housing, wealth, welfare, and community development. Government and budgetary practices are now spurring the creation of new groups interested in municipal performance and program effectiveness. Cutting across these groups and constituencies has been the growth of coalition movements around particular issues appealing to a large and diverse number of organizations.

The second type may be characterized as self-determining organizations that have been created to provide disadvantaged constituencies with those opportunities, services, and influences that have not been available through normal or traditional channels. They may involve a particular neighborhood or section of a city, a special minority community or portion of that community, or persons too poor and disconnected to care adequately for their family needs and rights. Their premise is that neither the public nor private sector will pay sufficient attention to their problems and plight, that they themselves must determine and direct their own development. Economic development corporations reflect this avenue for greater economic opportunities for poor and minority communities. So do many of the cooperatives and cottage industries formed in recent years. Other groups and organizations have turned to social and political strategies for greater power and influence. The traditional social services provided by United Way agencies and government institutions have often neglected disadvantaged communities or delivered services in an ineffectual way. New organizations, more responsive to and directed by these communities themselves, have therefore been created to provide more relevant services to those most in need. Alternative schools, food stamp outreach and sales, community-based health centers, many Head Start programs, and nontraditional manpower programs are examples of this corrective approach to social services.

Without a long tradition of experience and recognition, and premised on the need for and desirability of change, both types of organizations have found the task of supporting themselves extraordinarily difficult. Unlike many other institutions, their financial support has not necessarily been correlated to their performance level. Indeed, in some instances high productivity has insured inadequate backing. In a sense, they remain the financial stepchildren of the voluntary sector despite their crucial importance to the nation's economic and social programs.

Nowhere is this more evident than in their relationship with the governmental changes that have been introduced under the rubric of the New Federalism.

The New Federalism and Government Power

The New Federalism, introduced over the past few years, represented a tremendous challenge to institutions concerned with the strength of the voluntary sector. It is altering the relationship between the federal, state, and local governments, as well as the authority and power each exercises. It is redefining the responsibilities of the three levels of government toward the protection of the nation's minority and disadvantaged groups. It has concentrated much greater power in the executive branches of state and local governments without simultaneously strengthening the legislative branches. And it has changed the federal government's attitudes about and policies toward voluntary-sector organizations.

The devolution of governmental power and control has been implemented without due regard to the capacity of local governments to exercise these new responsibilities or their willingness to conduct business openly and to be held accountable. Nor have local and state governments been compelled to reform their archaic bureaucratic or procedural practices as a condition of receiving this new public trust. The New Federalism assumes that these governments have the competence to perform adequately or that, if they do not, the exercise of new responsibilities will somehow produce the necessary competence. There is ample evidence that both assumptions are fallacious.

The inroads of the New Federalism have been quiet, subtle, and slow. Much of its foundation has been laid by executive fiat without broad public awareness. Only after two years of operation is general revenue sharing, its most publicized program, beginning to be understood by the general public. The special revenue-sharing measures recently introduced are still mysteries to most people. A great deal of what has happened over the past few years has not been the subject of extensive legislative debate or public discussion, even though it will have an enormous impact on community life and priorities everywhere.

The operation of many local governments has traditionally been a relatively closed system. Citizens and community groups have enjoyed little or no opportunity to participate in and influence the priority-setting and decision-making government processes. Local budget procedures are still a mystery to most local organizations and individuals. Public information about city and county activities has been limited and often tightly controlled. A large number of elected and appointed officials have tended to treat the general public more as an obstacle to efficiency than as clients whose interests they are supposed to serve. Most citizens have never been involved in local government affairs except peripherally at election time. They view their governments largely as remote entities, divorced from their personal lives, secretive in their dealings, and callous to many of their needs.

As long as city and county governments were relatively weak, had to contend with strong independent local authorities and federal programs, and had limited control of much of the money channeled into their jurisdictions, this nondemocratic state of local government affairs was tolerable, if not particularly productive. Citizens, particularly minority constituencies, could look to the federal government and independent institutions and programs for redress and the protection of their rights and interests. Private nonprofit organizations financed directly or indirectly by the federal government and a few foundations could and did provide an outlet for active citizen involvement in local public activities. In short, a balance of power existed, which restrained local governments' influence over and control of its citizenry.

The New Federalism has upset this balance of power, tilting it heavily on the side of officialdom and government bureaucracy. Revenue sharing and other shifts have given chief executive officers of local governments much greater control over the funds entering their jurisdictions than they have ever enjoyed before.

Even in the areas of program planning and coordination the administration has made it clear that private-sector organizations are not to have a role to play. Representation on federal review and coordination bodies is limited to governmental representatives; there is no provision for citizen involvement or private-sector participation. Citizen involvement has been downgraded in all federal programs. In some it has become merely advisory; in others it has become so permissive a requirement that it is being ignored. The attempt to eliminate the Office of Economic Opportunity (OEO) and community action as well as the major cuts made in the Model Cities program attest to the difficulties experienced by independent citizen action in recent years in relating to government programming.

Adding momentum to this swing of the power pendulum has been the conscious decision by the administration to end direct federal support and encouragement of private nonprofit groups.

For disadvantaged and minority communities—either ethnic, class, or political—decentralization of government authority and the decategorization of federal grants represent a throwback to the 1940s. They cannot forget that categorical programs and federal strings were introduced precisely because state and local governments could not or would not protect their rights and guarantee them equal economic and social opportunities.

While the local political scene has changed in the past decade or two, it has not changed that much. Elected officials still make decisions based on majority opinion and pressure, and disadvantaged and minority groups know that where they are in the minority their interests and rights are likely to be ignored. The federal responsibility for and guarantees of minority rights and concerns that characterized the 1960s are being attenuated by the New Federalism and its programs. Redress and justice must be sought increasingly at the local level, which is difficult, or through the courts, which takes an inordinate amount of time.

A number of the reforms mandated by the New Federalism were necessary and potentially productive. The categorical grant system was in great need of consolidation and simplification. Local governments, lacking the means with which to be responsive to community needs, required additional resources and authority. Unfortunately, the doctrinaire way in which these reforms and other aspects of the New Federalism have been implemented has not corresponded to the requirements of a responsive government or an interested and active citizenry.

Government has been strengthened at the expense of the voluntary sector, not as a more effective partner to the voluntary sector. Greater power without commensurate capability or public accountability presents a dangerous potential for local corruption and tyranny. The federal government has refused to provide for checks and balances at the local level. Only the voluntary sector can fill this gap.

The Need for Community-Based Organizations

The manner in which general revenue sharing has been allocated and used reflects a number of the problems raised by the simultaneous increase in local government authority and reduction in federal responsibilities and controls.

Although touted as a mechanism for bringing power to the people, general revenue sharing has not perceptibly increased citizen involvement in local budgetary processes or local government matters, except in the relatively few communities that have had access to additional resources, technical assistance, and outside stimuli. Where citizen activity has occurred, it has usually been the result of citizen group initiatives, not those of elected or appointed officials. These officials appear to have little predisposition to open local government processes to greater citizen planning, participation, or evaluation. Despite a few notable exceptions, local officials have tended to neglect the public aspects of their public-service mission.

Nor does it appear that general revenue sharing has channeled a fair share of its funds to the disadvantaged and minority communities. Only 3 percent of the money spent by localities has been channeled into social services for the poor and the aging. Even less has gone into housing, community development, and other programs for the disadvantaged. This is an indicator of the problem that these groups are apt to encounter at the local level in attempting to gain priority attention and service.

Since priorities will be determined increasingly by local officials, mostly through local political processes, those constituencies that exercise the least influence or power will have to organize more effectively to press their case. Where desirable and possible, they will want to join with other similar groups to form more powerful coalitions capable of winning local government attention and programs.

Neighborhood and community groups are therefore assuming new roles: monitoring state and local government programs and performance; assessing community needs as a vehicle for more responsive government action; analyzing and intervening in the local budgetary processes; pressing for governmental reform; and assuming more adequate mechanisms for broad citizen involvement in government affairs. In many cases these additional functions will require capable leadership, specialized skills, and greater resources.

It is ironic that at the very moment when community-based organizations are more needed than ever, they should find themselves more financially strapped. A great number of community groups are dying on the vine. Others have either gone out of existence or are lying dormant, hoping that the trickle of funds can be turned on again. Numerous organizational efforts have died because of a lack of money, while ongoing organizations have had to reduce their program and staff levels and, consequently, their effectiveness.

There are a number of reasons for this state of affairs. The federal government's decision to reduce substantially the direct funding of private nonprofit organizations has taken a heavy toll. The recession has limited the money available through foundations. Churches and unions do not have the funds available for local organizations that they once did. The corporate world, no longer faced by the prospects of rioting and ghetto rhetoric, appears to have retrenched and weakened its commitment to community organizations and change at the local level. And few United Way affiliates have shown much interest in supporting community-based, issue-oriented, and activist organizations or coalitions. Given their broad structure, they are likely to continue the emphasis on traditional social service agencies and the volunteerism of the old school.

The financial prospects for community organizations remain dim. Only the foundations, despite their financial plight, appear to be a promising potential source of money for community groups in the short run. This potential, however, is dependent on the likelihood that the foundations can and will change their priorities.

National Problems and the Need for National Organizations

A vital, effective network of community organizations, ranging from neighborhood groups to local Leagues of Women Voters to antipoverty agencies to better-government groups, will depend not only on adequate resources but also on regional and national support systems that can provide a continual flow of information, contracts, and technical assistance. Local organizations, particularly those concerned with public-policy issues and intervention, are insulated from what is happening in Washington and from legislative and departmental decisions shaping federal programs. They find it difficult, if not impossible, to keep in touch with community development and model programs in other communities.

The national support and technical-assistance organizations, unfortunately, are facing a financial crisis similar to that of their local affiliate groups. Many have had to reduce their budgets drastically. Others that were planning to expand their services to meet new needs have had to curb these plans.

The significance of national organizations is not limited to local groups or local public policies. They have had and will continue to have an important bearing on national policies and the federal government. Just as local governments will require careful watchdogging on the part of community groups, the federal government and its bureaucracies must be held in check by public scrutiny and voluntary organizations.

The record of national organizations active in monitoring the federal government and checking its abuses is already impressive. Civil rights organizations have successfully kept pressure on the government to promote equal opportunity in certain areas and redress discrimination in others. A coalition of private groups succeeded in 1971 in preserving OEO and community action, and is once again fighting to maintain an independent federal antipoverty agency. Another coalition, with the help of Congress, forced the Department of Health, Education and Welfare to modify its restrictive guidelines for social services. And a few national organizations have been successful in bringing the major problems inherent in general revenue sharing to the attention of policy makers and the general public. More, not fewer, national groups must be involved in this continuing effort to keep the federal government open and honest.

In their efforts to influence public policies and satisfy their clients, the national voluntary organizations are constrained by a major deterrent, the provision that 501(c)(3) organizations are prohibited from conducting substantial lobbying. Business, unions, and the federal government itself, however, may lobby without risk to their corporate status. The constituencies represented by nonprofit organizations have equal legitimacy and should be heard by the Congress in its deliberations. Until the Internal Revenue Code is amended to permit voluntary nonprofit organizations to use a satisfactory percentage of their resources (15 percent to 25 percent) for lobbying purposes, these organizations and their constituencies will continue to be discriminated against.

The Foundations and Their Priorities

Although the foundations appear to be the only likely source of immediate financial support for local community organizations and national groups concerned with public policies, their record indicates that they will have to change their priorities drastically to meet this challenge.

Traditionally, the foundations have channeled their funds into established national and local institutions, such as universities, research institutes, cultural and artistic groups, old-line agencies, and professional organizations. They have generally avoided grassroots, neighborhood, activist, and social change–oriented organizations, either low-income or middle-class. Their stress has been far more on safe, respectable projects than on the cutting-edge of public issues and policy. While innovators in research and technology, they have for the most part lagged behind on social and governance problems.

In the 1960s, with the upsurge of community action and the growth of community groups, a relative handful of foundations began to take an interest in community-based organizations and social change. But their numbers never grew appreciably, nor did their priorities rub off on the world of philanthropy. Possibly twenty to thirty foundations, most of them in the East, have borne the burden of supporting community-based organizations. When the amount of money granted by the Ford Foundation is subtracted from the total allocated to these groups and their support organizations, the limited foundation involvement becomes readily apparent.

Two of the most frequently given rationales for not supporting community organizations are the memory of the confrontation strategies of local groups in the 1960s and the constraints imposed by the Tax Reform Act of 1969. The first is based largely on a myth about what actually happened in the 1960s. While a few community organizations did take to the streets to protest social conditions, most of these in an orderly and legal way, the great majority of them went about their neighborhood or community business in a normal manner. It is too easy to characterize the few hell-raising groups as typical of the genre. Moreover, the 1970s bear little resemblance to the 1960s. Community organizations today have different strategies and styles from their earlier counterparts.

The Tax Reform Act, in proscribing political activities by grant recipients, have set some limits on foundation activities. Yet it in no way impedes foundations from giving money to the hundreds of community-based organizations that are not actively engaged in political efforts. Why, then, has it been so difficult for these groups to obtain funds? Why have the League of Women Voters Education Fund and its affiliates been so hard-pressed financially? Why have other middle-class organizations interested in social action and government reform had trouble getting financial support? One reason may well be that many foundations have used the Tax Reform Act to cloak their own priorities and interests. Most were not interested in community organizations, social change, and government affairs before the Act and have not changed their priorities since.

The New Federalism, as has been mentioned, has realigned the relationships and responsibilities between the three tiers of government. Its implementation will affect tax policies, civil rights enforcement, and the services provided for low-income and working-class people. It will help determine the direction and nature of development for the next decade. One might reasonably have expected the foundations to take a great interest in this development and to have tested the assumptions behind revenue-sharing programs and the decentralization of government authority. Little such interest has been exhibited. Once again the foundations find themselves in the rear guard rather than the vanguard of the nation's institutional development.

If the family and community foundations have been reluctant to finance projects revolving around public policy and social change, the corporate foundations appear to have established an even more unimpressive record. As the corporations' commitment to urban and community problems wanes, their foundations' policies can be expected to become more, not less, conservative.

The unrepresentative nature of the majority of foundation boards may be one of the major reasons for the foundations' priorities and posture. Heavily weighted toward corporate representatives and family members, foundation boards cannot be expected to reflect either a broad perspective of the country's interests and needs or a progressive view of social and economic change.

The staffs of many foundations also leave something to be desired. Many are selected for those cautious qualities reflected on the boards. Others are appointed because of their corporate or family ties. Few appear to have been activists, community organizers, union officials, or persons with real public policy experience.

If the foundations are to meet the challenge of the 1970s and 1980s, their boards and staffs will have to become more diversified and representative of the society at large. Organizations such as the Council on Foundations will have to accelerate their efforts to educate the foundations about their responsibilities and obligations. Public-interest groups and research organizations will need to focus critical attention on the foundations and enter into a dialogue with them.

The Responsibilities of Other Voluntary Organizations

The traditional role of the individual volunteer providing program service time will remain an important social contribution and outlet for personal commitment and energy. That role, however, should be continually subject to analysis and redefinition in order to meet the tests of relevance and high priority. In areas with high concentrations of poor and minorities, the demand for volunteers is likely to be limited to persons with specific skills in business, law, and accounting, or other necessary specialties. In these districts, as well as in urban areas in general, the emphasis may be placed on group action rather than on individual service, on the need to work with and through powerful neighborhood or community organizations that can successfully influence public policies and equalize the distribution of resources. For such organizations, volunteers may prove most useful in soliciting support, both financial and political. More and more volunteers will want to turn from applying Band-Aids to the symptoms to attempting to change the system itself.

National organizations like the National Center for Voluntary Action and the United Way and community umbrella organizations, such as the local United Ways and Voluntary Action Centers, have a responsibility to help redefine the role of volunteers. They must help channel the energies of millions of Americans to meet changing societal requirements.

All too many local United Ways have not adapted to modern times. The funds they distribute are often not directed at their communities' gravest problems or to the neediest, most meritorious organizations. A large number are still reluctant to take on the most pressing public issues, even though these issues directly affect their client populations. More responsible and aggressive leadership will be required if the United Way organizations are to be a significant local force for progressive change.

The universities and colleges have a dismal record as providers of community resources and services. Endowed with a plentiful supply of trained researchers and student workers, the universities have the skilled manpower voluntary organizations are seeking. Their new rhetoric of community involvement and public service has not been matched by any collective commitment to action from the administration, faculty or, indeed, student level. At the very moment when they are most needed to provide community services, they are either unprepared or unwilling to respond to the challenge.

In general, the great majority of educational institutions have only involved themselves in community-related activities when they were well compensated to do so. The excuse for the "involvement only if paid" approach has been that universities are experiencing budget difficulties and that extra commitments require additional resources. This lame rationale is difficult to accept. Whether professors work with community groups, students become involved in social issues, or administrators encourage public service from the university are not matters of available dollars or additional resources. They depend instead upon educational values, institutional commitment and quality of leadership. A university or college has the right to decide if a professor's obligation stops with teaching and research or if it goes beyond these tasks to the needs of the community and society in general.

A good number of the problems reflected in the policies and practices of voluntary organizations, whether they are universities, local United Ways, or national organizations, can be traced to their board composition and board involvement. Like foundations, many universities and other institutions have trustees who are unrepresentative of the community at large, representing instead certain established interests. Such representation tends to cultivate caution and conservatism and to limit the fresh air injected into policy deliberations.

Frequently, the board members are trustees in name only. They may be too busy or uninterested, or they may be selected only for their reputation and prestige. Policy making and the affairs of the institution are left entirely in the hands of professional administrators, and the potential for intelligent lay direction and performance evaluation is thereby lost. There is a saying in Washington that the most unaccountable persons in town are the staff directors of the private national organizations. This could just as easily be said of many other administrators in the voluntary sector throughout the country. Until their boards are truly active and functional, these organizations will find it difficult to exercise the influence and produce the results we have come to expect.

Relationship Between the Private and Public Sectors

There has always been an element of tension and uncertainty in the relationship between the voluntary and public sectors. The voluntary sector has acted as a check on governmental excess and corruption, while the public sector has regulated the broad framework within which the voluntary sector has operated. This difficult but productive relationship must continue, particularly in view of the dangers inherent in the New Federalism.

There should, however, be a better understanding of what the voluntary sector can and cannot do as well as of the financial problems it can be expected to experience. It is clear, for example, that the economy may prevent philanthropy from raising its expenditure level over the next few years. Foundations, United Ways, and other institutions, therefore, will be forced to choose between maintaining their present priorities or, in order to move in new directions, transferring some of these responsibilities to public bodies.

As a general rule, philanthropic organizations should retain or adopt those programs and issues that cannot or should not be sponsored by governments. The arts and culture, for example, are receiving growing support from federal and state government agencies. Their activities should properly be considered an element of public education to be funded through public funds. There will thus be a decreasing need for foundations to support orchestras, ballets, and cultural institutes, thereby releasing funds for other purposes.

Having divested themselves of these projects, foundations will be in a better position to meet the challenge of supporting public issues development, community-based organizations and their national support groups, social change experiments, and the monitoring of government performance. For these are responsibilities that governments cannot undertake and with which they should not be entrusted. Science and technology are other activities that could and should receive greater government support and be less dependent on philanthropy, as long as steps are taken to ensure that such basic research will not be subjected to arbitrary political influence.

While citizens and voluntary organizations will have to bear most of the responsibility for holding local government accountable and for the development of public issues, governments should be expected, regardless of their party and philosophy, to put the New Federalism to the test by establishing effective mechanisms for citizen involvement in local planning, program operations, and evaluation.

If this is to be done, the federal government will have to take a strong initiative that it has so far been reluctant to take. Instead of reducing citizen involvement in federal programming, it will have to increase it substantially. If this does not happen, the gap between the voluntary and public sectors will grow, and dissatisfaction and despair with our public institutions will continue to grow dangerously. Guarantees of citizen involvement in government processes will not be sufficient to give many Americans equal opportunities to obtain their piece of the economic and social pie. Community action programs and community economic development corporations (CDCs) have successfully served as institutional vehicles for access to goods, services, leadership training and jobs previously denied to poor, working poor, and minority communities. They must be continued and strengthened, not undermined or eliminated.

Community action agencies and CDCs and related agencies, though funded by the federal government, remain one of the largest voluntary networks in the country. Over 200,000 persons, many of them poor with no previous record of community involvement, are serving on their boards and committees as unpaid volunteers. They deserve support from the voluntary sector. It is ironic that so little support for them has come from two organizations that are in the forefront of the voluntary sector movement, the United Way and National Center for Voluntary Action.

2

A Critique of the Philanthropic Process

OVERVIEW

The Filer Commission: A Critical Perspective

From Grantsmanship Center News, *December–January 1975*
This article helped prompt the Commission on Private Philanthropy and Public
Needs to pay special attention to the nonprofit groups. The commission was headed
by John H. Filer, an insurance company executive.

The Filer Commission on Private Philanthropy and Public Needs is likely to raise many more questions than it can answer by the time it issues a final report.

Many of these will be focused on the process of the study itself. What is the Filer Commission? Who sits on its board? What are its purpose and approach? From where does its financial support come? Who has conducted its research and analysis? What organizations, groups and constituencies have been involved? How effectively has the public's opinion been sought?

The nature, composition, and work of the Commission is little known throughout the country. Its outreach to those individuals, organizations and groups most involved in the future of philanthropy and the voluntary sector appears to have been minimal thus far. For a national commission studying public needs, this seeming lack of concern for an involvement with the public would seem to be a serious omission. It could undermine the accuracy and credibility of the Commission's findings.

Other questions will be directed more at the substance and relevancy of the research. What has been the study's major emphasis? Has the analysis of public needs received adequate attention? In what ways has the relationship between the public and voluntary sectors changed? Has volunteerism been redefined to meet changing socioeconomic needs? Have the priorities and impact of voluntary and philanthropic organizations been analyzed and evaluated? What organizations or individuals have been asked to do this research?

Information issued by the Commission itself indicates that the overwhelming amount of the Commission's resources, effort and time have been devoted to the analysis of philanthropic giving, the use of tax incentives, and strategies for increasing voluntary-sector funding. The inquiry, in short, is heavily weighted toward how and where money is raised. Very little research and energy apparently have been allocated to how effectively and equitably the money is distributed and spent. The questions, "Who gets what?" "What are the priorities of foundations and voluntary organizations?" and "Do current conditions meet society's changing needs?" have been either played down or largely ignored.

Only one-half of the voluntary sector–private philanthropy picture, therefore, is receiving substantial scrutiny. To put it another way, the donors of philanthropy have been stressed at the expense of recipients of philanthropy and the general public. Since an accurate assessment of the future direction of private philanthropy and public needs is dependent on both groups, the neglect of one is bound to have a significant influence on the outcome of the study.

If the Filer Commission were just another committee whose work and recommendations were slated for oblivion, there would be little need for public anxiety and concern. Its report would probably die a natural death on the unused shelves that line the offices and libraries of foundations, private organizations, government bureaus and the Congress. The Commission, however, is not just another committee. Its origin, composition, and support give some assurance that it will exercise a good deal of influence on future legislation and on the way policy makers view the voluntary sector and public needs.

Created in the fall of 1973 to launch "a broad-range, in-depth study of philanthropy, its relationship to government and its role in American society," the Commission is the baby of John D. Rockefeller III. It has received the encouragement of Wilbur Mills, chairman of the House Ways and Means Committee, ex–Treasury Secretary George P. Shultz, and the current Secretary of the Treasury, William Simon. Its director of research is Gabriel G. Rudney, a federal employee who is currently on leave of absence from his job as assistant director of the Office of Tax Analysis at the Department of the Treasury. It has also distributed over $1.1 million for research to a large number of prestigious academic institutions, research institutes, law firms, national organizations and individual consultants.

Equally significant is the fact that the Commission is today the only major public, quasi-public, or private body that is conducting what is supposed to be a broad, comprehensive study of private philanthropy and the voluntary sector. There is no potential competitor in the field. Its findings and recommendations are therefore likely to be taken seriously by those institutions, public and private, that have a responsibility for the future of the voluntary sector and are searching for information and guidance on which to base their decisions.

The composition of the Commission may help explain the emphasis and direction of the study to date. Contrary to the claim of one of its brochures, it does not represent Americans from all walks of life. It reflects very disproportionately the establishment side of both the voluntary sector and philanthropic organizations. Of the board's thirty-two members, twelve are corporate officials. At least another three have come from and have close ties to the corporate community. In contrast, one member comes from unions, while only two represent the religious community. There are no representatives from Spanish-speaking or Native American organizations, from community-based or grass-roots organizations, from neighborhood groups or from local social agencies. Nor do the ecology, consumer, and good-government movements have any representation. With two exceptions, the board has no members from national or local organizations that can be said to be primarily concerned with public issues and social change.

The Commission's advisory committee of over eighty members appears no more representative. The large majority are academics, lawyers, and professional consultants. A great many members are, in fact, paid consultants to the Commission, thereby raising some question about their value as independent advisors to the study.

The way in which over $1.1 million has been distributed for technical studies and research projects may also merit some critical analysis. Only a small portion of this amount is apparently earmarked for studies that will assess the effectiveness and relevancy of the current priorities and programs of philanthropy and the voluntary sector. Over 40 percent of all the funds have been channeled into two surveys of individuals and families concerning charitable and philanthropic activities and attitudes. The Conference Board, a research and trade association for the corporate community, has been given money to study corporate giving, its motivation and means of encouragement. Unless it is accompanied by other studies of corporate philanthropy and voluntary activity from different perspectives, it is likely to present an unbalanced picture of the corporate world.

A similar observation can be made about the $26,800 granted to the United Way of America for a study of volunteer services in the United States. If this is the only research commissioned on the role and future of volunteerism, the Commission may be in danger of reflecting the bias of the United Way and of ignoring other, equally important views.

The draft of the research study submitted to the Commission, moreover, calls into serious question the perspective on volunteerism of both the Commission and the United Way. The paper is limited to an assessment of the quantity of volunteer hours generated by local United Ways, based on short questionnaires returned from 184 local chapters. Considerations such as the quality of performance, the significance of the activity and the nature of the process have been totally ignored. Ostensibly a serious statement on volunteerism, possibly the only one to be contributed to the Commission, the study in its preliminary form is of dubious relevance and not worth the money allocated to it.

Who will look at the foundation world, its direction, priorities and problems? The Council on Foundations, a trade association representing the larger and some of the more progressive foundations, was asked by the Commission to submit a paper on the role and responsibilities of foundations in philanthropy. While the views of the Council will be an important and necessary contribution, they must be supplemented by other concerns and perspectives if a comprehensive and balanced picture of the foundation world is to be painted.

At least five of the nine basic areas marked for study and analysis by the Commission revolve around such issues as the relationship between the governmental and voluntary sectors, the adaptation of private philanthropy to changing social needs and the distribution of private resources among competing groups and organizations. Yet, despite this official concern, the Commission does not appear to have concentrated much of its effort on these essentially public functions of the voluntary sector. The distribution of its own resources, the limited perspectives it has tried to encompass and the relatively few contacts it has had with private national and local organizations would seem to indicate a traditional reliance on established institutions and views and an unwillingness or inability to tackle the tough problems of a changing society that is calling for major, often radical, changes in institutional behavior.

If the Filer Commission cannot or will not meet this challenge, it will have missed a unique opportunity to provide philanthropy and the voluntary sector with the information and framework they need to chart their future direction. It will have ignored a large part of what its original mission apparently was all about.

~

Vision of Philanthropy:
The Challenge to Foundation Trustees

*From a speech delivered to the annual meeting of trustees of the
Northern California Grantmakers, March 8, 1988. He spoke to the same
group in 1996, a speech that is excerpted on page 48.*

If there is one national characteristic that has distinguished our society from all others and has been the key to the preservation of our democratic institutions and pluralism, it has been the existence of a strong and unique nonprofit sector, fueled by private and institutional philanthropy. It has been an essential feature of our societal system of checks and balances, serving as a bulwark against the potential tyranny of both government and the majority. It has been a breeding ground for leadership. It has served as an instrument for necessary social and economic change. And the nonprofit sector has kept alive the American traditions of the public interest and volunteerism.

Today, unfortunately, our nonprofit sector faces problems and pressures unprecedented in its history.

The federal domestic budget cuts since 1981 have cost the nonprofit sector some $35 billion to $45 billion in losses, thereby weakening the programs of many organizations and causing many to go out of business. Disproportionately hurt have been those nontraditional organizations serving the poor, minorities, and other disadvantaged groups.

These enormous losses have not been replaced by private-sector financing. They never could have. Yet, the expectations placed on the private sector, either unconsciously or by commission, have soared, creating a huge gap between what many people want the private sector to do and what realistically the latter can accomplish.

The change in values over the past decade, with the new stress on money, "making it," and individual as opposed to community responsibilities, has tended to lower the status of nonprofit activities and made it more difficult for us collectively to forge a spirit of national unity based on social and economic justice.

Nonprofit organizations are experiencing difficulty in attracting the best and brightest of our young people. Nonprofit salaries and benefits are no longer competing with for-profit organizations and even government. In these tough times, financially and organizationally, many of the nonprofit sector's most effective people have left or are leaving.

Under fiscal pressures, a number of nonprofits are seeking desperately to become more self-sufficient and entrepreneurial, sometimes losing in the process the sense of mission for which they were originally established. The distinction between for-profit and nonprofit organizations is becoming cloudier, creating the risk that idealism and the sense of the public interest may be weakened or lost.

The threat to the health and vitality of the nonprofit sector during the coming decade poses an enormous challenge to philanthropy, to the way it does its business, to its capacity to change priorities and expand its vision. Our society's problems, and those of its nonprofit sector, have become so complex and demanding that philanthropy's past performance will not be good enough for the future. Philanthropy will have to spend its scarce dollars much more wisely and with much greater impact.

The Lack of Vision

In thinking about the challenges before us, I was struck again by the wise words of Benjamin Mays:

> It must be borne in mind that the tragedy of life doesn't lie in not reaching your goal. It lies in having no goal to reach. It is not a calamity to die with dreams unfilled, but it is a calamity not to dream. It is not a disgrace not to reach the stars, but it is a disgrace not to have any stars to reach. Not failure, but low aim, is the real sin.

If there is one overall criticism that I would make of American philanthropy, it is that it has lacked vision, a sense of its vast possibilities, its unlimited potential for helping to make our society a better and more just place for all our citizens. American philanthropy has aimed much too low and achieved far too little. It has, in a real sense, had far too few failures.

While its successes have been considerable, it has been, in general, lackluster, relatively safe, and not particularly innovative or experimental, except perhaps in the fields of science, medicine and, to a certain extent, education. Its burden of risk-taking has been shared by only a relative handful of donors.

Meeting Urgent Public Needs

Another area where philanthropy has not met its promise is in its failure to exercise its fundamental responsibility for meeting our society's most urgent public needs in a way that supports our democratic principles and institutions. Since the Filer Commission study (the informal name for the National Commission on Private Philanthropy and Public Needs) over a decade ago, we have come to accept this notion of the purpose of philanthropy, a purpose that is premised on a public obligation in return for the tax benefits conferred on donor institutions. Reflected in this concept is the view that philanthropy should do what governments cannot do, that it is positioned to try the new and untested without the constraints of bureaucracies and pressure groups and that it can and should provide the leadership for the changes that must come as our society develops and becomes more complex and difficult to manage.

Unfortunately, little attention has been paid to this critical issue, what I would call the public needs test of philanthropic relevance.

What are our most urgent and important public needs? The answer is neither obvious nor simple. What is clear is that social and economic conditions change; our most pressing problems are not those that existed thirty or forty years ago. Those changes, therefore, need to be reflected in the priorities of our foundations and corporations. Perhaps the key measure of a donor's success will be the extent to which it will have addressed those critical issues on which our national future and welfare depended.

When looking at much of philanthropy, I am reminded of Oscar Wilde's description of English country gentlemen galloping across the fields after foxes: "The unspeakable in full pursuit of the inedible." Translated into the philanthropoid's [a colloquialism for foundation officials] idiom, it could be stated as "the well-intentioned in full pursuit of the not so relevant."

Consider some of the country's most serious, current challenges. We have huge budget deficits and trade imbalances. Some of our economic institutions are not working effectively. The level of poverty in the country is higher than in 1980, and the gulf between the "haves" and the "have nots" has widened. By any reasonable definition of poverty, probably one-quarter of our population lacks the resources, opportunities, and support to "make it" in our society. We have a large homeless population and many more who are hungry. Many state and local governments are not functioning effectively: though they have more authority and power than ever before, they lack the capacity to govern well and are, in many cases, largely unaccountable.

Our rural areas remain depressed. There are troubling ethical and leadership problems among those who govern our public and private institutions. Self-help, bootstraps efforts, especially among our neediest constituencies, are dying for want of money. Americans are increasingly alienated from the electoral and political process. And there is growing concern about the way American foreign policy is implemented.

When we begin to identify these public concerns, we see that there is a serious mismatch with current philanthropic priorities. Very little money is being channeled into these vital areas of concern. While we need to respect the pluralism of giving, we should also be aware and disturbed that philanthropy, in the aggregate, is not meeting these urgent public needs. It is not preparing our country for its future. Is philanthropy being true to the public needs test? How can its performance in this respect be improved?

One specific response to this latter question is that, at a minimum, every foundation and corporation has the responsibility, indeed the obligation, of undertaking a serious process of reassessing its priorities on a regular basis in light of our most urgent public needs. Such a process should draw on the perspectives and resources of the community as well as on the views of the trustees and staff. This is a real challenge to philanthropy, for, to date, relatively few donor institutions have committed themselves to a disciplined reassessment of the extent to which their priorities are in line with perceived urgent public needs.

Unresolved Ethical Problems

A third reason for philanthropy's inability to fulfill its potential is its failure to resolve some serious ethical problems that determine the quality and fairness of its grant making. I am not referring to such matters as payments to trustees or conflict of interest issues among staff and board, although these questions are not insignificant. Of far greater consequence, in my view, are practices that affect the operation of the nonprofit community—for example, how grantees are selected, how they are treated, and how they are evaluated. A couple of examples:

The Neglect of the Poor

Every major national leader since Franklin D. Roosevelt has talked about the nation's urgent need to end poverty. Yet the persistence and enormity of the problem continues to undermine our democracy, to undercut our leadership internationally, and to waste the potential talent of one-quarter of our population.

Historically, philanthropy's response to poverty has been benign neglect. After the drastic domestic budget cuts of 1981, the growing holes in the safety net for the disadvantaged and the increased call for private-sector involvement, one might have expected a sizeable shift in philanthropic priorities. A number of foundations and corporations did slightly increase their contributions to the poor. On the whole, however, this increase was minimal. The poor, minorities, the disabled, women, and other disadvantaged constituencies are still receiving a shamefully small part of philanthropic resources. And, of this amount, very little goes to those organizing, capacity building, and advocacy efforts that are the key to real self-help and self-development. Often, capital expenditures continue while human needs go begging.

In a democracy, with its principles of individual dignity and social and economic justice, can philanthropy afford to continue to give so little to such a large number of the neediest in our society? Is it ethical for philanthropy to continue its neglect of the poor and the powerless?

The Double Standard

Probably nothing is so frustrating and infuriating to donees as the double standard by which many nontraditional organizations are judged much more rigorously according to higher standards than some of their more traditional or establishment counterparts. Let me give you an example.

Several years ago in a large metropolitan area, a popular amphitheater, located in the suburbs and catering largely to affluent city dwellers and suburbanites, burned to the ground. Without asking any serious questions about the nonprofit owning and managing the theater—for example, how accountable was the board, were there any major structural defects in the building—donors and the federal government mounted a massive fund-raising campaign which brought in millions of dollars in a very short period of time. Every major foundation, corporation, and individual donor, as well as the federal government, gave large sums of money without assessing whether the theater corporation was well run or accountably.

At the same time, a number of grassroots organizations serving poor and other disadvantaged families in the same metropolitan area could not raise a dime from many of these same donors, although their leadership, management, and programs were of the highest quality.

Many nonestablishment groups have been told by donors that in hard financial times they must become leaner, tougher, and more effective, yet we find that these arguments are frequently not applied to establishment organizations. Why should a fourth-rate orchestra, ballet, or museum be funded when it's so difficult to support first-rate community groups or alternative service agencies? Is there an inherent right for some organizations to exist and not others?

Excellence, it seems to me, has to be the standard for grant makers, whether the donors are dealing with establishment or nonestablishment groups. To do otherwise is to be unethical and, in the long run, to undermine the nonprofit sector itself.

These are only two examples of the ethical dilemmas philanthropy faces. You might add others: the lack of access to donor institutions by nontraditional nonprofits; the reluctance of donors to provide general operating support when such funding is crucial to the operations and integrity of nonprofit groups; the arrogance of some donors and the poor treatment often accorded to grant recipients; and the giving of general support to United Ways that are fighting to maintain their monopoly over solicitation at the workplace. Whatever their nature, these problems limit philanthropy's capacity to be equitable and more productive.

The Insularity of Philanthropy

The fourth area of weakness has been philanthropy's insularity and lack of public accountability. Although these characteristics have helped some donor institutions act constructively without public or political pressures, they have also lent an ivory tower quality to grant making, removed from the reality and complexity of community problems and the donee world. Small staffs and the limited time available to trustees have placed additional barriers to the donors' outreach. But probably the greatest obstacle to philanthropy's remaining in touch with the community and with current critical issues has been its relationship with the donee world.

For the most part that relationship has been one between beggars and givers, not one between equal partners in the philanthropic process. Because of this perceived imbalance of power, donors and donees generally communicate or meet only over the immediacy of a pending grant. The result is that a vital link to communities and the real world has been continually ignored by funding institutions. If donors would begin to deal with donees in solving problems outside the grant-making process, they would gain a much better sense of the major issues and problems confronting the community or country.

The traditional narrowness of many foundation boards and corporate contributions committees has not helped donors bridge the communications gap between philanthropic institutions and the rest of the community. While there has been a good deal of progress during the past ten years in adding minority, female, and non-family members to foundation boards, these additions have tended to come from a pool of professional elites. Where are the teachers, union members, social service workers and grassroots organizational representatives who, while not necessarily well known publicly, could provide perspectives and ideas that would significantly broaden and enrich the philanthropic decision making process?

The Challenge to Trustees

The four areas of philanthropic weakness that I have outlined pose a stiff challenge to donor institutions, to their staff and, particularly, to the trustees.

From where is the vision, the sense of possibilities, the excitement and the energy to come? I believe it can come—perhaps can only come—from the involvement, commitment, inspiration and hard work of trustees. Just as war is too dangerous to leave to the generals, philanthropy is too important to delegate entirely to professional staff. The latter will require leadership and support of trustees, as well as their ideas and criticism.

Developing a vision implies a commitment to try the untested and to risk failure. Some of the most urgent public needs I mentioned will have to be tackled. This will require some changes, in many cases some very difficult and often painful changes. Foundations, for example, will have to overcome their anxiety about dealing with governments if they are to confront the critical issues of local government reform and public accountability. They may have to create new mechanisms if the needs of rural areas are to be met. They will have to risk the objections of established professions and groups to initiate significant institutional reforms. The courage, support, and leadership of trustees will be essential for such innovation and experimentation. It cannot be done by staff alone.

Many of the ethical problems created by donors stem from the arrogance, poor judgment, and errors of omission of staff members. To counter this behavior, trustees will have to become more involved in evaluating staff performance on a regular basis and in exercising their oversight responsibilities as board members. Trustees have many resources they can call on to do this effectively. The perspectives and comments of donees, would-be donees, and community representatives could help trustees get a better overview of how well their donor institutions are run and perceived. Trustees must assume, if they have not already, a major role in the governance of their foundation- or corporate-contributions committee to insure that their priorities and policies are faithfully and effectively carried out.

And if the communications gap between donors and donees is to be bridged, trustees must become part of this new philanthropic partnership. It will not be enough for staff to interact more frequently with the community. Associations of grant makers will need to structure forums and exchanges between trustees, staff, donee representatives, and community people. Trustees will need to hear directly the views and recommendations of community constituencies. If this is not done, the we–they status between donors and donees, between donors and community, will be perpetuated.

Beyond Grant Making

Foundations and corporate donors are known and respected, or in a few cases disliked, for their grant making and little else. Almost all view their jobs as ending with the grant-making process. Is it surprising, then, that institutional philanthropy appears to have produced so few community or national leaders?

I, for one, believe that there is an important role for philanthropy beyond grant making. Because of the mystique it enjoys in many parts of the community, it has status and the respect of many. Its opinions would be carefully considered and its leadership would draw serious attention, if not always a following. It has the power to bring various community players together at the discussion or bargaining table. In this drawing power lies its potential for great community leadership.

If there is any missing element in our democratic system, with all its factions, interest groups, and government bodies, it is, ironically, the absence of common ground where such groups can meet to discuss mutual problems, stratagems and solutions, free of current conflict and impeding crises. Just as there is little or no common ground between donors and donees, there is often none between local governments and their citizens, between corporations and public interest groups, between various sectors of the nonprofit world. It is a void philanthropy can fill effectively.

As neutral conveners, donor institutions could make certain that the most significant issues are debated, and the discussions disseminated to as broad an audience as possible. Public educator, convener, catalyst, gadfly—these are the roles that are tailor-made for philanthropists. They are roles that go beyond grant making but could turn out to be much more significant than the giving of money.

The next few years could be exciting times for a philanthropy geared for change. But, as Benjamin Mays might have said, you must aim higher and have many more failures. Many years ago, G. B. Shaw captured the purpose and hope of philanthropy when he said, "If you live in the world of ideals, you will absorb some of their beauty. If you live in a world of facts, you will absorb some of their brutality. How I wish for a world in which facts were not brutal and ideals were not dreams."

∼

Philanthropy Under Fire:
How Foundations Should Respond

*From a speech delivered to the Northern California Grantmakers in San Francisco,
January 29, 1996. Mr. Eisenberg reflects on what has changed and what has not
since he spoke to the same organization in 1988 (see article on page 40.)*

Lately philanthropic institutions have exhibited a good deal of anxiety and concern about the growing criticism of the field in magazines, the media and by donee groups. In my view, this is the healthiest development that could have happened to the foundation world. Sunshine, analysis, and criticism, either from outside sources or from within, are the precursors of constructive change. For too long, the world of philanthropy has lacked these ingredients. Now, you will have to respond both to your critics and to your problems.

As public resources diminish, at least in the short run, increased attention will be focused on private resources. Criticism of the philanthropic sector will grow. Some of it will be sound and fair; some will be unfair and potentially damaging. Whatever its nature, I hope the response of philanthropy will not be defensive. It will be neither wise nor effective to draw the wagons in a circle in a state of siege. It is a time to listen to the message and not try to kill the messenger. Nor is it a time for effusive "mea culpas." What is called for is serious introspection, hard analysis, and an openness to real changes in the way you do business.

Lack of Intellectual Ferment in Philanthropy

The major reason that there has been so little introspection, self-criticism, and self-reform by foundations is that there has been almost no intellectual ferment in the philanthropic sector. In no other sector that I know of has there been so little concern for standards, performance, innovation, achievement, and change as in philanthropy. There has been little serious, internal debate among philanthropic colleagues and, certainly, no willingness to get any feedback from the donee world or the public. In the fields of education, health, and even business, professionals and lay people argue about ideas, criticize their peers, and conduct studies about their work all the time.

Not so in philanthropy, which seems to be a tight little island where collegiality has become a highly developed art form. There appears to be an unspoken rule that foundations should not be critical of one another, that a practitioner should be concerned only about his or her institution, and that there should be no questioning of the fundamental assumptions that govern the way philanthropy does its business. It may be a cozy and comfortable oasis but one that can yield little vision or change.

This atmosphere has been reflected in the Council on Foundations and all but a few of the regional associations of grant makers, entities which have behaved primarily as boosters and cheerleaders for the field, not as serious promoters of new ideas, higher standards, philanthropic innovation, and catalytic initiatives. They have not even made the effort to bridge the wide chasm in communications between donors on the one hand and donees and the public on the other, something that might bring greater reality and urgency to philanthropic priority-setting.

One of the causes for the inability of the Council and the regional associations to transcend their function of trade association, as well as for the lack of intellectual vigor in the field, has been the failure of foundation leadership, especially the heads of the large foundations. The latter's focus has been inward, that is, on their own operations, not on the interests of the sector as a whole. Most have played little or no part in the affairs of the Council or the regional associations. Look at the attendance record of regional association meetings and see how many heads of major foundations have been present and active.

In a strange way, the absence of major foundation leaders from these proceedings has created a peculiar caste structure within foundations, already viewed as elite in nature. The generals meet with their little cliques but rarely with the soldiers who do the work. Not good for morale nor for the notion of teamwork. And certainly not conducive to the development of a vision for the field. It is time that the heads of major foundations exercise their leadership responsibilities.

The Lack of Vision

The absence of intellectual ferment and critical self-examination is, I believe, what has created a "vision" problem for much, if not most, of philanthropy. Some years ago when I spoke at a similar meeting of the Northern California Grantmakers, I said that philanthropy had no vision or, at best, only a fuzzy notion of what it should do, where it wanted to go and how it could get there. In my view this is still true. At that time I mentioned many urgent social, economic, and governmental needs that had not been seriously addressed by the foundation community, including issues of poverty, the economy, and government performance. This is still the case.

With the exception of a small number of conservative foundations, which have a clear vision and know what they want to do, many of our large and midsized foundations fret about appearing "balanced" and nonpartisan, concerned about being perceived as political, intimidated by the possibility of some sort of retribution. Such a timid approach can only lead to a paralysis of vision, not to any solution of our urgent public needs. If our mainstream foundations are to be as effective as their conservative counterparts, they will have to develop a clear vision and goals.

If some, for example, want to attack and help reduce poverty, then they will have to promote the activism, self-help programs, research, organizing, and advocacy required to bring about this goal, regardless of how some people view these strategies. The commitment and focus must be on the vision and goals, not on the perception of "balance." And so it should be with other goals such as strengthening government and public accountability or the development of a sound and more equitable economy. Of course, there may be a few risks, but then isn't that what philanthropy is supposed to be all about?

This is a time for visionaries, not managers; a time for risk-takers, not the faint-hearted; and a time for goal-oriented programmers, not timid and conservative legal advisers.

The Need for Diversity

Conservatives and critics have attacked mainstream philanthropy for its trendiness and political correctness, as well as for its emphasis on diversity. While there is some truth in the former, there is no truth in the latter. The growing diversity in philanthropy is one of its greatest strengths and the promise of philanthropic renewal. It is the quality that will keep philanthropy in touch with the realities of our society, that will produce the public support it needs and that will tap the widest pool of human resources required for effective grant making. It is the ingredient in the makeup of both foundation trustees and staff that is essential for the nurturing of vision. What the foundation world needs is more, not less, diversity.

When I speak of diversity, however, I want to emphasize that this notion goes beyond race and gender. Over the past decade, there has been a notable and commendable increase in the number of people of color and women on foundation boards and staff. Unfortunately, this development has not always improved the direction and quality of grant making. The overwhelming number of newer board members who are women or people of color comes from the same elite pool of successful professionals and wealthy persons as their white male counterparts. What has been lacking in philanthropy, especially boards of directors, has been people representing a diversity of class and what I would call, for want of better terminology, temperament.

Take a look at foundation boards. Where do you find the teachers, social

workers, neighborhood and community leaders, ministers, artists, union members, and officials and small-business representatives? The answer: in very few
institutions. They are the very people who can best provide a sense of community problems, needs, and desires that philanthropy requires to be grounded
and relevant. They could and should play an essential role in developing a philanthropic vision.

So, too, could people who are diverse by what I have called temperament.
Too many foundation boards—not to mention corporate-contribution committees—are polite, clubby, and overly collegial groups, and not only because
of their class makeup. They prize the qualities of cordiality, getting along, and
restraint. They are uncomfortable with aggressively inquisitive minds, individuals who want to push new frontiers or who like spirited debate and questioning. Such people tend to be viewed as potentially troublesome and disloyal. Yet
they are the ones desperately needed by foundation boards in search of a mission and goals.

The same is true for staff. Too many seem to have been selected because
they are smart, credentialed, or a specialist in a given area, fit in with established
philanthropic procedures and won't create too many "waves." What Peter Frumkin [a faculty member who specializes in nonprofit affairs at Harvard Univer-
sity] has called "careerism" reaffirms their caution and lack of innovative
juices. What we need are program officers with imagination and courage as
well as an understanding of what communities and their institutions require.

The Response to Recent Social and Political Developments

It is precisely because so much of philanthropy has lacked a vision or point of
view about what it wants to achieve that many foundations to date have failed to
respond to the enormous changes that a conservative Congress and a rudder-
less [Clinton] administration have initiated.

Severe domestic program cuts and measures to balance the budget have
fallen disproportionately on the backs of low-income and other disadvantaged
constituencies. The federal system of government is undergoing massive transformation. Our tax policies are under assault by many who want to lessen the
burden on wealthy Americans. And drastic cuts in foreign aid are making it
difficult for us to maintain our global responsibilities. These and many others
are major public needs that have to be addressed. Yet philanthropy for the past
year and a half has remained on the sidelines wondering what it can or should
do. Where has it been?

For most foundations, it has been business as usual. Only a handful have
reassessed public needs, changed their priorities, or taken any action. Very few

even have bothered to consult with or listen to their donees or other nonprofits in the field.

Why has this happened? Foundations have given a number of reasons. These include: "We need to wait and see what happens"; "we don't know yet exactly what is going on"; "it takes us a long time to change gears"; and "we just have to continue to support our current donees with our limited resources."

For poor and disadvantaged people, for nonprofits that are hurting financially while experiencing greater demands from their constituents and for the general public that expects more from a privileged philanthropic sector, these answers aren't good enough. They don't justify inertia, paralysis, or inaction in the face of national crises. If neighborhoods and communities, nonprofits, and citizen groups know what to do, why don't foundations and other donors? Are they not listening, or don't they want to hear?

Part of the answer is that many foundations do know what is needed but are unwilling to take such steps. They do not like or are afraid of supporting organizing, activism, public-policy activities, and advocacy. They are much more comfortable with research and services. They often rationalize their unwillingness to promote action by citing administrative or procedural obstacles to such funding: "It's not our priority; we can't make small grants"; "our trustees don't like coalitions"; "such grants are hard to evaluate."

But part of the reason—I suspect the large part—is that many foundations are set in concrete, wedded to priorities, practices, and bureaucratic procedures that make it difficult for them to develop a vision, respond quickly to changing public needs, provide flexible grant making and avoid bureaucratic habits.

New Way of Doing Business

Behind much of grant making is a fundamental premise, perhaps largely unconscious, that impedes philanthropy from changing the way it does business. It is that donees or would-be donees must fit into the existing structure and procedures of foundations irrespective of the latter's appropriateness of relevance to the nonprofit world. It is a premise that says "do it my way or not at all." It is as though philanthropy exists for its own sake rather than for the communities and nonprofit groups it is intended to serve. The means have become an end in itself. This is not a real partnership between donors and donees. In a real sense, philanthropy remains a modern day version of noblesse oblige.

If foundations are to meet the test of philanthropic relevance, address society's most important issues in timely fashion, and provide what nonprofit organizations need to do their job, they will have to rethink and change the way they do business and relate to their grantees and would-be grantees. The following, in my view, are seven areas of philanthropic practice that require some serious modification.

1. Foundation agendas almost entirely determined by fixed program areas and budgets. Such categorical agendas with little or no discretionary funds hamstring foundation responses to major situations, crosscutting program efforts, new innovative approaches, emergency needs and targets of opportunity.

2. Lack of administrative mechanisms and the will to support important programs and organizations, such as small grants to local community groups, capacity-building grants to rural areas, or support to philanthropically underserved geographic areas.

3. Reluctance to provide what every nonprofit organization most needs: general support funds.

4. Unwillingness of foundations to increase their payout in grants, especially in times of crisis or scarce public resources. If the Federal Reserve Bank can adjust the interest rate to meet the needs of the economy, what is so sacrosanct about the 5 percent–payout requirement for foundations that, since operating costs are included, turns out to be under 4 percent in grants for a number of large foundations?

5. Failure of philanthropic institutions to maintain continual serious communication with the nonprofit world, except around the grant process, a process that actually distorts what little relationship exists.

6. Difficulty of acting in a timely way to crisis situations and to the changing needs of nonprofit groups. Administrative and procedural changes will be required.

7. Bureaucratic inefficiencies and arrogance in treating donees and would-be donees, making life unnecessarily complicated and painful for nonprofits. These actions range from rudeness and bad manners, to manipulation and control of grantees, to overly bureaucratic procedures, to a lack of sensitivity to the urgent financial needs of nonprofits.

With the help of nonprofit groups and the public, which have as much, if not more at stake than grant makers do, foundations can make a big difference in the way our nonprofit world responds to its charge of strengthening our democratic society and improving the lives of its citizens.

∼

HOW MUCH SHOULD FOUNDATIONS GIVE?

Congress Should Increase Amount Foundations Must Give

From The Chronicle of Philanthropy, *June 27, 2002*

Despite their enormous growth over the past twenty years, foundations are still required to distribute only 5 percent of their net assets each year—the minimal rate set by Congress in 1981. It is time for Congress to raise that figure.

In exchange for their substantial tax benefits, foundations have an obligation to share a fair burden of the costs of maintaining a vibrant nonprofit world and a healthy civil society. Unfortunately, foundations collectively have regarded the legal payout as a ceiling, not a floor.

In its obsession with maintaining the 5 percent–payout rate, the Council on Foundations has failed to ask and answer the simple question, "What is so sacrosanct about 5 percent?" If the most important economic indicator in the country, the interest rate set by the Federal Reserve Bank, can be changed several times a year, why shouldn't the payout rate be adjusted periodically to reflect changing public conditions and needs? Indeed, Congress probably should re-evaluate the payout rate every five to seven years.

Under the law, foundations are allowed to include in their payout expenditures not only grants to nonprofit groups but also all salaries and other administrative costs, the rental or purchase of office space, trustee fees, and legal and accounting expenses. In recent years large foundations have spent only 3.5 percent to 4.2 percent on grant making. They need to do much better than that to meet today's most-urgent public needs.

The National Committee for Responsive Philanthropy, supported by many members of the National Network of Grantmakers, an association of donors supporting social change, is undertaking an effort to persuade Congress to raise the payout rate to 6 percent in grants only. Such an increase would add more than $7 billion annually to the collective income of nonprofit organizations. It is the first time since the 1969 Tax Reform Act, which set a spending floor, that the payout rate has become the focus of serious public discussion among charities, foundations, researchers, and some politicians. It is an issue that the foundation world has tried to keep as its privileged domain.

Significantly, conservative grant makers have a better payout record than do big, mainstream foundations. A dozen conservative foundations cited by the National Committee for Responsive Philanthropy in a 1997 study reported that their average payout in grants in 1998 was 7.8 percent. That same year, twenty-three of the largest twenty-five mainstream foundations had an average grants payout of 3 percent, with a five-year average of only 4 percent. If the conservative institutions could distribute more, why couldn't the mainstream ones do the same?

What makes the matter worse are recent developments that have endangered our social welfare programs and the financial state of our charity world: serious cutbacks in many federal social programs, the recession, the loss of state revenue, massive tax cuts for the wealthiest citizens, the growing inequality of wealth and income, increases in homelessness, decreases in low-cost housing, and the growing competition for scarce funds among nonprofit groups.

For these reasons the expectations of and the demands on institutional philanthropy have grown. Whether grant makers will respond with more resources will be a serious test of foundations' relevancy.

Surely foundations can do much more. The growth in their assets has been phenomenal, far outpacing the increase in grants they have distributed to charities. Although their assets ballooned to $448 billion in 1999, or 9.4 times their value in 1981, grants as a percentage of assets declined from 7.9 percent in 1981 to 5.1 percent in 1998. The projected assets for 2000 climbed to almost $500 billion, according to the Foundation Center. Although the recent recession has reduced foundations' assets, the anticipated recovery will once again swell the coffers of the foundation world.

What's more, we can expect an enormous intergenerational transfer of trillions of dollars to charities and foundations during the next thirty years. Foundations will have more money than charities and grant makers dreamed possible. So why are foundations so worried about a possible increase in the payout rate?

The Council on Foundations, supported by many of its largest members, including the Carnegie Corporation of New York and the Ford and Charles Stewart Mott foundations, claims that a payout larger than 5 percent will inexorably lead to the depletion of foundation assets and the extinction of many foundations. Such a development, it contends, would violate many donors' wishes that their institutions should exist in perpetuity.

To justify its position, the Council cites a study of Michigan foundations commissioned by the Michigan Council on Foundations and conducted by Cambridge Associates, a consulting firm, that concludes that the current payout rate is necessary for the long-term preservation of foundation assets. It also refers to its own commissioned series of three studies by the consulting firm of DeMarche Associates.

Ironically, DeMarche's last study, a report that was issued in 1999, found that foundations could have maintained their portfolio purchasing power over the past forty-nine years with a payout of 6.5 percent, although DeMarche qualified that conclusion by stating that the high returns of the past fifteen years may have distorted its findings.

Those studies are contradicted by other research efforts that assert that foundations could maintain their principal over time with a much larger payout rate. Perry Mehrling, of Barnard College, for example, in a study commissioned by the National Network of Grantmakers, says that foundations could keep the value of their assets over the long term with a payout of 8 percent.

In the January 2002 *McKinsey Quarterly Newsletter,* two McKinsey analysts, Paul Jansen and David Katz, wrote that the current foundation payout rate isn't distributing sufficient funds to equal the value of their tax benefits. They suggested that foundations distribute at least 7 percent of their net assets. And they have been joined by a growing chorus of individuals, including the philanthropists George Soros and Ted Turner, the former senator Bill Bradley, the investor Claude Rosenberg, and the mutual fund executive Amy Domini, as well as a number of foundation executives who believe the payout rate should be increased.

The Council on Foundations' perpetuity argument falls flat because it is based on the premise that foundation assets must be in a state of continual expansion. If the "XYZ" foundation today has $10 billion in assets and only $15 billion fifty years from now, the foundation will still exist even if its inflation-adjusted value has gone down. No donors were ever guaranteed that their foundations would grow exponentially, just as they were never assured that their stock market returns would always increase. No major foundation will have to go out of business involuntarily in the long run with a little higher payout.

Some members of the Council seem so worried by the prospect of an increase in the payout rate that they have begun a whispering campaign of their own, one that accuses advocates of a payout increase of supporting conservatives who allegedly want major mainstream foundations to spend themselves out of existence. This is nonsense.

More cynically, it implies that conservatives can't have a good idea, regardless of motive, and that progressives and others should never agree with conservatives. "Guilt by association" is never a persuasive argument.

For too long, a small, elite group of wealthy donors and foundations has influenced the payout rate behind the scenes by quietly lobbying congressional committees without any public debate. The National Committee for Responsive Philanthropy and the National Network of Grantmakers are trying to broaden the discussion and to press for a long-overdue rate increase.

While a number of charities may be afraid to offend some of their foundation backers, it is nevertheless in the interest of all nonprofit groups to support an increase in the payout rate to 6 percent, and require that all of that be dis-

tributed in the form of grants. That rate should extend to community foundations and all donor-advised funds, which currently have no payout requirement.

The failure to support this effort would be a lost opportunity, not only to
obtain substantially more money for the nonprofit world but also to require
foundations to become more responsible partners in supporting civil society.

~

Don't Cry for Thee, Foundations

From The Chronicle of Philanthropy, *May 29, 2003*
Congress ultimately rejected the proposal discussed in this article.

From the anguished cries, wringing hands, and self-pity generated by foundation officials during the past few weeks, it sounded like the end of the philanthropic world is at hand. At least one journalist for a prominent daily newspaper says grant makers are so terrified that she has received frantic calls from foundation officials who say they need help in exposing what they call sinister threats to philanthropy.

But nobody has suggested that foundations be put out of business. All that has prompted this outpouring of anxiety was a proposal by two members of Congress that would, in effect, force most foundations to give more to charity each year.

The legislation, introduced by Reps. Roy Blunt, Republican of Missouri, and Harold Ford Jr., Democrat of Tennessee, would prohibit foundations from counting administrative costs—such as rent and staff salaries—when they determine whether they meet federal requirements to distribute at least 5 percent of their assets to charities. Leaders of many of the nation's wealthiest foundations, including the Ford, Annie E. Casey, and Northwest Area foundations, have all spoken out against the measure.

Since many large foundations spend 0.5 percent to 1 percent of their assets each year on administrative costs, the increase in grants to charities would be considerable, potentially adding several billion dollars to their coffers.

Poor foundation executives. One really has to feel sorry for grant makers who may be forced to provide more money to charity. The reaction to the Blunt–Ford proposal has been so intense it's almost as if foundation officials were asked to spend more of their own money. Instead of bemoaning their fate and fighting against a measure that is long overdue, foundations should be aggressively attacking issues that are truly important to nonprofit organizations and the public. Excessive compensation, conflicts of interest, and inattentive boards have plagued the foundation world in recent years, and no grant makers seem to be doing anything to stop that.

In their reactions to the Blunt–Ford plan, grant makers seem to have forgotten that foundation donors have received huge tax benefits in exchange for the privilege of giving away money to meet important public needs. They have overlooked the obligation of foundations to support nonprofit groups struggling with big budget problems, brought on by enormous cuts in federal and state program funds and reductions in foundation grants.

What's more, grant makers conveniently forget that during the fifteen boom years of the market through 2000, when their assets ballooned to almost $500 billion, the aggregate sum distributed by foundations decreased rather than increased. When times were good, they somehow weren't good enough to give nonprofit groups the money they deserved. Foundations' banking instincts pre-empted their grant-making responsibilities.

And many well-intentioned but misguided foundation officials are still belaboring the spurious contention that foundations will become extinct if they have to distribute any more than the minimum share of assets now required by the federal government. Several studies prove them wrong, as do foundations that have distributed more than 5 percent annually and survived in good health.

Some grant makers are also arguing that the proposed legislation would force foundations to reduce their support for management training for nonprofit groups and accountability activities, such as publishing annual reports. That assertion belongs in a joke book. The proposal in the House doesn't say that foundations have to stop putting money into administrative activities; it just says that that money can't be counted to meet the payout requirement. If foundations stop spending on administrative activities that are vital to charities, then it isn't because Congress forced them to do it. The onus for this irresponsibility falls directly on the foundations themselves, not on the legislation.

Foundations should also realize that all their whining about the proposed change to the payout rules is just going to attract more scrutiny of their activities by the news media, and ultimately by lawmakers. In particular, journalists are likely to look more carefully at some of the administrative spending that foundations are so zealously trying to preserve.

Plenty of foundation directors are overpaid and the recipients of special perks. The *Chronicle*'s most recent survey of compensation at twenty of the nation's largest foundations, for instance, found that six chief executives of foundations make more than $500,000 annually, and six others make between $400,000 and $500,000. Some foundation CEOs sit on corporate boards, for which they receive trustee fees and are subject to potential conflicts of interest.

Many foundation CEOs are also responsible for their institutions' high administrative costs: sumptuous offices often renovated at enormous costs, such as the $2 million in expenses incurred by the James Irvine Foundation to move into offices with spectacular views of San Francisco and its bay; lavish expenditures on meals and entertainment; and first-class air travel and expensive hotels. While no one expects foundation executives to wear hair shirts, their high living cannot be justified.

Conflicts of interest are a continuing problem at many foundations, and often lead to an abuse of tax-exempt funds. For example, the Yawkey Foundation, in Boston, is being investigated by the state attorney general's office for its $15 million grant to Boston College because of the close ties of five of the foundation's trustees to the college. Foundation boards of trustees all too often exercise little oversight over their institutions' activities. Some accept high CEO compensation packages as a way of philanthropic life, reinforced by the view of numerous business executives who serve on foundation boards and expect any CEO to be highly paid. Other trustees, often family members and friends, are neither aware of nor concerned about conflict-of-interest problems or the potential that top foundation officials are getting overly generous financial rewards through their philanthropic connections.

The prevalence of large trustee fees is another matter of concern, especially because such fees can be counted by foundations that want to prove they have given away the minimum required 5 percent.

American foundations are spending many millions of dollars each year on fees to their trustees, who are among the wealthiest and most highly paid professionals in our country, money that could otherwise be spent on nonprofit organizations and their programs.

In a study of 238 foundations—including 175 of the wealthiest foundations—that two of my former Georgetown University colleagues, Christine Ahn of Food First and Channapha Khamvongsa of the Ford Foundation, and I are completing, we found that the foundations in our sample spent more than $44 million in 1998 just on trustee fees.

Many of those foundations have subsequently raised the amount they give to their trustees. Why should trustees of foundations receive any money for their charitable work, while board members of charities, many of whom are poor or middle-class, get no money for their charitable efforts?

It is time that grant makers, led by the Council on Foundations, take a tough stand on trustee fees, either by recommending their elimination or urging reasonable limits on their amounts.

The Council on Foundations and the regional associations of grant makers, not to mention foundation leaders, must do far more. They have been too slow to blow the whistle on their colleagues who abuse the public trust.

At the annual meeting of the Council in Dallas last month, Dorothy S. Ridings, president of the Council, and Emmett Carson, president of the Minneapolis Foundation, expressed concern about recent foundation scandals and urged members to take more effective action in assuring public accountability. The Council and the regional associations should discuss these concerns more regularly and candidly in their publications and public statements. They should highlight examples of bad behavior as a lesson that foundations need to learn.

It should be clear by now that self-regulation by foundations has not worked. Public accountability and the eradication of abuses will be achieved only if state and federal governments do an adequate job of oversight. Although the council has stated that the Internal Revenue Service needs more resources to do its job, it has not forcefully pressed Congress to provide those resources.

Aggressive lobbying by foundations and nonprofit groups could prompt Congress to earmark the excise taxes that foundations pay to be used for stepped-up state and federal oversight of nonprofit groups. That would be a far better use of foundations' political capital than the effort now under way to beat back the change in the payout formula.

Foundations need to deal with a wide array of issues if they want to become more accountable and worthy of the public trust. Trying to maintain a tightfisted approach to grant making at a time of national need is not one of them. Swarming over members of Congress and invoking the specter of extinction is not only fraudulent, but also a disservice to our needy and hardworking nonprofit organizations. The American people expect, and deserve, more from the foundations they subsidize.

~

Penetrating the Mystique of Philanthropy: Relations Between Fund Raisers and Grant Makers

From the Fall 1999 issue of Nonprofit Quarterly

For most of us who work for community organizations, there is a mystique about foundations and corporations and the way they give away their money. This air of mystery and awe is a major reason we have such a hard time raising money from them.

We are not familiar with their history and how they operate. We know few if any of their board members. We are not likely to meet them or their professional staff at the local supermarket or anywhere else where we work and socialize. When we do meet, it is almost always about a proposal we have submitted to them for funding.

Since they have the money we desperately need, we naturally view our relationship with them as inherently unequal, an imbalance of power. We also know or have heard about their "establishment" priorities, their relative lack of accountability and the problems encountered by organizations similar to ours in getting a fair hearing. And we are aware that charitable giving, unlike the political and judicial systems, does not provide any legal avenues for appeal. A foundation or corporate donor's decision is final.

These perceptions and experiences have combined to create a picture of philanthropy that is deadly in its impact on so many of our organizations. It is a portrait of an elite group of givers to whom respect and obedience must be given by a host of petitioners asking for philanthropic handouts. It is like the worshipers in ancient Greece pleading with the Delphic Oracle for good fortune.

While the attitudes and actions of those who give money have helped shape this nature of philanthropy, those of us on the receiving end—the donees—must share some of the responsibility for perpetuating the mystique of philanthropy. By accepting the premise that donees are unequal partners in the philanthropic process, we have helped to create the monster we so greatly resent.

In general, we have traded our rights as donees for the hope that by being cautious we might win over the donors. We have sought to be loved and adopted rather than respected. In seeking safety, we have not gained either the respect or love of contributors. Nor have we helped close the wide gulf of communication and understanding that separates us from the giver community.

By approaching fund raising apprehensively and passively without confidence we do not attack the problem of raising money in an organized and strategic way as we would an important community problem. We appear uncertain, frequently leaving the donors with the impression that we are disorganized, undependable and weak. How many times have we seen some of the toughest organizers, who sport several institutional scalps on their belts, turn to Jell-o when faced with a foundation?

Until we stop acting as beggars in the philanthropic game, we will not be able to eliminate this mystique. The first step is to adopt an attitude that says, "We are at least as good as the donor." This should not be an assertion of arrogance but a recognition of our own qualities and strengths.

We must remember that donors need us as much as we need them if their giving is to be of high caliber. Many of us are more experienced and skilled in our fields than our colleagues in philanthropy. Many have had the kind of learning experiences in poor communities that most donors will never have. Given that many corporate and foundation people want to do a good job, they often view productive relationships with donees as an important part of their work. By assuming we are equals, we can be treated as equals. If we can have solid working relationships with local politicians, Congressmen, union officials, and nonprofit colleagues, we can enjoy similar contacts with philanthropoids.

Part of the beggar's mentality is to think in terms of what the donors want, not what we need to fulfill our objectives. Since foundations and corporations have varied priorities, we have often tried to be all things to all people, cutting and tailoring our interests and programs to fit those of the donors. In many cases, the result has been dismal. Either we undermined our mission or initiated programs for which we were ill suited. And donors are seldom fooled by our flexibility.

A donee community less submissive, more determined to maintain its integrity and more aggressive in its posture with donors would lead to greater respect and receptivity for our cause in the philanthropic world.

If we look at ourselves with confidence and at donor institutions more realistically, we will find that the task of requesting and receiving money will become easier and less stressful.

The proposal, for example, should loom less ominously. For many, it has become part of the philanthropic mystique, filled with expectations of excellence that cannot be met. We become paralyzed when we try to write the perfect proposal. The proposal should be considered for what it is, no more and no less: the means by which we state why we need the money and what we will do with it. It is not meant to be a jewel of prose.

Although most foundation and corporate professionals understand the limitations of proposals, they often do not have the background, experience, or motivation to judge or be excited by the activities of nonestablishment organizations. For this reason, we cannot afford to let them evaluate us by our proposals alone. We need to see them in their offices, get them to know us as individuals and persuade them to visit our organizations. By meeting personally with donors, we can help break down the barriers between donor and donee that have fueled the mystique of philanthropy.

The inaccessibility, lack of accountability and bad manners of many foundations and corporations are trademarks of philanthropy that many of us have resented and criticized for years—unfortunately mostly among ourselves. Few of us have actively fought back to demand accountability, fair access, due process in grant-making procedures and equitable treatment in decision making. We have accepted unreturned phone calls, unwillingness to meet applicants, rudeness, arrogant behavior, decisions without explanation and double standards with a complacence that we would not tolerate in our dealings with other sectors and people.

This pattern of behavior, although it has improved somewhat in recent years, will not change unless we decide to do something about it. In other words, we need to insist on the attention of donor staff directors and trustees, monitor the activities of the giving world more closely, and be prepared to appeal to the public in extreme cases. Of course we also must make sure that we meet the standards we set for donors—too often we are as unaccountable as those we criticize.

Some people worry that challenging donors will lead to anger and retribution. The experiences of those organizations that have challenged donors do not bear out such anxieties. A few may have been hurt in the short run, but most have gained the respect and additional support of philanthropic institutions. We who are mistreated by donors have very little to lose and everything to gain by refusing to accept unfair procedures and practices.

But we can't do it alone; we need to act collectively. In certain cities and states, coalitions of nonprofits can be formed to monitor donor institutions and push for public accountability.

If we do not start to work together on fund-raising, we will never reform philanthropy, and those organizations that are the best financed and can afford to take the most risks are frequently the ones not willing to rally on behalf of colleague organizations. We will have to do a better job in pushing ourselves and our reluctant friends to join in a common effort. Only then will we be able to put to bed the mystique of philanthropy and open new opportunities for future funding.

∼

A Lack of Guts and Intellectual Vigor
Hobbles the Foundation World

From The Chronicle of Philanthropy, *February 21, 2002*

The foundation world has long been a backwater of lazy thinking, uncritical attitudes, self-satisfaction, and backslapping. In recent months, a few top foundation executives have written thoughtful speeches and articles challenging institutional practices and encouraging more effective performance. But their work stands out precisely because most of American philanthropy suffers from intellectual torpor and a lack of critical analysis.

The inability or unwillingness of most foundation officials to tackle the most challenging problems facing grant makers has left the task to a handful of academic researchers and practitioners. The result: a field that is poorly equipped to deal with its weaknesses and future role.

Part of the reason for this failing can be attributed to an exaggerated sense of collegiality that suffuses the field and stifles internal criticism. The lack of transparency, media scrutiny, and public accountability are other factors. But the major culprits are the chief executives of foundations, especially of the large ones, who appear to have thought little and written even less about their world—its performance, standards, problems, and challenges.

The grant-making scene bristles with important—and controversial—issues. Should government in a democracy limit the asset size of foundations to ensure that the billions of tax-exempt dollars they hold are used effectively to meet the most urgent public needs? Should the governance decisions of foundations be open to greater public scrutiny? Should foundation boards be more representative of the constituencies that grant makers purport to serve?

The list of issues goes on, but few foundation executives are willing to take them on.

What is so surprising about this state of affairs is that a large number of these foundation executives come from the academic world. Many of them have been presidents or deans of universities and colleges. Most of the former academic officials have doctorate degrees. Presumably, they have taught, done research, and written tracts and books, however illuminating or boring, to maintain their former academic positions. Have they lost their cerebral capabilities and writing skills since making the transition to philanthropy? In many cases, they are receiving salaries that are double or more than the amount of money they earned in academe. Not a bad trade-off: more money for probably less time-consuming work.

Former academics are not the only ones to have jumped on the philanthropic gravy train. Business executives, consultants, members of various professions, and nonprofit practitioners have also been recruited to fill major foundation positions. They, too, must have been required to think critically and write persuasively—or at least have others write for them—to have been successful at their former jobs. Why, then, have they also joined their academic colleagues in an atmosphere of silence once inside the world of philanthropy?

Whatever the reasons for this phenomenon, it is encouraging to see a trickle of philanthropoids bucking this trend. For several years, Ed Skloot, executive director of the Surdna Foundation, has been writing about foundation priorities and the reasons that foundations do not perform better.

Likewise, Gara LaMarche, director for U.S. programs at the Open Society Institute, has, in articles and speeches, questioned the responsiveness and accountability of foundations. He has pointed to grant makers' timidity in addressing controversial public-policy issues, to their intrusiveness in their grantees' programs, and to their lack of self-criticism.

Lance Lindblom, president of the Nathan Cummings Foundation, in a speech to the annual conference of Independent Sector last fall, called for a new vision on the part of philanthropic institutions.

Bruce Sievers, retiring executive director of the Walter and Elise Haas Fund, has produced thoughtful articles on venture philanthropy, while Thomas G. David, executive vice president of the California Wellness Foundation, recently wrote a strong piece on the need for foundations to provide general operating support to grantees—and not just program money. And a few executives, such as Vartan Gregorian, president of the Carnegie Corporation, have written opinion articles on the mission and work of foundations.

On the right, foundation executives such as Chester Finn, president of the Thomas B. Fordham Foundation; William Schambra, senior director of programs of the Lynde and Harry Bradley Foundation; and Heather Richardson Higgins, president of the Randolph Foundation, have written in recent years about the impact and shortcomings of philanthropy.

But this sprinkling of thoughtful writers will not be enough to provide the foundation world with the intellectual vigor and critical faculties it needs.

One might have thought that the Council on Foundations would be an important leader in encouraging more introspection and critical analysis within philanthropy, at least among its members. Unfortunately, the Council appears to be far more concerned about its public-relations effort to sell foundations to the American public than about improving and strengthening foundation performance, accountability, and relationships with grantees. The Council has done little in its day-to-day activities to advance the relationship between foundations and grantees; it sat on the sidelines during congressional debates over phasing out the estate tax, and it refused to take a position on using the excise tax on foundations to help pay for expanded enforcement activities by the Internal Revenue Service and state attorneys general.

The more conservative Philanthropy Roundtable [an umbrella association of donors and foundations] has seemed to be a more exciting venue for the discussion of substantive and challenging ideas. It has been less afraid to tackle controversial problems and issues than has the Council on Foundations.

Unless the Council on Foundations makes a 180-degree turn, the responsibility for thinking and strategizing about philanthropy will have to fall on individual leaders in the foundation world, a group that to date has shown little interest in or aptitude for the task.

We can only hope that the events of September 11 will prompt a new phase of introspection and analysis among foundation executives. The gravity of the episode and its impact on nonprofit groups have put a spotlight on a number of issues that foundations should be concerned about: Has foundation money been used efficiently and fairly to aid victims of the tragedy? Are foundations adequately supporting small charities that have experienced declines in donations because of the public's outpouring of gifts to nonprofit groups set up in the wake of the attacks? And what of the long-term issues that arise from the attacks and the simultaneous economic recession: Should foundations be paying out more of their assets in grants, especially during times of national crises? Foundations have had plenty to think and write about.

If the momentous events of September 11 don't move foundations to abandon their ivory towers and become engaged in the issues of the day, nothing will.

Bill Moyers, speaking at a meeting of the Environmental Grantmakers Association in October, issued a call to action that should apply to every foundation leader in the United States: "We're survivors now, you and I," Mr. Moyers said. "We will be defined not by the lives we led until the 11th of September, but by the lives we will lead from now on. So go home—make the best grants you've ever made. And the biggest—we have too little time to pinch pennies. Back the committed and courageous people in the field—and back them with media to spread their message. Stick your neck out. Let your work be charged with passion, and your life with a sense of mission. For when all is said and done, the most important grant you'll ever make is the gift of yourself, to the work at hand."

Amen.

~

Desperately Seeking Leadership

From Foundation News & Commentary, *November–December 1998*

At least six top foundations—Hewlett, Packard, MacArthur, Rockefeller, William Penn, and the Howard Hughes Medical Institute—will be appointing new chief executive officers this year or next year. Each has an opportunity to select a new leader of vision, substance, and courage. To put it more bluntly, right now each of those foundations has a chance to bring on the kind of strong leadership that the philanthropic community has been sorely lacking.

Many top foundation executives in recent memory have been intelligent, hard-working people. They've come from a variety of backgrounds—business, nonprofits, health and, often, academia. A few had broad visions that captured the possibilities of creative philanthropy and, to the extent their boards permitted, actually practiced risk-taking grant making. Some have been excellent managers and talent scouts, attracting to their institutions energetic program officers willing to think outside the box. At least one or two of these executives had their careers cut short by unappreciative boards.

Yet, for some reason, in the aggregate foundation executives have failed to provide a critical assessment and debate aimed at raising the sector's performance standards or to creating better rapport with the grantee community. They have not left their individual imprimaturs on the Council on Foundations or the regional associations of grant makers. Most of them couldn't be bothered to spend much time in the affairs of their own trade associations. For too many, their professional lives don't extend much beyond their own foundation doors.

Maybe it's safer that way. "Don't worry about what my foundation does, and I won't worry about yours," is an attitude that might foster a warm collegial approach, and might make everyone happy. But is it good for the field? I dare say not.

In short, we have had plenty of smart executives, but few leaders.

Tall Orders

Where are the voices today that can speak out with credibility about the many challenges facing philanthropy in the twenty-first century? Who serves as the conscience of the field? Are there executives who have as much passion for what is going on in the field in general as they have in the internal operation of their own organizations?

The problems facing the nation in the next decade are daunting. Much of the responsibility for reinvigorating our society and its democratic institutions will fall on the nonprofit sector, and grant makers will have to fuel much of it. Add to this thought the projection that billions of new dollars will be added to America's philanthropic assets launching hundreds of foundations in the next two decades or so. These new foundations will require strong executives. It is important that foundations begin now to set a high standard of leadership that can guide future grant-making institutions as they make their own leadership decisions.

One might think it will be pretty easy to fill the top jobs at the half-dozen top foundations currently looking for a new chief. A prestigious position with a high salary and plenty of perks should attract the best and the brightest from all over the country. If the searches resemble many of those conducted in the past, then finding someone to fill the job shouldn't be too demanding.

But then again, that's the point: the searches should not resemble those conducted in the past. If the foundations are willing to raise the bar and look harder for people with extraordinary vision and courage, their task will be much more difficult.

Same Old Searches

The problem with traditional recruitment efforts has been the narrow lens through which foundation boards of directors have looked at prospective candidates. Overwhelmingly, the latter have tended to be university or college presidents or past presidents; high-profile names from government, business and academia; and establishment insiders known personally by the boards.

Almost totally overlooked have been nonprofit executives, professionals, and foundation personnel from smaller institutions who are as (if not more) capable than most of the candidates seriously considered by the major foundations in the past. Several reasons, I believe, account for this practice.

Boards

First and foremost, perhaps, is the nature of large foundation boards of directors. They are composed primarily of an elite; people who are accomplished professionals, business leaders, wealthy family members and well-known educators. They seem to prefer candidates who resemble themselves and belong to their own professional and social circles.

They also tend to place a highest priority on "getting along." Aggressively inquiring minds who want to push new frontiers, take philanthropic risks, and support community interventions are not likely to be their serious candidates. Such people are often viewed as potentially troublesome.

The word on the street is that the large foundations are looking for big names to fill their posts. If this is true, their boards of directors need to remind

themselves that the most important big names are those of the institutions—
MacArthur, Hewlett and Packard, and the like—and not those of the potential
candidates.

But foundations don't need another "name." They need a savvy, energetic
and creative leader who can do a terrific job.

Headhunters

Search firms are another reason for the failure of many major foundations to
recruit the most talented candidates. In their desire to please clients, headhunters frequently recommend only those candidates who are highly credentialed and who, they think, will get along nicely.

Furthermore, few headhunters have worked at nonprofit organizations
themselves. Few have a real understanding of the nonprofit sector as a whole,
and few have a feel for the type of leadership that is needed in it. The qualities
of vision and courage are rarely found in headhunters' Rolodexes, or even in
their own backgrounds.

Search firms often do a poor job of checking references beyond those actually suggested by potential candidates themselves. Unsolicited references can
be the most important part of a search, testing whether a candidate has provided leadership in his or her previous organizations, worked cooperatively,
and avoided serious mistakes of judgment. Meaningful reference checking requires certain investigative skills. Too often, this factor is overlooked.

In a recent *Washington Post* article highlighting the large salaries and compensation packages of top foundation executives, foundation officials commented on the extraordinary difficulty of recruiting talented people to top jobs
without high salaries and benefits. Where have they been looking? The answer:
in the same limited talent pool from which they have drawn past directors.

If the foundations are really committed to seeking the best possible talent
available, boards of directors and their search firms will have to transcend their
old habits and focus on a much broader array of candidates than they have in
the past.

There are a number of directors of small- and mid-sized foundations, as
well as a few program officers in the top institutions, who could make fine chief
executive officers at major foundations. Nonprofit organizations, including the
foundation's own donee groups, know of many highly qualified potential candidates. They should be consulted.

Key Qualities

What are the special qualities that the major foundations should be looking for
as they seek their new directors? I would include the following six:

Vision. The candidate should be aware of both the strengths and weaknesses of the field of philanthropy and have a personal commitment to help improve the standards and effectiveness of not just one foundation but the field as a whole.

Broad understanding of and respect for the nonprofit sector. Candidates should view nonprofit organizations as equal partners in the philanthropic process who deserve respectful treatment. Implicit is a commitment to find nonprofit groups in a manner that is best for the donee, not what's best for the donor or—more to the point—what's convenient for the donor's bureaucracy.

Willingness to communicate with donees and the public. Foundations have an obligation to communicate with their donees and would-be donees beyond the framework of a pending grant. Continual consultation with donees, other nonprofits and the public should be an important influence in the development of foundation priorities, policies, and practices. Candidates need to have the desire to bridge what is currently a wide gap between donors and donees.

Commitment to creativity and innovation. Any new executive should be able to encourage new ideas and approaches to tough problems, to identify outstanding talent to implement innovation and to energize other institutions to collaborate in such ventures.

Creativity, however, should not be confused with a disposition toward trendiness. Sometimes giving continued general support to a "true and tested" creative grantee takes more courage than hopping from one new project to the next.

Willingness to take risks. Although philanthropy prides itself on being the cutting-edge sector, it is programmed for safety, not for risk or possible failure. Candidates for major foundation posts should have the courage to support organizations and projects that take risks, or have the potential for programmatic or policy innovations.

Capacity to work effectively with the board of directors. Directors should have the experience, tact, flexibility, and toughness to work well with their boards. They need to be willing to engage board members in, not isolate them from, the affairs of the foundation. This means exposing them to outside critics as part of an educational process. The directors should also take the responsibility for strengthening their boards by helping diversify them both in perspective and in composition.

While there are, of course, other important criteria for selection, the above six seem to be directly related to the potential for real leadership, as well as good grant making. The top foundations currently looking for leaders could, with the right choice, help re-energize our sector.

Five outstanding new leaders might even put to rest Mrs. Cheveley's observation in Oscar Wilde's *An Ideal Husband:* "And philanthropy seems to me to have become simply the refuge of people who wish to annoy their fellow creatures. . . ."

∼

The Left Doesn't Have It Right on Grant Making

From The Chronicle of Philanthropy, March 12, 1998

In recent years, mainstream foundations have come under increased scrutiny on a wide set of issues, from the inflexibility of their grant making to their limited accountability. Although the criticisms come from across the political spectrum, people generally are more familiar with those from the right, partly because they have tended to be more strident, persistent, and ideological than those from the left.

Even if one disagrees with the criticism from the right, however, at least it is consistent with the conservatives' view of what constitutes a better and more productive society: smaller government, untethered capitalism, an emphasis on traditional values, policies that aren't based on race, and increased volunteerism.

That does not seem to be the case with the left.

In a recent issue of *The Nation,* for example, Michael H. Shuman, former director of the Institute for Policy Studies in Washington, complains that mainstream foundations are not supporting progressive think tanks and research institutes that could match the intellectual vigor of those on the right. Instead, he claims, foundations are dissipating their money by giving it to thousands of disparate grassroots organizations. How brazen—and inconsistent with the progressive vision—can one be?

There is, no doubt, a need for additional funds for progressive think tanks. But critics on the left should take care to make a distinction between those think tanks that, by their practices, share the progressive vision and those that do not.

At the heart of progressivism is a vision of an America that is non-elitist, where people of all races and nationalities can participate in the processes of democracy and be treated equally, and where the poor have the resources to lift themselves up by their bootstraps.

While a few of the progressive think tanks—including the Center for Budget and Policy Priorities, the Center for Law and Social Policy, and the Applied Research Center—are connected to the grassroots, many others are not. Instead, they tend to be elitist, with ideas emanating from the top down. They have few ties to local nonprofit groups and little direct contact with poor, working, and middle-class citizens, whose interests they purportedly serve.

More serious is Mr. Shuman's claim that mainstream and liberal foundations have squandered vast amounts of money on thousands of grassroots groups. Contrary to Mr. Shuman's view, community organizations that serve the poor have received a very thin slice of the philanthropic pie. Only a handful of mainstream foundations have been willing to underwrite groups for their organizing, public-policy, and advocacy activities, let alone provide them with general support for their operations. Individual donors have an even worse track record of giving to organizations that help low-income people and of supporting grassroots advocacy efforts.

As government decision making shifts from the federal to the state and local levels, grassroots organizations should receive more support for their efforts, not less. Not only are grassroots groups well connected to the needs of their constituents, but historically they have also been the most effective in improving people's lives.

Perhaps Mr. Shuman and other critics on the left have forgotten that the Community Reinvestment Act—which has done more than any other piece of legislation to bring renewed investment and credit to poor neighborhoods—was the direct product of a national grassroots campaign. Or that the same can be said of many of the victories posted by consumers and environmentalists over the past two decades.

In the end, the achievement of the progressive vision will depend more on the success of such organizations than on whether a think tank can generate more ideas, research, books, and conferences.

To be sure, some of Mr. Shuman's observations are on the mark. He faults the large, liberal foundations for their support only of those programs that fit within narrowly defined categories, for their fear of being viewed as partisan or political, and for their reluctance to give long-term or general support to nonprofit organizations. It is surprising, however, that he takes the Public Welfare Foundation to task in this area. Few, if any, large foundations have provided more money for advocacy work and general support than has the Washington philanthropy.

Mr. Shuman concludes by saying that most foundations do not realize their weaknesses because grant recipients are too afraid to "rock the boat" or "nibble on the hand that feeds." But that is not entirely fair. Some progressive nonprofit organizations have taken money from philanthropic sources and criticized them without having caused irreparable damage to their institutions—which is more than I can say for many so-called progressive think tanks.

Mr. Shuman calls for an honest dialogue between grant makers and grant recipients, something that is long overdue. What is equally in demand—and in very short supply—is a strong dose of courage and candor by all nonprofit organizations, whatever their ideology.

～

The Case for General Support

From Nonprofit Quarterly, *Winter 1999*

Ask any nonprofit organization what its fund-raising priorities are and almost without exception the answer you will receive is: general operating support. Yet according to data compiled by the Foundation Center, in 1997 only 13.1 percent of all grant dollars distributed by foundations actually went to general operating support. The irony of this situation is that while the foundations are currently touting the importance of "capacity building," they are at the same time denying their grantees the general support that is essential to the work of building strong organizations. [For more on capacity building, see article on page 76.]

Foundations are a crucial source of support for community-based organizations. Much of the latter work does not appeal to corporate donors, nor do they find it easy to attract individual givers. Although grassroots fund raising and fees for services do provide some income, foundation money is often crucial to rounding out budgets. Unfortunately much of that money is not targeted at real needs.

Why is this the case? Are foundations simply not listening to what nonprofits have been saying? Have donees or would-be donees not articulated their needs vigorously enough to donor institutions? Or perhaps foundations have chosen to ignore both the needs and requests of nonprofit organizations? I suspect that it is the last question that largely informs grant making.

By now, there should be no question about the fundamental importance of general support to the development of strong, independent organizations, whatever their mission, nature, or size. This type of funding enables organizations to recruit and maintain first-class multipurpose staff, to ensure solid planning and administrative services, to conduct staff training on a continuing basis, and to launch new initiatives without waiting for an infusion of special project money. It provides the flexibility to respond quickly to changing environments, to emerging needs, and to targets of opportunity. It permits nonprofits to integrate public policy and advocacy work into their overall activities, since few foundations appear willing to target money specifically to advocacy functions. And it is the means by which organizations can participate in and contribute to significant coalitions, as well as embrace an agenda that may be broader than their original mission.

Adequate general support is also an essential ingredient of many foundation-funded special projects. Without it, many organizations could not afford to initiate new programs, many of which are never fully funded by targeted funds. For example, several years ago the Center for Community Change [which Mr. Eisenberg headed] calculated that to run a four-year community leadership development program supported by the Kellogg Foundation, it would have to contribute a substantial amount—$500,000—of its own general support money. Fortunately the Center had the "flexible money" to invest, ensuring the success of the program.

So what can we do to ensure that general support funds are available and used appropriately? Venture capital philanthropists, citing the experience of successful venture capitalists, have argued forcefully that long-term investment of flexible funds is the best way to build strong nonprofit organizations. So, too, concur the largest conservative foundations, which have achieved a notable track record of creating and supporting many of the most stable and influential conservative institutions in the country over the past thirty years.

Defending Foundations' Reluctance

In spite of all the evidence proving the importance of general operating support, foundations defend their reluctance to provide flexible funds on a number of grounds. Yet many of them simply do not stand up to scrutiny.

Boredom. Barry Karl, the noted historian of philanthropy, has observed that many program officers want to do more than merely respond to requests for flexible operating funds. They are bored with general support.

Activism. As a growing number of young and talented people have joined foundations, foundation staff members have increasingly taken an activist role in shaping and being more directly involved in the specific programs they are supporting, thereby reducing the amount of money available for general support.

Impact. This trend has been exacerbated by foundations' mounting concern that they produce a measurable impact within a short period of time. This reflects a lack of trust in the ability of nonprofits to achieve results without the guiding hand and control of the foundations themselves.

Public policy avoidance. In addition, by targeting money to special projects foundations can disassociate themselves from the general operations and, especially, the public-policy and advocacy activities of their donee organizations.

Time limits. Some foundation executives claim that it is much more difficult to terminate general support grants than special program grants. While the latter always operate within specific time limits, there is no reason why such limits couldn't apply equally, as they most often do, to the former as well.

Accountability. Other foundations believe it is much easier to evaluate special projects and to hold them accountable to a certain set of standards. There is no reason why competent program staff and evaluators shouldn't be able to evaluate the general performance of nonprofit organizations as effectively as they can the results of special projects. In any case, while foundations increasingly talk about evaluations, few seem to have the capacity or energy to carry out meaningful evaluations of their grantees, nor do many of them even spend much, if any, time conducting site visits.

Trustee responsibility. Some foundation staff members say that trustees don't like general support grants, preferring projects that have a beginning and an end. It is difficult, however, to tell when this is really the case or when it is actually just a matter of staff preference. Many trustees have told me that they support or would like to support flexible funding. It is the responsibility of foundation employees to inform trustees about the urgent need and requests for general support by nonprofits. Unfortunately, they often fail to carry out this responsibility.

Power. Probably the major reason for the lack of general support is the issue of power and control. As Steven Burkeman, secretary of the Joseph Rowntree Trust in Great Britain, succinctly put it, "The transfer of money is also the transfer of power . . . Maybe this is one reason why core funding is valued so much—more of the power of choice remains with the grant holder."

Through special and project funding, foundations retain a much greater measure of power and control over grant making and their grantees than they do when they provide core funding. They are essentially helping to determine the direction, agendas, and programs of nonprofit organizations, which are properly the responsibility of nonprofit boards and staff. Foundation personnel do not publicly acknowledge it often, but a number of program officers have commented off-the-record that this desire for control is implicit in a good deal of grant making and underlies much of the opposition to general support.

Disguising General Operating Funds

Complicating the already serious problem, many foundation officers have taken to encouraging their would-be donees to tailor requests for core funds into proposals for special project money. Nonprofits, desperate for money, have often willingly complied with such suggestions. The result is sheer sophistry.

The hypocrisy of the process has undermined the integrity of both foundations and grantees.

Moving On

The time has come for foundations to put aside their concerns about control and their excuses for not providing general support. They must concentrate instead on what is best for their grant recipients and for nonprofits in general and listen carefully to what grant seekers have been telling them for many years. That does not mean giving up funding for special projects, but it does mean that a substantial portion of foundation dollars should be channeled to general support. Fifty percent for this purpose would not be an unreasonable goal.

Yet nonprofit organizations also bear some responsibility for this state of affairs. They have been reluctant to push foundations for core funding, preferring instead to ask for what they think foundations are willing to give. A more aggressive posture would produce much better results. Once foundations are faced with greater and more forceful demands for general support, the more likely they will be to change their priorities.

There are positive signs that foundations are slowly beginning to change their practices. A number of large institutions, such as the Charles Stewart Mott, Irvine, Ford, and Public Welfare foundations, have given general support for many years and continue to serve as examples to their colleagues. Others seem to be increasing their flexible support. And a growing number of smaller foundations have aggressively adopted policies stressing the importance of general support. Finally, fueled by the advocates of venture philanthropy, this is now becoming a "hot" topic for discussion within philanthropic circles, prompting a growing number of nonprofit organizations to push harder and more successfully for general support. Greater internal debate by foundations and more outside pressure could shift the pendulum in the other direction.

The purpose of philanthropy is to make our society a more enlightened and better place for all its citizens. It tries to achieve this mission by funding the activities of nonprofit organizations, the strength of which is dependent on the availability of general operating support. As long as foundations are reluctant to give this flexible support, they will undermine the very purpose for which they were created.

$\sim$

Capacity Building: Beware the Easy Fix

From Nonprofit Quarterly, *July 2001*

"Capacity building" is the largest philanthropic buzzword generating interest among foundations wanting to strengthen the structures and organizational performance of grantees. Promoting this concept, a number of foundations have created yet another affinity group—perhaps more aptly termed *infinity* groups—Grantmakers for Effective Organizations. Led by the David and Lucile Packard Foundation, a growing number of foundations are making more grants for this purpose.

Building strong, highly skilled, and sustainable organizations that can deliver the highest quality service and advocacy programs should be philanthropy's highest priority. Yet it is not clear whether many foundations that appear committed to capacity building know much about how to increase the capacity of their grantees. Too many funders make capacity-building decisions without asking the organizations in question for an assessment of their needs. This directive approach not only irritates the grantees, but often misses the problems most in need of correction. Barbara D. Kibbe of the Packard Foundation had it right when she said, "We'd never set the priority."

The reliance of foundations on management support organizations and independent consultants is often a major obstacle to effective capacity building. A growing and thriving industry of management assistance organizations has emerged over the past decade to provide support, often very expensive, to groups and their donors that are wrestling with nonprofit management, programmatic, and fund-raising problems. Too many of them are not competent to do the job, lacking the values, professional skills, and political judgment required by the organizations they profess to assist. While many support groups can address specific needs such as financial management, personnel policies, or a narrow program initiative, few excel in the complexities of building healthy and productive organizations.

In fact, private consultants are rarely the answer on a long-term basis. While some are highly skilled, others offer only mediocre assistance, which can be worse than no help at all. Moreover, the good ones are expensive, and few organizations can afford to retain them for long periods. Many management support organizations lack the skilled people needed for effective assistance: staff members who have run both small and large effective organizations, fund raisers who actually have extensive experience in raising money and can do more than write proposals, people who understand leadership development. There is no substitute for demonstrable skills and successful experience.

Others, especially those that are for-profit, have neither the resources nor the commitment to stick with an organization over the long haul. Sadly, they exhibit little interest or appreciation for the values and organizational missions of their nonprofit clients. By contrast, organizations such as the Environmental Support Center, the Center for Community Change [the organization Mr. Eisenberg headed] and the McCauley Institute build enduring relationships with their clients lasting many years. They emphasize the primacy of mission and values in their assistance programs, while at the same time providing the needed management help. These assistance groups—committed to the work of their clients, comprehensive in their approach, and dedicated to providing long-term assistance—deserve encouragement and support from funders.

Most management support groups lack the capacity to tackle public-policy activities, advocacy, organizing and lobbying. Nor are they comfortable in doing so. Yet a growing number of nonprofits, even service organizations, are addressing these very issues. Increasingly, strategic planning, budgeting, staff expansion, and public-policy priorities require the type of assistance that is more policy and activist oriented than has previously been the case. Management support organizations, technical-assistance centers, and consultants each have a role to play in capacity-building initiatives. For the most part, however, they are less effective than the direct provision of general operating support to organizations wanting to strengthen their operations and grow their programs.

Core support is at the heart of capacity building. It can cover a wide range of important functions such as planning and evaluation, board–staff relationships, technological improvements, public accountability, and measures and reserve funds with which to launch new programs or policy initiatives. With flexible money, nonprofits can hire the management program and policy staff members they need to be viable and productive. This approach is decidedly more cost-effective in the end than a dependency on protracted management assistance and consultants.

Years ago when the Center for Community Change wanted to address management and fund-raising problems, the Ford and MacArthur foundations gave the Center a large, three-year general support grant to address these issues. With this money, we hired the needed management and fund-raising staff. It was a much cheaper and more long-term solution than the use of support organizations and consultants. Similarly, when the Packard Foundation recently granted the *Nonprofit Quarterly* $535,000 to become national in scope, the foundation said, "Here's the money, spend it on staff and resources you think you need to do the job."

Old habits die hard. Foundations are still reluctant to provide core support, even to their favorite grantees. In 1997, for example, only 13.1 percent of all money granted by foundations went to general operating support. If foundations are serious about capacity building, they will have to reconsider their policy of not funding the infrastructure needs of grantee organizations through core support. By funding the most effective strategy for creating strong non-profits, foundations, ironically, will find their own capacity for effective grant making enormously enhanced.

~

Redrawing the Map of Philanthropy: Addressing Inequities

From The Chronicle of Philanthropy, *September 9, 1999*

Friendships, personal contacts, reputations, visibility, access, and poor judgments too often serve to undermine the fairness of foundation giving.

So does geography. Many of the poorest areas of the country, often home to large minority populations, are grossly underserved by foundations. States in the South, Southwest, Great Plains, and noncoastal Northwest—and rural areas everywhere—have relatively few foundations and philanthropic dollars to deal with enormous social and economic problems.

By contrast, states in the Northeast, the Midwest, and on the West Coast house 31,428 of the 44,146 foundations in the country, or 71 percent, according to the most recent statistics compiled by the Foundation Center. Grant makers in those three regions gave approximately $12 billion of the $16 billion expended in grants in 1997—fully three-quarters of the total.

As a rule, foundations tend to give to charities located in their own regions. When you consider the paucity of foundations in certain regions—and combine that with the fact that foundations everywhere provide few resources to rural areas—the inequities of distribution are magnified.

And there is no sign that that imbalance is changing. Of the 9,158 new foundations created in the 1990s, the same share—71 percent—are located in the Northeast, Midwest, and on the West Coast. Foundations in those regions account for 72.5 percent of the total giving of new institutions.

While those figures indicate a very slight narrowing of the gap in giving between regions, the expected explosion in the next thirty years of large foundations worth trillions of dollars is likely to continue the geographic maldistribution of foundations and giving, if not exacerbate it.

The recent addition of $6 billion to the assets of the Bill and Melinda Gates Foundation in Seattle is a case in point. Although the fund has a global reach in areas such as technology and health care, it also plans to focus much of its giving on charitable causes in the Pacific Northwest, where the Gateses live. As other new high-tech millionaires in Silicon Valley and elsewhere pursue their philanthropic interests—and as the older, established foundations receive new infusions of money and reap the benefits of the soaring stock market—the greatest expansion of foundation assets and foundation giving will undoubtedly take place in the three already dominant regions. Simply put, that is where the big money is.

The growth also will take place predominantly at large institutions, and that does not augur well for local or state charities in underserved regions. Most large foundations resist channeling funds to local or regional nonprofit groups, preferring instead to give relatively big grants to large, national nonprofit organizations. For most large grant makers, the increased cost of making smaller grants to local communities, including the need to expand the size of their staffs to serve more grantees, has proved to be a serious deterrent to more decentralized grant making. And it is unlikely that the new large foundations will be any different.

To be sure, the assets of community foundations, which tend to support local charities, are growing impressively in many regions of the country, including underserved ones, and there has been tremendous growth of new wealth in states like Colorado, Florida, and Nevada. But the greatest growth still is taking place at large institutions in the states and regions that already benefit the most—meaning that the current geographic gap is likely to widen.

To make matters worse, foundations in the South and Southwest tend to be very conservative, reluctant to support grassroots organizations and social change. Texas, for example, boasts 2,181 foundations, but only a relative handful of them support serious efforts to attack problems of poverty, race relations, community development, and the environment. Disproportionately poor and burdened by transportation problems, rural areas are in desperate need of assistance to build a working system of nonprofit organizations, to stimulate economic development, and to improve their educational programs and social services.

A few national foundations have given blocks of money to smaller foundations like the Foundation for the Mid-South, in Mississippi, as well as to a few large nonprofit organizations to then distribute to local grant applicants. That practice, however, is still in its infancy and is running into considerable opposition from many foundations.

What's more, underserved regions do not need "pass-through" foundations, or those that operate their own programs. They require foundations with large asset bases that can distribute a great deal of money to local and regional groups.

What, then, can be done to remedy this inequitable distribution of foundations and their assets?

Most foundation executives merely throw up their hands and shrug their shoulders. Yet with some creativity and boldness, the large foundations could easily create several new major philanthropic institutions for regions like the South and Southwest, and for rural areas.

Just recently, the David and Lucile Packard Foundation gave away $1.6 billion—11 percent of its assets—to endow a foundation, the Packard Humanities Institute. There is no reason why many of the large foundations like Ford,

Rockefeller, MacArthur, Kellogg, Lilly, and Pew couldn't create similar entities to concentrate on philanthropically neglected areas of the country.

Alternatively, those and other large foundations could pool their resources to create new institutions with large endowments. With the growth of their assets far outpacing their grant making, the big foundations are in an excellent position to make long-term investments to benefit a large population that currently is beyond the reach of philanthropy's benevolence.

Foundation officials talk a great deal about collaboration. Here is a wonderful opportunity for them to "walk the talk."

∼

Why Foundations Should Aid Local Charities

From The Chronicle of Philanthropy, *February 8, 1996*

As the federal government cuts spending and gives more authority to states and localities, small and medium-size nonprofit groups will face increased burdens.

The problems will hit groups in a wide range of areas, from the arts to social services to economic development to health. Not only will many charities have to find new sources of support for their programs, but they will have to learn how to work more effectively with state and local government officials. And they will have to monitor local and state governments and hold them accountable.

What's more, organizations of all kinds will be forced to deal more and more with public policy matters. To be effective, they will have to work in concert with other groups that want to satisfy the demands of their low- and moderate-income constituents.

To cope with all those new demands, many local groups will need help paying their operating expenses. It will not be easy for them to find the money they need. Very few foundations are willing to make small or moderate-size grants to local organizations, despite the increasingly urgent problems facing so many neighborhoods in this country.

Foundations offer numerous reasons for their unwillingness to help local groups. They say that making small grants is not cost-effective. They note that it takes more of their staff's time and effort to distribute small grants than large ones, and they say they would probably have to hire more staff members if they started making small grants. In addition, they contend that it is too hard to evaluate how much is achieved with a small grant and to make sure that the money is used wisely.

Unlike business, philanthropy is not primarily concerned with the health of the bottom line. Cost effectiveness should not be a roadblock to meeting critical public needs. Nor should the need to add one or two staff members be an obstacle to starting a small-grants program. In fact, an increasing number of foundations have started their own costly special projects—and many have hired new program officers to formulate and manage them. Is a foundation's pet project more important than helping local groups and coalitions?

Philanthropic resistance to small grants stems from a dangerous combination of bureaucracy, inertia, and unwillingness to listen to or even consult with community activists. Some foundations do have the courage to make small grants, and their efforts could easily be emulated. The John D. and Catherine T. MacArthur Foundation makes grants of $25,000 to $50,000 to dozens of community organizations in Chicago. For fifteen years the Charles Stewart Mott Foundation has been making grants of $10,000 or less to hundreds of community groups throughout the country. And a few consortia of foundations have established emergency loan and emergency-grant programs for charities.

Foundations and corporate donors do not have to stake out new territory to make small grants. If they wanted to try approaches that have already succeeded, they could:

- Run a small-grants program through an intermediary organization. The Center for Community Change [which Mr. Eisenberg headed until he retired] is one of six groups that has worked with Mott over the years to help distribute its small grants. This approach involves little or no additional cost for a foundation. Grant makers simply provide the intermediary organization with a sizable sum to redistribute in small amounts to local community groups; the intermediary organization then provides management advice to grantees and monitors the work of each charity.

- Make small grants directly to local organizations. It would take one or two additional staff members to do this, or a redistribution of work assignments. To reduce the burden on staff members, the foundation could pay an outside organization to provide management advice to the recipients of small grants.

- Collaborate with other foundations to set up a small-grants fund. Several foundations could pool their resources and share the costs of hiring one or two staff members to distribute money from a joint fund. Participating foundations could have a representative on the grants-allocation committee of the fund and share all the expenses of managing the program.

- Create a new foundation. A group of grant makers could jointly establish a new foundation that would provide small and moderate-size grants to local groups in special areas. For example, charities in rural areas have long needed money to strengthen and expand their operations. By creating a new rural-oriented institution, foundations could work together to do something they have been unwilling to do individually.

Leaders of grassroots groups across the country face similar problems. They all need money to deliver services and conduct advocacy efforts to help their constituents. Why aren't more people, especially those who work at foundations, listening to their cries for assistance?

The way many foundations now do business is not adequate to meet the challenges nonprofit groups face today. Grant makers must find a way to muster their creativity, competence, and courage if they want to respond to the problems confronting these groups. After all, isn't that what philanthropy is supposed to be all about?

~

Foundation Grants Shouldn't Mix with Politics

From The Chronicle of Philanthropy, February 6, 2003

In October the Boston Foundation pledged $1 million to help the city of Boston raise enough money from private and nonprofit sources to sponsor the 2004 National Democratic Convention.

The award, rare if not unprecedented for a community or private foundation, raises a number of serious questions about the appropriateness of such a grant. Should a tax-exempt institution give money for a partisan political event or activity, thereby endangering the credibility of that foundation? Don't more suitable, needy nonprofit causes exist, especially in these economically difficult times, that deserve to be higher priorities than political conventions? Could such a grant set a bad precedent for other foundations to follow?

The city's fund-raising campaign for the convention, led by Boston Mayor Thomas Menino and Senator Edward Kennedy, also enlisted the support of such groups as the Barr Foundation, which pledged $250,000 to underwrite arts activities during the convention, the nonprofit Blue Cross and Blue Shield of Massachusetts, which will donate $1 million, and State Street Corporation, whose foundation will also contribute $1 million.

The grants are contingent on the receipt, from the Internal Revenue Service, of tax-exempt status for the convention's nonprofit arm, Boston 2004, which is controlled by the mayor's office. The groups have declared that their money would not go to political activities or causes, but be used for economic, educational, and cultural programs tied to the convention.

In a letter sent to various people who questioned the appropriateness of the grant, Paul Grogan, president of the Boston Foundation, said the grant was made "primarily on the basis of the economic impact the convention will have, both short-term and long-term." He added that "the working poor, immigrants, and minorities are populations that historically are of special concern to the foundation. It is precisely these groups that are most heavily represented in the service industries that will benefit most from a major convention."

Mr. Grogan acknowledged that the foundation's board engaged in a spirited debate before deciding to make the grant. Still, he said, putting $1 million toward the convention, rather than spending it directly on the foundation's traditional grantees, is worth the risk. He was emphatic in asserting that the money would not go into a general pool of funds collected by the city to support the convention, but would be used specifically to help strengthen minority businesses and economic development projects. Boston's mayor promised to honor that priority, Mr. Grogan said, although it is not yet clear what mechanisms will be in place to ensure the foundation's money will be used as intended.

Mr. Grogan also said that support for the convention would enable the foundation to gain a higher profile in the Boston area and make it easier to raise money from big donors.

The Rev. Ray Hammond, chair of the foundation board, said in an interview that the grant was an opportunity for the foundation to help catalyze economic development in Boston and set a standard by which foundations in other urban areas could be involved in big, broad events that spur economic development, such as commercial conventions, civic celebrations, and political gatherings.

Both Pastor Hammond and Mr. Grogan, who is widely believed to harbor political aspirations, insisted that Democratic partisanship had not played a role in the foundation's decision. "We would have made the grant had it been the Republican National Convention," Mr. Grogan said, a point echoed by the pastor.

The Boston Foundation's commitment to the convention does not appear to have caused serious concern in the Boston area. If anything, a number of academic, nonprofit, and other observers think the award is a good one that can help the city.

Still, some nonprofit and community representatives, who did not want to be named, are critical of the grant. They argue that, at a time of increases in hunger, homelessness, and poverty, the $1 million could have been better spent on direct benefits for low-income and minority recipients and on an array of other social services, including low-cost housing and job-creation and -training programs. Some say that investments in long-term economic development projects, rather than short-term convention activities, would do the most good for the poor. Others say foundations should avoid supporting political activities, especially at the expense of the needy.

Of the several dozen nonprofit officials and observers interviewed for this column, John Bonifaz, executive director of the National Voting Rights Institute, in Boston, was the only one willing to speak for attribution. He said the grant to Boston 2004 is "too closely tied to overtly partisan political activity," and that "even the appearance of political partisanship can undermine the credibility of philanthropy."

The Boston Foundation's decision, no doubt, was made all the more difficult by the aggressive fund raising for the convention by the mayor and Senator Kennedy. But a few foundation representatives from the Boston area said that, had their foundations been asked to contribute to the convention, they would have turned down the requests. They said they believe their guidelines preclude political events. They also said there were more important projects and charities to support.

Besides the Boston Foundation's decision, philanthropic support for the

Democratic Convention has some other questionable elements worth noting. The State Street Corporation channeled its donation through its tax-exempt foundation, not as a direct business expenditure from the corporation. One possible reason for following this approach is that the bank can draw on accumulated foundation money rather than spend new corporate funds. The choice, however, could reduce the amount of money that otherwise would go to charities that serve the needy in the Boston area.

The more serious question that State Street's approach raises is whether tax-exempt funds of corporate foundations should be used to finance political events. While it is common for corporations to give money to politicians and political parties, they normally do so with taxable funds, accounting for the donations as business expenses.

No doubt, corporate-foundation grant making is motivated largely by self-interest and the bottom line. But that is different from using philanthropic funds to respond directly to politicians in whose jurisdictions a corporation is competing for business. Taxpayers should not be supporting that kind of corporate self-interest.

In 2000, the California Community Foundation, the community foundation for the Los Angeles area, gave a $25,000 grant to the mayor's office to help recruit and train volunteers for the Democratic National Convention. The city requested $100,000, but the foundation board felt that amount was inappropriate. That grant appears to be the only precedent to the Boston Foundation's award.

What, if any, are the long-term implications of the Boston Foundation grant for philanthropy? Is it a unique opportunity to improve the economy of a major city and the visibility of the foundation? Or is it merely a large amount of money that Boston could have raised another way? Could it set a precedent for community and other foundations that want to extend their civic and political influence? What if 10 or 15 other foundations decide to make large contributions to partisan political events? Wouldn't that endanger foundations at large? Doesn't the grant draw too fine a line between politics and philanthropy?

If foundations want to support partisan political activities and events at the national, state, or local levels, they should realize the potential consequences that such grant making may bring. After all, donors to foundations receive tax benefits because those institutions support a range of nonprofit programs and activities, including advocacy as well as services and research, not because they help support or conduct political activities. The latter could lead to increased government intervention and regulation.

Nor should we forget that the Ernest Istooks of this world—a reference to the Republican representative from Oklahoma who unsuccessfully sought to bar from political activism tax-exempt groups that receive federal money—are still lurking in Congress, waiting for the opportunity to pounce on the so-called liberal foundations and other nonprofit groups.

Foundations today face an enormous challenge in meeting the country's most urgent public needs. They don't have nearly enough money to meet the demands placed on them by charities and the public. They are cutting back on money for their grantees and refusing to support new programs and projects. They should continue to channel their grants to charitable and educational activities. The last thing they should do is wade into the swamp of politics at the expense of tackling important social problems.

The Boston Foundation made a tough and risky decision that it believes will help the city of Boston. One hopes it will. But it would be foolish in the long run for other foundations to follow suit.

∼

Grant Makers Should Turn the Evaluation
Spotlight on Themselves

From The Chronicle of Philanthropy, *September 4, 2003*

In recent years, foundations have been falling all over themselves trying to measure the work and effectiveness of their grant recipients. Yet, by and large, those same foundations have ignored the need to evaluate their own perform- ance using the same standards they set for the charities they support. What's good for the goose is apparently not so good for the gander.

That not only is unfair, but it also shows a contempt for the efforts of a wide variety of people and institutions to improve the effectiveness and ac- countability of philanthropy in this country.

Because foundations play such an important role in sustaining and strength- ening civil society, they have a duty to monitor and improve their perform- ance. The nation needs foundations that can learn from their failures as well as from their successes, that can more effectively meet the needs of charities, and that can reinforce democratic processes and institutions. By refusing to assess their own performance on a regular, systematic, and unbiased basis, founda- tions are failing to meet the urgent needs of grant recipients—and, by exten- sion, the public at large.

Not surprisingly, foundations are gung-ho for evaluating the performance of their grant recipients and the specific projects they carry out. They appear obsessed with the search for objective measurements and quantitative analy- ses, despite the skepticism about such an approach by leading evaluation re- searchers over the past thirty years. As the Harvard University philanthropy historian Peter Dobkin Hall has observed, "Evaluation as used in foundations today generally appears to have more to do with managing legitimacy than with any genuine concern with efficiency." In other words, if grantees can jus- tify their programs and document their progress, foundations believe, then who can cast stones at the grant makers themselves?

At the root of grant makers' search for legitimacy is their growing fear that the foundation world may not be producing maximum results and that its control over grant recipients may not be adequate to ensure desired objectives. This anxiety seems to stem from several factors: the wish to avoid risks, the pressure of trustees seeking verifiable results from nonprofit programs, grow- ing foundation mistrust of charities and their ability to carry out their mis- sions, and a longing for the warm comfort of objective measurements.

It also reflects foundations' loss of confidence in their own intuitions and judgments. That loss of confidence is one reason many foundations are increasingly insisting on negotiating goals and objectives with charities, calling the approach strategic philanthropy. It is why some are embracing a more hands-on relationship with charities—a practice often termed high-engagement philanthropy. Never mind whether such approaches help nonprofit groups maintain the independence they need to fulfill their missions.

To be fair, a handful of foundations have commissioned evaluations of their own activities. With few exceptions, however, those have been narrow in focus or conducted by friendly consultants, often as concerned with securing future contracts as with the stringency of their examinations.

What is needed is a commitment by the foundation world—starting with the Council on Foundations, Independent Sector, Philanthropy Roundtable, regional associations of grant makers, and other umbrella groups—to a new system for evaluating the performance of grant makers.

Such a system would mean assessing how well foundations individually and collectively are meeting the needs of charities and, ultimately, the people the nonprofit organizations seek to help. Are the foundations organized internally so that they can quickly recognize and deal with emerging social service and public policy needs? How willing are the foundations' boards and staff members to hear the voices of grantees, policy makers, and others? Are grant makers spending their resources wisely, and in ways that justify the preferential tax treatment they receive?

To insulate such an evaluation system from foundation pressures, it could be financed by a new organization supported by foundations themselves, as well as by other private sources. This organization could be governed by a broadly representative independent board that includes not only foundation officials but also grant recipients. To carry out the evaluations, the organization should finance nonprofit consulting groups, some established especially for this purpose, that could recruit teams composed of foundation representatives, grantees, scholars, community leaders, and independent writers and researchers who can conduct tough and fair assessments of philanthropic institutions.

In recent years many foundations have been criticized—often legitimately—for such faults as excessive executive compensation, high administrative costs, poor relationships with grantees, and neglect of major public needs. It is time foundations took a closer look at such failings, as well as at some of the best practices that have enriched the nonprofit world. A good start would be for several foundations, both large and small, to set an example and commission evaluations of their own operations.

But that would be just a start. The time has come for foundations and the umbrella groups that represent their interests to play by the same evaluation rules they have set for the nonprofit groups they support. To do less would be simply to prove the grant-making world's insecurity and fear of accountability.

∼

CORPORATE SOCIAL RESPONSIBILITY

Corporate Philanthropy More "Self-Interested" Than "Enlightened"

From The Chronicle of Philanthropy, January 26, 1995

Corporations have long characterized their philanthropy as a form of "enlightened self-interest," the notion that charitable contributions benefit the company as much as the community. But lately companies seem to be focusing much more on the "self-interest" and much less on the "enlightened." Some troubling examples:

- The ARCO Foundation abruptly fired its widely respected president, Eugene R. Wilson, who was responsible for much of the oil company's positive national image. In his seventeen years at ARCO, he had put the company on the philanthropic map, yet he was dismissed while on vacation without so much as a public "thank you." Loyalty, leadership, and excellence apparently had counted for nothing, not even at Atlantic Richfield.

- The Philip Morris Companies threatened to leave New York—and thus withdraw financial support for the city's arts organizations—if the city council passed a proposed antismoking ordinance. The company pressured arts organizations to intervene with the council. In asking for political favors from grantees, Philip Morris demonstrated blatant disregard for the spirit of philanthropy. Some observers were quick to criticize the arts groups but slow to condemn Philip Morris, as if it were acceptable for corporations to act this way.

- The new breed of CEO lacks the vision and long-term commitment to the local community shared by many of yesterday's corporate giants. A new generation of CEO's emerged in the 1970s and early 1980s with a broad vision of corporate responsibility. People like the Dayton brothers of the Minneapolis retailing family, John Filer of Aetna Life and Casualty, Andrew Heiskell of Time, Inc., Donald McNaughton of Prudential, J. Irwin Miller of Cummins Engine, William Woodside of American Can and Sky Chefs, and James Ross of BP America were imbued with a vision of corporate leadership that went beyond the bottom line. Today, by contrast, we are hard-pressed to identify socially aware executives who are willing to take on the mantle of community and national leadership.

This view of the state of corporate philanthropy is in sharp contrast to the "new paradigm" of social responsibility now gaining currency in the field.

In an article published in the *Harvard Business Review,* Craig Smith, a long-time observer of corporate giving, argued that more and more companies are using philanthropy to "increase their name recognition among consumers, boost employee productivity, reduce R&D costs, overcome regulatory obstacles, and foster synergy among business units." What the community and nonprofit groups get, he maintained, are corporate leadership in tackling social problems, companies' long-term commitment to finding solutions, and valuable noncash support—from management advice to employee volunteers.

So what's new?

Before the era of "downsizing" and mergers and acquisitions, companies used their giving programs to further their bottom-line goals. That was "enlightened self-interest."

Companies such as Aetna, Levi Strauss, Prudential, ARCO, and BP America started long-term programs in community and economic development. The insurance industry made some commitments to combat AIDS. Even before, in the 1970s, companies like Xerox lent their executives to charities to improve their operations—although the practice seemed to have little effect.

The "new paradigm" puts a good face on the same efforts going on today, but fails to explain other changes that are less flattering to corporate philanthropy.

Economic hard times in certain industries, acquisitions and mergers, and global competition have all tended to weaken corporate philanthropy. Over all, corporate giving has failed to keep pace with inflation for six straight years, according to the Council for Aid to Education.

Much of this real decline in corporate contributions can be attributed to companies' having to cut back in the face of operating deficits. But, disturbingly, some of the cutbacks have come from companies that are still making a sizable profit. When ARCO initially decided to "downsize" its philanthropy by drastically reducing its grants budget and firing the foundation staff, the company's profits had declined but still amounted to $269 million, with the prospect of better years ahead. Why didn't ARCO and other corporations that have reduced their giving programs instead cut corporate frills, such as club memberships and other executive benefits and privileges, rather than grants to strengthen community programs and organizations?

Sagging profits are not the only factor responsible for reductions in corporate giving over the past few years. Not that long ago, many companies viewed their charitable contributions as a means of stabilizing and strengthening the communities in which they would operate for many years to come. It was a long-term approach, motivated by enlightened self-interest, that aimed to create and strengthen nonprofit organizations, as well as ameliorating social problems.

But that was before the recent frenzy of mergers and acquisitions, the musical chairs–quality of executive turnover, the sky full of CEO parachutes, and the shift in corporate focus and planning to the immediate, rather than the long-term, future. It is not surprising that corporate philanthropy has followed suit, becoming a tool for short-term gains and objectives.

The "new paradigm" stresses what the company can achieve today, not tomorrow. As such, it is often not compatible with good citizenship.

Several other developments are putting up obstacles to good corporate citizenship:

- The increasingly global nature of the economy has given many companies another excuse for not paying much, if any, attention to domestic needs.

- The business community is riding high, enjoying greater popularity and credibility as government and politicians fall into disrepute.

- Many of the best corporate-contributions directors have retired or resigned in recent years, leaving a leadership void. Some have left because they did not like the direction in which corporate philanthropy was headed, or because they saw themselves as an endangered species. The firing of Gene Wilson at ARCO sent a clear warning signal to other corporate-contributions officers.

The shrinking of corporate philanthropy and its changing priorities are being felt throughout the nonprofit world. Large, established, and popular charitable organizations have generally held their own. But small, local, little-known, and activist groups have been hurt, which in turn has hurt the disadvantaged people whom those organizations tend to serve. While never known for either innovation or risk-taking, corporations today seem even more reluctant to support this type of grant making.

There is even some danger that a growing number of companies may be tempted to violate the boundaries of charitable giving and philanthropic ethics. In the Philip Morris case, the written grant contracts between the company and its grantees presumably did not include any requirements other than the conventional reporting and accountability obligations. By requesting political favors, Philip Morris converted philanthropy into business lobbying— regardless of whether the grantees approved. If not strictly illegal, such actions are clearly beyond the acceptable limits of charitable giving. Perhaps Philip Morris's poor judgment and the negative publicity it received will discourage other companies from similar efforts.

The importance of philanthropy to corporate operations is more in question today than it has been for many years. In a sense, corporations have been at least partially liberated from the bonds that tied them to charitable giving and their communities. They are in the driver's seat. They can do what they want with more impunity than ever.

The Philip Morris incident, the reluctance to get involved in the community, and the added pressure to make profits and further short-term interests all point to a potential danger: corporate grant makers may find it difficult to maintain the proper balance between market concerns and enlightened philanthropy, between business activities and good citizenship, between donor influence and grantee independence.

Occasionally, a community will loudly protest the downsizing of corporate philanthropy, as Los Angeles did in the ARCO case—a protest that, to the credit of ARCO's new CEO, led the company to affirm its commitment to the city, if not to restore the foundation's former grants budget.

Both corporations and nonprofit groups must be vigilant in protecting the equilibrium between community and corporate interests. Much will depend on the extent to which tomorrow's CEO's will have the leadership, vision, and dedication to good citizenship that is so vital to the nonprofit world.

~

The September 11th Attacks Challenge
Philanthropy to Stand Up to Corporate Opportunism

From The Chronicle of Philanthropy, *November 29, 2001*

If foundations are concerned about promoting democracy and curbing the corrosive power of big corporations, as some of them profess, they will have to become more activist and risk-taking than they have ever been. This fall's terrorist attacks have thrown them the gauntlet. How they respond will say a lot about their sense of responsibility, their values, and their capacity for change.

The terrorism of September 11 and, later, in our postal system, should have shattered any illusions we may have had about many of our corporate institutions. Banks have campaigned against new laws to restrict overseas money-laundering activities, and airlines have tried to hold on to their customary role of providing airport security on the cheap—despite the deaths of thousands of Americans stemming from the terrorist hijackings.

But what is good for banks and airlines is not always good for the country. It should be clear by now that corporations, while crucial to our economy, have only one major goal: making money. To them, everything else—national security, public health, environmental protection   is secondary in importance.

The attacks also have demonstrated how important, indeed essential, government is to our national life and well-being. Much maligned as too big, bureaucratic, and inefficient, the federal government, along with state and local jurisdictions, has labored in recent years to maintain public confidence. The role played by government and political leaders since September 11, however, appears to have reversed the long slide in the public's confidence in civic institutions, one hopes permanently.

Both those developments have profound implications for nonprofit organizations, as well as for foundations that support them. Their challenge will be to make certain, on the one hand, that corporate greed is held in check and, on the other hand, that government institutions not only regulate corporate excesses but are accountable and serve the public interest.

Nonprofit groups have, in the past, demonstrated that they are capable of accomplishing those tasks, if they have adequate resources and the courage to challenge established institutions. More than fifteen years ago a coalition of grass roots organizations challenged the policies of banks that refused to grant home mortgages and business loans in neighborhoods with large numbers of low-income people and minority-group members. With sound documentation and strong organizing pressure, the coalition, with a little foundation money, persuaded Congress to pass the Community Reinvestment Act, which affirms the obligation of banks to be fair in their lending policies.

Similarly, with the help of the Ford Foundation, environmental groups in the 1970s began their sustained research about and pressure on corporate polluters, efforts that have resulted in much higher standards of air quality, cleaner rivers, and the elimination of many toxic waste dumps.

Our growing laissez-faire economy has given rise to a corporate world that, having amassed unprecedented political influence by bankrolling elections and politicians of both parties, has run roughshod over the needs, rights, and safeguards of American citizens. It is fair to ask what the business schools at Harvard, Stanford, and other universities have done to inculcate a sense of ethics among their graduates.

Even after the September 11 disasters, big corporations, abetted by the shameless politicians who support them, are continuing their relentless push for tax breaks and subsidies, thus depriving the nation of the income needed for assistance to those most affected by the depressed economy. As Robert S. McIntyre, director of Citizens for Tax Justice, recently said, "Who would have thought that a national emergency would set off such a feeding frenzy by corporations and the wealthy? And who could have imagined that so many of our nation's elected officials would eagerly go along with this monstrous demonstration of greed."

That is not to say that we should abandon our free-enterprise system, which has proved to be superior to any other economic system. But it does speak to the need to repair capitalism as currently practiced, to place limits on its ability to undermine national interests.

Now is the time for nonprofit organizations to reassert themselves and fulfill this crucial responsibility. But that will be difficult because so many federal agencies—the Federal Aviation Administration, for one—as well as state and local governments remain the champions or prisoners of the very industries they are supposed to regulate. Their task will be made all the more difficult by the possibility that foundations, in the face of recession and September 11 humanitarian concerns, may reduce their grant making for these activities.

Contrary to their claim as the cutting edge of the nonprofit world, foundations are deeply afraid of examining and challenging the performance of both government and corporations. Over the past twenty years, only a relative handful of grants have been earmarked for that purpose. Foundations are grossly undersupporting organizations like Common Cause, the Center for Public Integrity, Citizens for Tax Justice, and the National Campaign for Jobs and Income Support that are doing effective advocacy work.

Nonprofit organizations have shown how effectively they can conduct research and monitor the policies and activities of corporate and government institutions, as well as the nation's electoral and political systems. They have the capacity to mobilize people and create powerful coalitions. And they have formidable lobbying skills. All they lack is the money with which to carry out those tasks. That, in the post-September 11 world, will be the responsibility and challenge of foundations.

~

Bad Research on Corporate Philanthropy

From The Chronicle of Philanthropy, *June 29, 1995*

The Capital Research Center is giving research a bad name. Its annual publication, *Patterns of Corporate Philanthropy,* is a piece of sloppy scholarship that demeans the integrity and intelligence of American corporate leadership.

The report's thesis is that America's largest corporations give too much money to liberal and left-leaning nonprofit organizations that supposedly are doing work that threatens the free-enterprise system, seeks to expand the role of government, or undermines respect for individual rights and responsibilities. In short, the book argues, major corporations are sowing the seeds of their own destruction.

To make things worse, it says, big businesses gave left-leaning policy groups more than three times the amount of money they gave to right-of-center policy groups.

Patterns of Corporate Philanthropy has always won a good deal of publicity from conservative-leaning publications. However, it has recently received more attention than usual. House Majority Leader Richard Armey has been criticized for sending a copy of the latest edition to eighty-two chief executives of major companies, along with a letter complaining that too many corporations were supporting left-wing causes.

The notes of alarm and danger sounded by the publication make it seem as though the Four Horsemen of the Apocalypse were once again on the rampage, destroying the very pillars of capitalism and our democratic society. But behind its anxiety and stridency are many false assumptions, fuzzy and simplistic definitions, a tiny amount of research, and a heavy dose of arrogance.

In making its case that corporate philanthropy is endangering free enterprise, Capital Research tracks 129 corporations and the approximately $36 million they contribute to nonprofit organizations involved in public policy, a minuscule portion of the more than $6 billion that corporations give to charity.

The center wrongly assumes that only those grants awarded to public-policy groups are used for advocacy purposes. That is not the case. Most of the establishment institutions that are the recipients of the overwhelming majority of corporate philanthropy—such as universities, hospitals, United Ways, arts groups, cultural institutions, and social service organizations—devote at least some of their budgets to advocacy work.

With some exceptions, those are not left-of-center organizations. The universe of corporate-supported nonprofit public-policy activity, therefore, is much larger and more conservative than that seen through the center's narrow viewfinder.

The Capital Research Center's results are also distorted by another false assumption: that all the money donated by corporations to the nonprofit groups cited in its report is actually used for public-policy and advocacy purposes. That is not accurate. While some of the organizations are primarily engaged in policy and advocacy, many others devote only a small portion of their funds to influencing government.

Groups like the National Urban League, the Enterprise Foundation, the Council on Foundations, and the National Council of La Raza spend most of their money on charitable programs and providing support to other nonprofit groups. Others spend their funds on nonpartisan research or scientific studies.

My own organization, the Center for Community Change, which is listed in the report, allocates the vast majority of its resources to helping antipoverty groups in urban and rural communities strengthen their organizations, improve their self-help programs, and revitalize their neighborhoods. Our on-site technical assistance to community groups, along with leadership training and fundraising help, is primarily what corporations and other grant makers support. Of our forty-eight staff members, only one works full time on public policy.

The Capital Research Center has not done its homework. It does not really know what most of the groups it has surveyed actually do or how they allocate their resources. Its so-called researchers have never spoken to us nor visited us to inquire about our operations. Yet they have not hesitated to classify nonprofit groups into eight broad categories ranging from "conservative" to "radical left." They label organizations' goals with vague phrases, accusing some groups of pursuing "collectivist public policies" and defending "government's role as a problem solver" and others as "defenders of individual liberty and responsibility" and supporters of "government-initiated restructuring of American economic and social institutions."

The center does not attempt to explain or clarify the meaning of those terms. Its leaders believe that change-oriented right-wing groups are champions of individual liberty and responsibility, but they do not feel the same way about organizations like ours that run self-help programs and promote economic opportunity in low-income communities. That is ideological claptrap, not research.

Runaway ideology prompts the Capital Research Center to paint all the groups it considers liberal as anti–free enterprise and anti-business—once again reflecting its ignorance of those organizations.

On the contrary, the nonprofit groups cited in the report are strong supporters of the free-enterprise system and the crucial importance of business in our democratic society. Yet those organizations also believe that individual rights must be protected, that the environment must be preserved, that discrimination should be eliminated, that the workplace must be safe, and that all institutions, private and public, must be accountable and free of corruption.

When those essential features of our democracy are undermined, those groups feel they have a responsibility to criticize institutions that have failed to play by the rules of the game, whether they be governments, nonprofit organizations, the press, or businesses. Those checks and balances afforded by free speech and debate are the strength of our American system.

Unfortunately, the Capital Research Center does not really believe in the give and take of a democracy. It automatically ostracizes any institution that criticizes some business practices or would like to see greater corporate responsibility in areas like environmental protection or community revitalization. Those who seek reform and improvement are lambasted as destroyers. Those who understand and support the important role of the federal government in a representative democracy are derided as big-government proponents and critics of big business.

The Capital Research Center's approach is a hangover from the Cold War mentality of "if you're not with us, you're against us." It fails to reflect the complexity of our society and institutions. It may be the stuff of Tom Clancy novels, but it is not research.

Of the 129 corporations surveyed in its report, only one, the Eli Lilly Company, wins an A for its record of not supporting anti–free enterprise and business-bashing groups. No company receives a B, only nine earn a C, and the rest get D's and F's.

The center's conclusion is that big-business support of advocacy groups "flies in the face of conventional wisdom." It adds, "It is clear that too many corporate executives just don't get it."

It's the Capital Research Center that doesn't get it. Its indictment of corporate leadership flies in the face not of conventional wisdom but of thoughtful judgment. Its presumption that it knows better than experienced corporate leadership what is best for American business reflects both arrogance and ignorance.

The center shows its failure to understand the nature of corporate philanthropy by excoriating corporations that have made charitable contributions during a year in which they lost money. Corporations give money because they know that the favorable publicity they get from supporting good works helps to sell their products. It is good for business—just as lobbying costs and capital investments are good for business—even during a losing year. Another example of amateurs second-guessing the professionals.

A careful reading of the Capital Research Center's work should silence the alarm bells about the state of corporate philanthropy. Despite the center's efforts to build a mountain out of a molehill, the molehill still stands. The free-enterprise system is still alive and well. The only danger to big business comes from so-called friends like those at the Capital Research Center. *Patterns of Corporate Philanthropy* has been, and remains, "much ado about nothing."

Drucker on Philanthropy: Without Foundation

From The Chronicle of Philanthropy, *July 29, 1999*

Peter F. Drucker, the guru of corporate management, is considered by many to also be a guru of nonprofit management. Yet the widely acclaimed nonagenarian has once again demonstrated how out of touch he is with philanthropy.

In an interview in the March–April issue of *Philanthropy,* a magazine published by the Philanthropy Roundtable, Mr. Drucker observed: "Well, let's be indiscreet. Name a single major foundation that has done a good job for more than five or eight years, without turning into a grant-making machine where grant requests come in and the money flows out. The Ford Foundation had this one accomplishment—the Green Revolution in India—but otherwise, all their spending has had absolutely no results. When is the last time the Carnegie Foundation [*sic*] made a difference? Not in my lifetime. Rockefeller made a difference—a tremendous difference—in the 1920s and 1930s, but since then what have they done?"

On what planet has Mr. Drucker been living? Were he more earthbound, he might have noted the enormous contributions made by those three major foundations, as well as others, to the arts, the environment, consumerism, community development, civil rights, opportunities for members of minority groups, women's issues, education, health, and housing—not to mention the building of civil societies overseas and economic and community development activities to help the poor around the world.

Those contributions were made over four decades. There is absolutely no evidence that foundations can't go beyond five to eight years before becoming routine and uncreative in their grant making.

Were it not for Mr. Drucker's distinguished career as an analyst of and expert on corporate management, his opinions on the nonprofit world could simply be discarded as just plain silly and ignorant. But they can't. They deserve critical attention.

Mr. Drucker's notion of philanthropy appears in large part to reflect—and is as misplaced as—the attitudes toward philanthropy that emanate from the Manhattan Institute, the Capital Research Center, and other conservative think tanks. According to that view, the major foundations performed well as long as they were sponsoring scientific and medical research, building libraries and other university facilities, underwriting established cultural and arts programs, combating diseases, and promoting education. In the 1960s, when they started focusing on new social and economic issues—the problems of poverty, race, and gender and the need for new organizations and mechanisms to adapt our democratic society to a rapidly changing world—those foundations, according to conservative gospel, lost their way.

But while most conservatives decry the so-called activism of major foundations, they don't say that those philanthropies haven't made a difference. That observation is left to the less ideological and more ingenuous Mr. Drucker. If only he had actually looked at the foundations' records, talked to some of their staff members, and asked nonprofit executives for their opinions, he might have found the following:

The Ford Foundation has had a profound impact on American society during the past thirty-five years. It has provided crucial support to many, if not most, of the major minority and civil rights organizations in the country. More than any other foundation, it has been responsible for the creation and growth of the community development movement and the nonprofit financial and other organizations that sustain a large portion of that movement. The Police Foundation, one of its creations, has done much to improve policing throughout the country. Its generous support of community foundations has been one of the reasons behind the rapid growth in the number and size of community foundations nationally. Its creation of the Public Education Fund (now the Public Education Network), its support of the influential magazine *Youth Today,* and its establishment of the National Arts Stabilization Fund have all had impressive results.

The Carnegie Corporation can point to similar high spots in its philanthropy. Its Commission on Public Broadcasting led to the creation of the Corporation for Public Broadcasting. It sponsored Gunnar Myrdal's monumental work, *An American Dilemma,* a book that not only shed new light on the nature of race relations in this country but also was instrumental in advancing the arguments that resulted in the historic Supreme Court decision that declared the doctrine of "separate but equal" to be unconstitutional and ended legal segregation in the American school system. With other foundations, Carnegie was responsible for helping to establish and sustain the Children's Defense Fund and a number of other legal-defense organizations. Its promotion of quality early childhood education, including children's television through *Sesame Street* and other programs, has left its distinctive mark on the field. And it developed the National Board for Professional Teaching Standards.

As for Rockefeller, we certainly shouldn't forget the major role that that foundation played in the Green Revolution. What's more, Rockefeller, along with Carnegie and Ford, supported anti-apartheid activities in South Africa, which Nelson Mandela and others have credited with helping the nation make a peaceful transition to a democratic, black-led, multiracial society. Other foundations can also trumpet success stories that have positively affected our society.

While I and other observers of philanthropy have been—and still are—critical of many of the priorities and grant-making activities of major mainstream foundations, we have to recognize that they have helped to establish, nurture, and sustain many of the most important nonprofit organizations and programs of the past four decades. Indeed, they have made a substantial difference. Mr. Drucker, I'm happy to say, is dead wrong.

~

Hospital Offers Glad Tithings to South Bend: Supporting Community Groups

From The Chronicle of Philanthropy, *September 10, 1998*

A five-year grant of more than $1 million to a grassroots organization for general operating support seems almost unbelievable in the current grant-making climate. Yet the South Bend Heritage Foundation, an Indiana charity that works to fight poverty, was recently the recipient of just such a philanthropic rarity.

What makes the gift even more astounding is that the donor is Memorial Hospital, a nonprofit institution in South Bend that "tithes" 10 percent of its operating surplus each year for grants to community programs and projects run by the city's nonprofit organizations.

According to Brooke Rosman at the American Hospital Association's Health Research and Educational Trust in Chicago, some twenty hospitals currently commit about 10 percent of their operating surpluses for grant making in their communities. A few others, while not tithing, are also acting as grant makers to support local nonprofit organizations.

Virtually all of the hospitals that participate in such programs are nonprofit institutions, though there is nothing to prevent for-profit hospitals from getting into the act as well. At a time when so much attention has been focused on the philanthropic foundations being created with the assets of nonprofit healthcare entities that convert to for-profit status, another source of philanthropic funds has often been overlooked. Indeed, tithing by hospitals represents a potentially rich vein of support for needy charitable organizations.

The philosophy behind tithing is both simple and pragmatic: it rests on the belief that community health is as much a social, economic, and environmental matter as it is a medical one. Major community problems like health, crime, and poverty, tithing hospitals believe, are interrelated and cannot be resolved in piecemeal fashion. By investing in community partners, those hospitals realize that they receive an extremely positive return: more productive nonprofit groups and programs from which they can learn and through which they can extend their outreach and effectiveness in the health field.

"Tithing doesn't cost you a penny," says Phil Newbold, president of Memorial Hospital. "You get much more back than you put in."

Memorial Hospital, part of the area's Memorial Health System, established its Community Benefit Fund five years ago from the previous year's excess operating revenues. At the time, it distributed about $1 million to worthy nonprofit groups that were working to improve the health of the community.

This year, the Community Benefit Fund will distribute more than $3 million in grants to charitable organizations in South Bend. In a departure from previous grant making, the fund will provide large, multiple-year grants to a few of the city's most effective groups, including the South Bend Heritage Foundation. The fund will also award smaller amounts to many other institutions.

The five-year commitment from Memorial Hospital will provide the financial stability that the twenty-year-old South Bend Heritage Foundation requires. One of the most productive and impressive community organizations in the country, the charity, headed by Jeff Gibney, boasts a formidable track record of accomplishments, including the development of more than five hundred units of low- and moderate-income housing, the construction and management of a major youth center and shopping center, the establishment of a community health clinic, and success in persuading city government, through advocacy, to devote more of its resources to the poorest parts of town.

Despite its impressive record and importance to the city, however, the charity has continually struggled to maintain its operations and small core staff of nine people. South Bend and its environs have few foundations. The large foundations in Indianapolis, such as the Lilly Endowment and the Moriah Fund, have been somewhat reluctant to spread their bounty to the northern part of the state, while the major national foundations haven't demonstrated much interest in supporting grassroots organizations, especially those located in small or mid-sized cities. Were it not for the charity's creativity in earning revenue from its community development projects, including housing, it could not have survived.

The financing of nonprofit organizations through hospital funds represents a wise use of community and private resources, especially in small and mid-sized cities and regions with few foundations and corporate headquarters. The payoff for participating hospitals in terms of credibility, community outreach, and sounder community health programs can be considerable. South Bend's Memorial Hospital has blazed a noteworthy trail that others, one hopes, will soon follow.

~

PHILANTHROPY IN THE TWENTY-FIRST CENTURY

The "New Philanthropy" Isn't New—or Better

From The Chronicle of Philanthropy, *January 28, 1999*

Various publications recently have been touting "the new philanthropy," which, they say, promises to make grant making more effective and accountable.

The new philanthropy, according to those accounts, includes two types of grant making. The first is the emergence of new large donors, many of them from the prosperous field of technology, who want to apply their business skills to giving away their money. The second is the increasing number of foundations that are directly and intimately involved in the development and implementation of their grantees' projects and programs.

So what's new in the new philanthropy? Not much. Such practices have long been common. But their growing frequency and size are a disturbing development that raises the fundamental question of who should control the mission, goals, and agendas of nonprofit organizations: donors, or the boards and staffs of the nonprofit groups themselves?

For the wealthy newcomers to philanthropy, grant making generally is viewed as a hands-on process in which individual donors are involved from beginning to end. Like venture capitalists, they want to insure that their investments pay off, that there is a measurable product, and that the recipients of their munificence are good and accountable managers. Being intimately engaged also gives the donors an added sense of personal satisfaction. It does not seem to matter that they may not have any skills, experience with charitable organizations, or other qualifications beyond their business background.

While some commentators are calling this approach new, it is nothing of the kind. Large donors like John D. Rockefeller, Andrew Carnegie, and Walter Annenberg took a close personal interest in the way their money was distributed, at least in the initial stages of their philanthropic ventures. Nor can it be said that a concern for accountability, good management, and measurable results are novel qualities that big donors, individual and institutional, are bringing to the grant-making table.

Responsible foundations and program officers have traditionally insisted on their grantees' accountability, made grants that have produced results, and helped nonprofit organizations improve their performance. How else can one explain the many successes in many fields of which foundations can rightfully boast?

Of the two types of "new philanthropy," programs that are both inspired and controlled by foundations—or what might be called frontline philan-thropy—is the more disturbing. Such philanthropy is often characterized by the heavy involvement of foundation staff members in the gestation and man-agement of a program, by the selection by the foundation staff of consultants to grantees, by evaluators from foundations who assess the results and success of the project, and, in some cases, by the creation of new nonprofit groups with little legitimacy in a community or in a particular charitable field.

To justify their strategy of increased control, many foundations cite the importance of their having more of an impact. As a senior program officer from a major New York foundation told me, "We have a limited amount of money to spend on domestic social programs. We therefore want to make sure that this money is well spent and targeted to meet our institutional objectives. In order for us to have an impact, our staff must play a key, active role as a partner."

Given the imbalance in financial power between foundations and their grantees, it is not surprising that those "partnerships" are usually controlled by the grant makers.

There are other reasons for foundations' wanting to be involved in the im-plementation of programs. Many bright program officers have their own ideas about how things should be done and are not content merely to respond to proposals by nonprofit organizations. They want to set goals and objectives and shape new programs and public policy.

Then, too, some foundations that specialize in a particular field have one or more experts on board who believe that they know what to do about cer-tain problems. It hardly matters to them that the nonprofit world has hun-dreds, if not thousands, of experts for every one in the foundation world.

The Annie E. Casey Foundation, for example, spends almost all of its large grants budget on its own programs. Although grant applicants may have other needs and priorities, they do not have the option of asking for such funds. Ei-ther they buy into the foundation's program, or they get no money.

The same is true for the Equal Opportunity Program at the Rockefeller Foundation, and at other foundations as well. In the environmental field, the Pew Charitable Trusts has built a reputation for pouring millions of dollars into its own environmental projects and creating new organizations. In large measure, Pew has ignored much of the environmental movement, especially the grassroots organizations, that over the past thirty-five years have provided outstanding leadership on environmental issues throughout the world.

That is not to say that all foundation-inspired projects are manipulative and controlling. Many have been eminently worthwhile, and many foundations have been properly mindful of the independence of their grantees. Among them are the Charles Stewart Mott and Public Welfare foundations.

But the more money that is devoted to such efforts, the less is available for desperately needed general operating support, for unsolicited proposals, and for other important special projects. For too many nonprofit organizations, which often struggle to make ends meet, the lure of money has unfortunately led them to sacrifice some of their independence, flexibility, and institutional creativiity.

Behind many of these programs is a lack of confidence and trust by foundation executives in the ability of grantees to run successful programs. That attitude, which reflects the views of a small group of elitists who presume to know what is best for communities and charitable organizations, has done as much as anything else to arouse the deep suspicion, frustration, and resentment that so many nonprofit executives have long felt toward their colleagues in the philanthropic world.

There is nothing really new in this state of affairs. The new philanthropy is nothing more than the old philanthropy, except that it is occurring more frequently and involves greater amounts of money. As such, it deserves to be analyzed, questioned, and challenged, both by donors and by grantees. Unchecked, it could threaten the vibrancy, creativity, and independence of nonprofits at a time when such qualities are needed more than ever before.

～

Raising Some $25–Trillion Questions:
Making Sure the Wealth Transfer Benefits Society

From The Chronicle of Philanthropy, *December 16, 1999*

It's hard not to be ecstatic about recent projections that indicate that $25 trillion or more could be donated or bequeathed to charities and foundations over the next fifty years. Such numbers are breathtaking, more than anybody ever dreamed would go to philanthropy.

Too few people, however, have begun to grapple with the obligation to insure that this Niagara-sized bounty is used to improve the lives of all Americans—especially those left behind by the current economic boom. If the new donors give in old ways—and some early indications are that they will—then those trillions of dollars may not make much of a difference in shaping a better future for our society.

Traditionally, giving by both individual donors and foundations has been safe, convenient, and conventional, with individuals giving to their places of worship, alma maters, and favorite cultural groups, and foundations giving overwhelmingly to well-established institutions in the health, education, arts, and social services fields. Very little philanthropic money has supported local and small grassroots social services organizations. Even less has supported organizing, public policy work, and advocacy by groups that represent low-income people, minorities, and other disadvantaged constituencies.

Partly as a result, substantial poverty and other social woes undermine the fabric of our society. Faith in the benefits of government wanes. And the issue of race and racism continues to divide us. To be truly effective, a substantial part of the philanthropic assets of the forthcoming transfer of wealth must be used to deal with those vital issues and needs.

Now that the federal government is shifting more and more power and money to states and cities, the capacity and willingness of philanthropy to make resources available to local nonprofit organizations will help determine the success of "devolution." Many local charities and government agencies are in desperate need of funds to become more competitive and effective at both the local and state levels.

Like today's foundations, many of the new large foundations are likely to give mostly to national or international groups, claiming that distributing small grants is not cost-effective. At the same time, they will be reluctant to provide large grants to nonprofit intermediaries for regranting to smaller local organizations.

However, there are ways that large amounts of money can be distributed to local communities. Gifts to community foundations, for example, are an easy and effective means of accomplishing that task. So are gifts to other national and regional organizations that are experienced in distributing the funds to local groups. Or, the donors could take part of their funds and create a number of smaller new regional foundations in areas that are underserved by philanthropy.

But even if they do so, some nagging questions remain. The new foundations will represent staggering amounts of money. The Bill and Melinda Gates Foundation is now worth more than $17 billion, the David and Lucile Packard Foundation is now worth $13 billion, and the William and Flora Hewlett Foundation, which is valued at $2.3 billion, is soon expected to triple or quadruple in size. Indeed, it is not inconceivable that during the next three or four decades, U.S. foundations could reach $50 billion to $100 billion in assets—more than the economies of many nations.

Consequently, it may be time to re-evaluate the role that philanthropies play in a democracy. At what size, for example, do foundations—institutions that are cushioned from the electoral process and the market's bottom line—begin to arrogate too much power and influence over the nation's policies and priorities? What actions should be taken to insure that the boards of the large foundations are representative of the nation and its diverse interests? When, if at all, should antitrust measures be invoked?

In our democracy, representative government has the responsibility for determining public policies and priorities. It grants tax advantages to philanthropy so that the country's charities and other institutions of civil society can be maintained and strengthened. If we determine, however, that the public's best interests are not being served, then we have to alter these institutions.

For example, to get the most from philanthropy, the government might need to consider applying antitrust measures. It is hard to say how big a foundation can reasonably be without violating the public interest, but that is something the government and its citizens will have to study and decide. If foundations are found to be too large, they will have to be broken up into smaller institutions that are governed by separate and representative boards of trustees.

Making would-be mega-foundations smaller will not be enough to insure accountable and enlightened philanthropy. Who serves on foundation boards will be crucial. Trustees should not be just family members or friends of the family. Nor should they be other foundation staff members. They should include people with experience in running nonprofit groups, community representatives, civic leaders, and others who can bring to the boards a keen perspective and understanding of public needs. Boards that are more diverse in terms of class, race, and temperament are likely to lead to better grant making.

Thinking about such issues now is crucial. It's not good enough for us to lay back and wait for the gold to pour into our philanthropic coffers. We must begin now to discuss and debate where the money will go. Those conversations will provide some much-needed guidance to the nation's future big donors, as well as help many of today's foundations figure out how to become more effective and relevant.

3

How Best to Help the Needy

After the Los Angeles Riots:
The Solution Lies in Neighborhoods

From The Chronicle of Philanthropy, *June 16, 1992*
*This article was written after Los Angeles was torn by rioting following a
court acquittal of four white police officers who had been charged with
assaulting a black motorist, Rodney King.*

The anger, violence, and destruction that engulfed parts of Los Angeles in May
stemmed from many interrelated causes: chilling poverty, the lack of available
jobs, police brutality, racial inequalities and tension, easy access to automatic
weapons, disaffected gangs of young adults, and poor social services. And that's
just the beginning of the list.

At the heart of the social cyclone was a feeling of frustration and despair
about life in South-Central and other neighborhoods, a sense of hopelessness
about the future, and a conviction that nothing much would be lost through
rash action. It was a desperate reaction to a desperate set of urban conditions,
to which we Americans, despite our occasional rhetoric of sympathy, have become largely impervious.

The lessons of the 1960s explosions in Detroit, Watts, and elsewhere seem
to have been lost on us after years of government neglect, the rapid growth of
suburbia and a smug middle class, and a collective refusal to provide the investment needed to rebuild our neighborhoods and cities.

To those lessons of what for many appear the distant past, Los Angeles
added a few new twists. Serious urban problems are no longer just a matter of
black and white. They are now issues of class and poverty. They are multiethnic
and multicultural. Racial tensions in an increasing number of communities involve Hispanics and Asian Americans as well as whites and blacks. The looters
we saw on our television screens were a rainbow coalition. So were the victims.

117

What do we make of all this? What can we do to help rebuild our urban neighborhoods, not to mention our severely depressed rural areas, which we continue to neglect?

If we have learned anything over the years, we should realize by now that the same problem afflicted Watts and Detroit and South-Central and Long Beach: Without a human infrastructure of strong community-based organizations and mediating institutions such as churches, fraternal organizations, merchants' associations, and other groups, communities are likely to lose cohesion, become chaotic, and produce fewer leaders. Without strong organizational structures, those communities cannot apply pressure on government and the political leadership for equitable services, resources, and treatment. And so they become second-class areas, the residual repositories of voiceless and powerless people, the tinderboxes from which explosions can be expected tomorrow and twenty years from now.

A dozen community development organizations and other neighborhood-based groups in South-Central could serve as the nucleus of citizen power, providing neighborhood residents with a real stake in the community. But with the exception of Watts Labor Community Action Center, their resources have been minuscule and their staffs severely limited in number because of a lack of philanthropic support.

Most Los Angeles–based foundations and corporations, like their counterparts in many other cities, have been reluctant to support community organizations in their self-help, organizing, housing and economic development, and advocacy efforts. In avoiding the tough issues of poverty, race, and the empowerment of community organizations, those grant makers have not met the test of responsive philanthropy. In a real sense, they have let down their city. In seeking safety, they have attained mediocrity.

The initial response to the riots by Los Angeles philanthropies appears uncertain and muted. An initial meeting with community-based organizations, social service groups, and other nonprofits called by several grant makers seemed to generate more frustration and annoyance than optimism on the part of community representatives. As one of the community group leaders observed, it is likely to be business as usual.

In contrast to the reaction by Los Angeles philanthropies, several large national foundations, such as Ford and Charles Stewart Mott, have already committed substantial funds to community groups in the city. And several foundations in the San Francisco area, such as the James Irvine and Tides Foundations, have indicated that they want to support rebuilding activities by grassroots organizations in Los Angeles.

But foundations and corporations outside the city can't be expected to carry the burden either in the short or long term. That will fall on those philanthropic organizations within the metropolitan Los Angeles area. The California Community Foundation, chartered to provide for the public needs of the city and county, will have a special responsibility in meeting the challenge of rebuilding South-Central and other low-income neighborhoods.

What happened in Los Angeles and Long Beach could happen in other cities throughout the country, tomorrow or a year or two from now. Dozens, if not hundreds, of neighborhoods in this country suffer from the same level of poverty, racial tension, and hopelessness as South-Central does.

Fortunately, many of them have community organizations in various stages of development. They are the seeds of community renewal, the building blocks for a revitalization process. Despite their track record of success and their promise, they are starving for a lack of staff and resources. They are philanthropy's neglected stepchildren in a society that proclaims the virtue of self-help and bootstrap approaches but refuses to provide the bootstraps.

Although foundations, corporations, and a few United Ways have increased their giving to low-income and minority community-based organizations during the past ten years, those donations still represent a tiny, almost imperceptible, sliver of the philanthropic pie. Perhaps the shock of Los Angeles will prompt a rethinking and reordering of priorities. A substantial amount of new money will be needed for community-based efforts to develop and stabilize urban neighborhoods. The next few years will not be time for business as usual.

While locally based community-development efforts will have to be the frontline in the rebuilding process, they cannot be expected to succeed in isolation from macroeconomic and other national public policies that shape and determine local activities and resources. We cannot afford to create expectations at the local level that cannot be fulfilled.

Local community-development programs must be accompanied by national and state public policies that provide jobs, undertake long-neglected public-works programs, reduce the number of dangerous weapons on our streets, increase the amount of money for low-income housing, provide capital and insurance for small businesses in inner cities, and give literacy and Head Start education to all eligible recipients. Local grassroots activities must also be complemented by serious efforts to reform and strengthen local governments. If the legitimacy and authority of city governments are not restored, it will be impossible to govern our urban areas, let alone rebuild them.

This presents an enormous challenge to foundations, which favor safe and traditional grant making over risk-taking and innovation. Few grant makers have been willing to underwrite the public-policy and advocacy activities of nonprofit organizations. Fewer still have shown any interest in government reform, citizen monitoring, and public accountability issues. Yet if we are to forge a multiracial and multicultural society based on economic opportunity and social justice, those are the very efforts that will have to be supported financially.

Is there any reason to believe that our philanthropic institutions will be able to rise above their past principles and priorities in the public interest? It is too early to tell. Strong support for community-based organizations, for public-policy and advocacy coalitions, and for improved and accountable local governments would be a radical departure for all but a few of our foundations, corporations, and United Ways. But if the serious concern, conversation, and contemplation now under way in the philanthropic backrooms are any indication, we might have some reason to believe that change, albeit slow, might take place.

If no changes are made, then philanthropy will have failed in its purpose of meeting the nation's most urgent public needs. More than a few people will seriously wonder whether the benefits of philanthropy still outweigh its costs in tax expenditures and its implicit support of establishment institutions and an increasingly unjust and divisive society.

∼

Time to Remove the Rose-Colored Glasses: Community Groups Demand Scrutiny

From Shelterforce, March–April 2000

Though outwardly positive and peaceful, the community development movement has been marked from the beginning by sharp philosophical differences, disputed achievements, and serious tensions. The rarity of public airings of community development corporations' problems and weaknesses is due to the absence of critical analysis of these organizations. The literature of the movement is almost pure exegesis, written by cheerleaders, not objective observers. Only recently have any analysts begun to focus on the movement's problems and limits.

In recent years a number of established and seemingly successful CDCs have either shut down or suffered serious setbacks. Many others walk a fine line; they are undercapitalized, overextended, and poorly managed, and they lack general operating support.

Perhaps most surprising of CDC failures was the 1997–98 collapse of Eastside Community Investments in Indianapolis. With more than eighty employees and a multimillion-dollar budget, ECI had gained a national reputation as one of the community development movement's pilot ships. It became the darling of city officials and large foundations like the Lilly Endowment. Despite early warnings of financial disaster before it spun out of control, the organization continued operating without foundation oversight or public scrutiny. When ECI finally went belly-up, the Lilly Endowment, which had poured millions into its operation, chose to look the other way. Neither it nor city government appointed a team of evaluators to investigate what happened, lessons that might have benefitted other struggling CDCs. The same was true for foundation funders in other cities where CDCs died or lay on their deathbeds.

The reason for this "ostrich head in the sand" approach is that foundations, financial intermediaries, and CDCs themselves have collaborated in a conspiracy of silence in an attempt to maintain an "all is well" image to the outside world. No one has had the courage to take the responsibility for the movement's failures.

Shaped by Funders

A look at the movement's history provides another explanation. Funders' philosophies and priorities have largely shaped CDCs. Private foundations, corporate donors, and the federal government are not institutions often known for their courage, tenacity, and risk-taking.

The community development movement's roots lie in earlier economically oriented organizations such as city booster corporations, community unions, Southern low-income co-operatives, and some of the early grantees of the Office of Economic Opportunity's Research and Demonstration Division. But modern CDCs began in 1967 with the Labor Department's Special Impact Program's launching of the Bedford Stuyvesant Restoration Corporation. A year later, under the same program, the Office of Economic Opportunity funded its first CDC, the Hough Area Development Corporation in Cleveland. By mid–1971, OEO, which had taken over SIP, had funded eighteen urban and nineteen rural CDCs. In the 1970s the number of CDCs grew rapidly.

Initially, CDCs were to be more than generators of housing and economic development. Behind the Special Impact Program—later Title VII of the Economic Opportunity Act—lay the notion that comprehensive efforts were needed to attack the problems of poor neighborhoods and communities. Community development corporations would assist in the economic, social, and physical revitalization of low-income communities. They would develop jobs, improve services, build indigenous leadership, and involve private enterprise in the rebuilding process. Neighborhood residents would be an integral part of this work, both serving on CDC boards and as an active constituency.

Many of the early CDCs did undertake a balanced program of economic development, services, public education, and advocacy strategies. But the pressure to focus almost exclusively on housing and economic development intensified by the end of President Nixon's first term. Joseph Halbach, who then headed the Office of Economic Opportunity's Economic Development Division, claimed that social goals conflicted with economic objectives. He insisted that CDCs should be profitable enterprises, not concerned with resident participation or community control. When Gerald Mukai took over the unit during the Carter presidency, he took Mr. Halbach's philosophy one step further, informing CDCs that they were to operate like businesses. He encouraged and condoned some of the questionable practices they modeled after their business counterparts.

In the 1970s, foundations found CDCs attractive alternatives to more activist local organizations and pressured them to more narrowly focus on housing and economic development.

The Ford Foundation, with a large investment in CDCs, provided much of the philanthropic leadership that steered community development in this direction. Ford's philosophy, espoused by Mike Sviridoff, the foundation's capable and energetic vice president for domestic programs, was based on a hierarchical view of community-based organizations. At the apex of the pyramid were large CDCs that enjoyed close, friendly relationships with business and local governments; at the bottom were the activist groups involved in community organizing and issue advocacy. The fact that an organizing group like Citizens Organized for Public Service in San Antonio had been responsible for shifting hundreds of million of dollars in federal and local money to the impoverished did nothing to shake Ford officials' belief that organizing and development were incompatible. Indeed, only in the last couple of years has Ford begun to support community organizing and constituency building.

Corporations also found CDCs to their liking. CDCs fit the corporate image of bottom line, results-oriented organizations with which they could easily relate, as long as the groups did not attack established community institutions or cause too much trouble. The Reagan years accelerated this tendency of CDCs to follow a straight housing and economic development path.

Paying the Price

But this departure from the Special Impact Program's original vision came with a price. Lured by the siren call of funders, many CDCs dropped their organizing, advocacy, and community leadership development activities. Perhaps none was so dramatic as the shift in the Mississippi Action for Community Education's efforts that had built a strong constituency in sixteen counties through community organizing. In eliminating its organizing and advocacy projects, the group lost much of its constituency, influence, and power—a development from which it has yet to recover. Other organizations like Telecu in Los Angeles, the Spanish Speaking Unity Council in Oakland, BUILD in Buffalo and the Mexican American Unity Council in San Antonio experienced similar changes.

This more narrow agenda often proved self-defeating for CDCs. In many cities, universities and hospitals destroyed thousands of affordable housing units without any opposition from their neighborhood CDCs. This often resulted in a net loss of affordable housing in these communities, despite CDCs' efforts to produce new housing. And it was not surprising that the battle to win passage of the Home Mortgage Disclosure Act and the Community Reinvestment Act was won by community-organizing and advocacy groups, not CDCs, which had the most to gain from this legislation but did little or nothing to promote it.

In their push to become more business-like, many organizations appointed business people and professionals to their boards, limited the size of their boards, and reduced the role of community residents in their operations. Community accountability lost its cachet with CDC directors and staff. In the face of enormous pressures to narrow their efforts, it is a tribute to certain organizations like the Bickerdike Redevelopment Corporation in Chicago, the Northwest Bronx Laity and Clergy Concerned, Los Sures and the Fifth Avenue

Committee in New York, the Coalition for a Better Acre in Lowell, Massachusetts, and the South Bend Heritage Foundation in South Bend, Indiana, that
they continued their comprehensive approach to community development.

The emergence of the large intermediary organizations, especially the
Local Initiative Support Corporation, the Enterprise Foundation, and the National Congress for Community Economic Development, further abetted this
narrow development. It also perpetuated the view that all was well in the community development world. NCCED issued periodic reports on the movement's impressive expansion, based on the assertions of the organizations
themselves, without any objective analysis. Wishing to maintain the confidence
of donors, Enterprise and LISC became the national public relations advocates
for community development. They were neither anxious to stir and encourage
the growth of advocacy nor cause the problems and tensions many organizations were experiencing to surface.

It was in the intermediaries' self-interest to zealously promote the Low Income Housing Tax Credit without modifications, even though the program in
many places increased the cost of affordable housing, lengthened the building
process, provided a public service employment program for technicians and
lawyers, and increased CDCs' dependency on them. Nor did it seem to bother
them much that the complex tax credit made it increasingly difficult for CDCs
to provide housing for very low-income people. In stressing CDC housing
production almost exclusively, the intermediaries failed to provide an alternative to this approach, namely the management and control of production by
private developers in cases where CDCs might have found such a strategy better suited to their needs and those of their constituents.

Shift to Comprehensiveness

In the early 1990s, more comprehensive community development approaches
once against started coming into vogue. This was partly due to many CDCs' re-
alization that effective community revitalization required a broader focus.
Probably the major cause of this reversal, however, was that major foundations
"discovered" that comprehensive approaches to community building were important. New foundation initiatives gave legitimacy to the notion that CDCs
could and should assume responsibility for a broader range of activities and
greater community accountability, even though most of the initiatives, unfortunately, were foundation inspired, manipulated, and controlled, often with
questionable results.

The historic debate about comprehensive versus narrow approaches and the
proper balance between organizing and development should not obscure the
community development movement's enormous achievements in many cities

and rural areas. The nonprofit community development field has developed hundreds of thousands of housing units, financed innumerable businesses and commercial enterprises, and improved many neighborhoods, or parts thereof. Many CDCs have become technically more competent and capable of going to greater scale. These successes have been well publicized. What hasn't received much, if any, attention are the problems that beset community development and threaten its future.

Both LISC and the Enterprise Foundation have conducted informal assessments of CDC failures and problems, but these have been carefully guarded in-house documents. Foundations and other donors, with a real stake in community development, have continually hesitated to evaluate either the field's failures or problems. For example, when the Enterprise Corporations, which were supposed to finance the Enterprise Foundation's low-income housing programs, all went out of business, foundations that had donated millions were unwilling to sponsor an evaluation of why it happened. Further, no foundations, though aware of the weaknesses of the Low Income Housing Tax Credit, have been willing to evaluate its impact and the ways it could be improved.

It is just in the past year that journalist Carol Steinbach and Robert Zdenek, former executive director of NCCED, have commendably written about ECI and the problems other CDCs are facing. Yet even their critical look is tempered by a reluctance to assign blame for ECI's demise, to place the responsibility where it should lie, on the funders, intermediaries, and the executive director who suddenly left town by the midnight rail without taking any real responsibility.

If the community development movement is to profit from its mistakes and tensions, it will require a tough, ongoing objective analysis, one that takes into account issues of responsibility, accountability, and integrity. That assessment will have to deal with the challenges of organizing and advocacy, alliances with other community-based groups, the question of production versus the management of production, the role of the large intermediaries, matters of leadership, the extent of community accountability, and the limitations of CDCs themselves. The community development corporations deserve better treatment from their funders and boosters. They need the truth about the movement, their potential, and their options.

If community development's enormous accomplishments are to be perpetuated and strengthened, we will need a body of observers, evaluators, and critics who will put the lie to the good old public relations myth that only good news, even if incomplete, is the sure path to success.

∼

Philanthropy Community Building

Excerpted from National Civic Review, *Summer 1998*

Despite great odds, low-income neighborhoods and communities in urban and depressed rural areas are beginning to show encouraging signs of revitalization. In large part, these signs of progress are due to the hard work of grassroots community organizations, with the support of local governments, other nonprofit groups, and philanthropic institutions. These groups are rehabilitating and building new affordable housing, launching commercial and economic development projects, working with police to eliminate drugs and violent crime, pushing for educational reform, and creating community leadership. The hope of creating stable and productive neighborhoods rests on the work of effective community organizations.

At long last, we have learned some hard lessons about building strong communities. The first and most important is that such efforts cannot be successful unless residents themselves are a major part of the processes of planning, implementation, and evaluation. In very poor neighborhoods, where disinvestment, discrimination, institutional breakdowns, and municipal neglect have been rampant, strong community-based organizations, churches, and other nonprofits are especially important. They are the key to enabling these neighborhoods to come to the community bargaining table with the resources, power, and influence to make a real difference. It is a sad fact, unfortunately, that real participation of this kind is often not encouraged or practiced.

The second lesson is that community building or revitalization cannot be achieved in a scattered, piecemeal fashion. Our efforts must be comprehensive and strategic. At the grassroots level, this means that the old tensions and separation between organizing and development, between one-issue and multi-purpose organizations, between social services and advocacy, no longer can have as much currency as in the past. They are all part of a low-income community strategy, and these organizations must learn and be encouraged to work together and fight for the common good of their low-income constituencies. Local grassroots coalitions offer a strategy whose time has come, but they are also the hardest organizations to sustain financially.

The third lesson we have learned is that neighborhood and community building takes money—big money. Embedded in our history or sense of individualism is a seeming unwillingness on the part of Americans to invest sufficiently in our social fabric or in our communal activities. We have watched neighborhoods disintegrate without mounting corrective efforts to remedy the situation.

In order to make money, businesses and corporations raise large amounts of capital to invest in research, equipment, plant facilities, and personnel. They do so because they know it is necessary for profit making and success. Somehow, our political leaders and citizenry have not gotten this message. We continue to delude ourselves that significant changes can take place with little investment, either in infrastructure or people.

Fourth, we now know that real community building cannot take place without a productive partnership between community organizations and local governments. Governmental revitalization activities can no longer be restricted to downtown development. Many governments have neglected the needs and views of their low-income constituents, while the latter have not been very successful in mobilizing their potential power to influence and shape government policies and programs. The tension and alienation between low-income communities and governments must be overcome. How to develop common ground between the two factions remains a major obstacle in community building and a perpetual challenge to philanthropy.

New Developments and Problems in Community Building

Low-income neighborhoods and community groups have learned and now know how to build or rebuild their communities, if only resources are available. But three recent developments have occurred to make their job harder: persistent poverty, federal budget cuts, and devolution. Our country continues to experience deep, persistent poverty, especially among people of color and recent immigrant populations, despite its enormous economic wealth. Persistent poverty has been accompanied by a pronounced widening of the gap between the rich and the poor. For millions of Americans, real wages have gone down over the past two decades. Cut it any way you like: class lines have become even more rigid.

To make matters worse, we have seen that a rising economic tide no longer lifts all boats. Despite our economic boom, there are not enough low-wage jobs to absorb the people coming off the welfare rolls. We now have a two-tiered economy, one with highly educated and skilled workers, the other with poorly educated, low-skilled and periodically unemployed workers. The two tiers rarely converge. Those on the bottom tier find it increasingly difficult to climb to the second tier. Since so many people locked into the bottom tier and in inner cities are of color, our economy is creating a confluence of race and class differences that poisons our notion of a social compact and a sense of civil society. These conditions of deep poverty and the lack of jobs have made community building all the more difficult.

Moreover, during the last few years we've seen a growing meanness of spirit on the part of many Americans toward their less fortunate fellow citizens, partly inspired by, but not restricted to, the increasing influence of conservative ideology. Many of us have lost our sense of compassion and communal spirit. This is reflected in the deep federal budget cuts for programs of assistance to low-income people, while the military budget has been preserved or even slightly increased, and taxes for middle-income and wealthy citizens have been substantially reduced. The deep cuts for affordable housing, nutrition and health programs, and social services have hurt those most in need of help. They have also had a negative impact on local grassroots organizations and social service organizations in low-income areas, thereby reducing their budgets and their programs. The very infrastructure of low-income communities has been seriously weakened.

Winds of Change and the Grassroots

A few years ago, when the winds of conservative change swept through the halls of Congress and the White House, there was virtually little or no opposition by local low-income grassroots organizations, social service groups, and other nonprofits to the proposed budget cuts and other measures that would impact low-income people. Democrats and liberal Republicans reported that they had been overwhelmed by calls and letters from conservative nonprofits and lobby groups but had heard little from constituencies and organizations concerned with the poor. In typical congressional fashion, they went with the tide despite some reservations. What happened?

Historically, local low-income grassroots organizations, social service groups, and other nonprofits have had little interest in—or capacity to—become public policy players and tough advocates at the local, state, and national levels. For many of them, it was all they could do to survive or deliver services well. Local nonprofits were often hesitant to alienate local and regional funders who, they knew, did not like public policy and advocacy activities.

Lack of public information was also a barrier to their active involvement with these issues. If one did not read the *New York Times,* the *Los Angeles Times,* the *Wall Street Journal,* or the *Washington Post,* one had little idea what was happening to the federal budget, national policies, welfare reform, or devolution. One could learn little or nothing from television or radio.

The experience was a painful but important lesson to local nonprofits. They realized that they had to build a capacity for public policy participation and advocacy if their low-income constituents were to have any influence in the policy debates at all levels of government. They had to tap into or build better information networks that could alert them to what was happening in Washington, as well as in the state capitols. No longer could they afford merely to deliver direct services. Part of their agenda had to be devoted to policy efforts to gain for low-income people their fair share of public resources and economic opportunities. This agenda, they now know, had to include forging coalitions to gain greater power and influence.

Devolution is confirming this growing concern and need in poor communities. The transfer of money and responsibility to state and local government jurisdictions has meant that grassroots organizations and their low-income constituencies can no longer depend on the federal government for protection and redress. They have to access state governments, many of which have been beholden primarily to rural and suburban constituencies that historically have been relatively insensitive to the needs of inner cities and barrios and the poor. Community-based organizations have had little or no connection to state governments, have rarely lobbied on state legislation, and don't have a presence in the state capitols. In a real sense, they have enjoyed less access to state governments than to the federal government. Nor have they been tied to statewide networks such as chambers of commerce, labor unions, Leagues of Women Voters, and other groups.

The rhetoric of devolution has included the shibboleth that decentralization would bring government closer to the people. The irony, of course, is that for low-income and other disadvantaged populations, decentralization in fact has made government less accessible and farther removed from these citizens.

Welfare reform has been the pilot ship or test case of devolution. It could turn out to be a very mixed blessing indeed. On the one hand, it has inspired creativity and innovation as well as new resources on the part of some state and local governments. It is demonstrating what good governments can do to create jobs, provide additional day care and transportation costs, and sustain other key social programs. On the other hand, many states have been punitive, showing a concern for getting mothers off the welfare rolls but not for eliminating poverty. They are implementing harsh welfare reform plans, not creating jobs or providing adequate funds for day care and other supportive services. A number of states have used their surplus funds to build roads and lower taxes, not to promote the welfare of the mothers coming off the rolls.

One of the unintended consequences of welfare is that it has spurred organizing efforts by community organizations around the country. Where they have had resources, they have successfully pushed for innovative job creation programs, more day care funds, and greater transportation support. They have joined and organized state coalitions to influence state governments.

Unfortunately, many community organizations do not have the resources to mount effective policy campaigns. They have not been able to secure funds for additional staff, travel, and logistical costs. Few foundations and corporations have been willing to provide money for these purposes.

Need for State and Local Government Reform

The efforts of low-income people and their grassroots organizations have been impeded by local and state governments insensitive to their problems and in need of serious reform and capacity building.

Too many state and local governments have demonstrated little concern for providing the public with policy and program information. Many still resist calls for greater sunshine. As local nonprofit groups become more involved in state policy formulation, the clamor for greater public accountability and citizen participation grows. At a time when everybody is crying for evaluations, only a relative handful of state and local governments have any serious process for assessing the impact and effectiveness of their programs. Only a few have an official evaluation unit within their systems. The many civic or community groups that could be contracted to help provide this information are never used. Many state and local government executives have little idea how their midlevel officials are performing.

The executive branches of state and local governments have increased their authority and power over the last fifteen years. Devolution is adding to their strength. By contrast, state and local legislatures have become second-class or third-class citizens in the government process. In many if not most states, legislatures meet too infrequently, their legislators are woefully underpaid, they lack staff resources, and few successfully exercise their oversight functions. They and their local government counterparts cannot compete effectively in the budget process. In short, state and local governments are in need of structural and procedural reforms, as well as capacity-building resources.

Under the imperative of devolution, governments are, hopefully, forced to rethink the way they do business, relate to their citizens, deliver services, and develop their low-income neighborhoods. It is this type of rethinking and restructuring that helps restore public confidence in government.

4

Philanthropy's Global Role

How Philanthropy Could Improve Foreign Policy

From The Chronicle of Philanthropy, *February 9, 1993*

Now is the time to take a fresh, independent, and thorough look at our foreign policy establishment and the way this country carries out its diplomatic, economic assistance, intelligence, cultural, and information missions overseas.

The Clinton Administration is already overwhelmed by the foreign crises it has inherited in Bosnia, Iraq, Somalia, the Middle East, Haiti, and many other places. Under pressure to act and resolve problems in those parts of the world, it will not have the luxury of undertaking a comprehensive review of the more generic problems that have plagued our foreign policy and Foreign Service for some time.

Nor should it. Government commissions and studies have generally not offered tough evaluations, creative recommendations, or scrupulous candor. Those that have reviewed our foreign policy agencies during the past thirty years have not been exceptions to this rule.

What we need is a well-financed private commission that could do for foreign policy what the Commission on Private Philanthropy and Public Needs did for the nonprofit world in the 1970s. That commission asked hard questions and did a thorough job of assessing why foundations were not doing enough to deal with the nation's most serious problems. Our foreign policy establishment needs that same kind of scrutiny.

Although it would consult with government agencies when possible, a private commission would be independent and objective. Such a commission could bring sunshine and greater clarity to a network of foreign policy agencies that have largely been unaccountable. Its findings could help both the President and Congress develop badly needed reforms and improve the conduct of American policy.

Over the past three decades the structure, policies, and practices of our foreign policy establishment have come under serious criticism, yet little or no change has occurred beyond a reshuffling of the proverbial "deck chairs."

Why, for example, has our intelligence apparatus so often failed in detecting and helping us prepare for serious crises? Why have we supported so many dictatorships for so long against our long-term self-interest and that of democracy? Have institutional traditions and vested interests blocked essential reforms in the way in which agencies operate and relate to one another? And why are so many of our most talented young people turned off by the prospect of a Foreign Service career?

Questions about the recruitment, training, and promotion of Foreign Service personnel should be a priority item for the commission. Simply put, are we attracting and retaining the right people with the appropriate character and skills needed for the 1990s? Do we still have too many officers who are bright but uncreative, articulate but lacking in candor, driven more by caution than by integrity and courage? Does the culture of the service and the criteria for promotion stifle those very qualities that are necessary for effective policy making? Why do so many of our ambassadors continue to be political appointees with no other serious qualification than a $100,000 contribution to the party in power? Such an entrenched practice does little to strengthen the morale and practice of the Foreign Service.

Political and economic reporting and analysis should be the foundation of good diplomacy. Is the current system working? Are the thousands of dispatches regularly sent to Washington by the various agencies overseas read, digested, correlated, and used by top policy makers? Is there a more effective way to guarantee that people who are making decisions are well informed?

The Foreign Service, or at least the State Department, seems to assume that young career officers, either through training or osmosis, can become first-rate political and economic reporters and analysts. Is that view valid, or should the service use more talented and experienced people, such as investigative journalists, to provide analysis? In any case, what can we do to get more fresh air and creativity into the service?

Our foreign aid, including economic assistance programs, has often been ill-conceived and ineffectual. Large-scale and showcase projects in third-world countries have often contributed to unplanned urbanization and the degradation of rural areas. Economic aid to Eastern Europe and the former Soviet Union could become the basis for a "how not to do it" manual for future assistance programs. Politics has often influenced which nonprofit groups and consulting firms receive contracts to do foreign work.

Given the absence of rigorous evaluation, it is difficult to tell how much bang for the buck either the recipient nations or the United States has received. Should the Agency for International Development be restructured, eliminated, or merged with another entity? Should more or all of our aid be multilateral and channeled through the United Nations, World Bank, and other international agencies? What should the balance be between bilateral and multilateral assistance?

The United States Information Agency's mission has been to tell America's story to the world. We need to know how well it has done its job, and what it must do now that the Cold War has ended. Is there still a need for a USIA? Are the libraries and cultural centers around the globe worth preserving? If so, how can their activities be improved and reach more people? Should the agency have a seat on the National Security Council? How can it relate more effectively to the other agencies?

For many years, some observers have urged the transformation of the Voice of America into an independent entity like the British Broadcasting Corporation. Is it now time to do so? Would such a move enhance Voice of America's objectivity and credibility?

And, finally, how can we make sense out of the multiplicity of agencies that are involved in the conduct of foreign policy? Lines of authority are not always clear. The overall structure is awkward, burdensome, and inefficient. How can it be consolidated and reshaped to be more effective?

Those and many other questions beg immediate examination. They are too important to be left to a small group of foreign policy professionals and a few members of Congress who have inadequate time and resources for serious oversight activities.

A private national commission, financed by foundations, could bring together a broad and diverse group of outstanding people, not just prestigious names, to at least begin the process of evaluating our foreign policy establishment. It should be composed of representatives from government, business, academe, charities that do work abroad, and public-interest organizations; it would also have to have a staff of competent professionals.

The commission could do what government will never be able to do: Look at the foreign policy establishment objectively, critically, and nonpolitically.

It would be a big and challenging job. But foundations have set a precedent. They have supported important commissions that focused on and helped to reshape medical education, hunger in America, public broadcasting, and philanthropy itself. They could do the same for our foreign policy and Foreign Service. The Commission on Private Philanthropy and Public Needs defined the purpose of philanthropy as meeting our most urgent public needs. Can there be a public need that is more urgent? We cannot afford to wait much longer for this work to begin.

$\sim$

The Problems and Challenges of
International Philanthropy

From Foundation News and Commentary, *July–August 1991*

During the past few years, international grant making has come increasingly into the philanthropic spotlight.

The environmental hazards posed by global warming, the easing of the Cold War and developments in Eastern Europe, the depressed economic conditions in third-world countries and the international dimensions of large refugee populations, have piqued the genuine concern and interest of a growing number of foundations, corporations, and individual givers. Such problems have also attracted several of the more trend-oriented donors who have never met a new, hot, and safe issue they didn't like.

As a result of these new interests, philanthropic globe-trotting has attained impressive proportions. Delegations of foundation representatives have visited the Soviet Union, Eastern Europe, Western Europe, Africa, and Latin America. The Council on Foundations has sponsored several of these excursions. A number of foundations and individual grant makers have toured abroad on their own.

Some sponsors also believe that the value of these visits goes beyond exploring the potential for grant making. In their view, raising philanthropic consciousness about international issues, developments, and problems is an equally significant purpose.

While much of this outpouring of international curiosity and concern is timely and most commendable, some of it smacks of philanthropic adventurism. Many of the donors who have made official trips overseas would and will never make a grant to the countries they visited.

A number have taken advantage of the opportunities offered by official delegations, guided tours, and tempting invitations. Were these philanthropists just tourists, no one could question the purpose or impact of their travels. But they are not. They come in their official capacity as donors with, potentially at least, considerable money to spend. To nascent nonprofits in Eastern Europe, the Soviet Union, Africa, and elsewhere, where indigenous philanthropic resources are either small or nonexistent, their visits have sparked and will continue to spark enormous expectations. When these visits are not followed by grants—even a couple of years later—disappointment and disillusion are bound to follow.

A number of Eastern Europeans and Soviets have already complained about the incongruity between the large number of foundation representatives they have seen and the lack of philanthropic funds they and others have received. As one of them commented not long ago, "We have seen some of these people several times and have spent a lot of time with them and yet we have received nothing. Why do they bother with us?" If their hopes are not to be further dashed, only those foundations and other funders who are truly serious about giving overseas should venture into the international arena.

The new burst of philanthropic activity internationally does not seem to have involved practitioners from the American nonprofit world in any significant way. This is surprising in view of the continual, explicit demand by emerging nonprofit groups in Europe and in developing countries for assistance from and exchanges with American nonprofit practitioners. The latter, not philanthropoids, are the ones who can be most useful in helping local groups overseas organize their programs, build effective organizations, strengthen their policy and advocacy work, and introduce sound financial and management systems.

Practitioners generally seem to have been excluded even from the initial assessment process overseas. Although it is common practice domestically for donor institutions to use skilled practitioners to evaluate community needs and programs—especially in areas where donors lack expertise—the donors usually have chosen not to do so when exploring the international scene. The delegations of touring American philanthropists sponsored by the Council on Foundations, for example, have not included any nonprofit practitioners, even though the latter might have enriched the groups' observations and findings.

A few foundations have used nonprofit representatives to advantage in making initial assessments overseas. The New World Foundation, in New York, sent a small group of community organizers to Eastern Europe to discuss the need for and potential of American-style organizing in the region. The Pratt Center was commissioned by the Ford Foundation to test the validity of community development corporations as effective mechanisms for housing and economic development in Africa. Yet such efforts are atypical, not the rule.

In short, those who have the most to offer foreign nonprofit organizations other than money, and the most to learn from such interaction, are unfortunately those who cannot afford to pay their own way, namely, the grantee groups.

The growing enthusiasm for international grant making also poses several dangers for American philanthropy.

The first is the potential for deflecting the attention of donors from our most urgent domestic problems. It is all very well to talk about the need to attack poverty in developing countries, but what about the enormous poverty problems in this country, which have been neglected by philanthropy for years? There have been suggestions that major foundations provide a substantial percentage—25 percent has been cited—of their contributions to international efforts. Why haven't we heard similar pleas that one-quarter of major foundation giving be allocated to disadvantaged constituencies and their struggles in the United States?

Perhaps under pressure to find new resources both for domestic and international giving, and not to substitute the latter for the former, grant makers may want to consider more seriously than in the past raising their payout rates to less conservative levels.

The siren calls from overseas are alluring and exciting. They beckon from new philanthropic worlds to conquer. They often offer even fewer risks and less public accountability than is the practice here at home. After all, it is one thing to give money to an unknown organization thousands of miles away protected from scrutiny by the American public; it is quite another to provide grants to institutions and groups under our very noses.

All this is not to argue that a greater emphasis on overseas grant making is inappropriate. On the contrary, given the increasingly global nature of economic, environmental, and other problems, international philanthropy is more important than ever. But it should not be permitted to serve as an excuse to reduce the already scarce resources being channeled to such massive problems here as poverty, malfunctioning units of local government, and the need for leadership development.

If anything, new ventures into international giving should prompt donors to look even harder and more objectively at their own domestic track records. Those about to support antipoverty efforts or environmental programs in developing countries but who do little or nothing on these issues domestically will remain justifiably vulnerable to the criticism of hypocrisy.

The second danger is that in their zeal to encourage the growth of nonprofit sectors and philanthropy overseas, Americans will be tempted to export their existing philanthropic models without much, if any, consideration of the their strengths and weaknesses.

Many of our donor institutions have elite, nonrepresentative boards of directors. The large majority of them do not issue periodic public reports or make much information available to would-be grant recipients. Access to their grant-making process is often limited to those with contacts on the boards or staffs. A great number of funders work hard to avoid innovation, experimentation, and risk-taking. Only a relative handful give a substantial amount of their contributions to low-income, minority, and other disadvantaged constituencies, not to mention activist and advocacy organizations.

Are these the kinds of philanthropic institutions we want to see born and nurtured in other countries? Or do we want to help create new philanthropies that take the best of the American experience and discard its worst features?

The model of community foundations, for example, is being actively promoted abroad by American donor institutions. They could be enormously productive in supporting new nonprofits and attacking the most serious community problems. But their effectiveness will be limited if they pattern themselves after those American community foundations that do not have boards representative of the total community, do not give a substantial amount of money to those most in need, stress fund raising over good grant making, have little contact with their communities and are characterized by dull and safe contributions. There are plenty of good community foundations that could set a positive example for newly emerging community foundations overseas.

Who from American philanthropy and the nonprofit sector are being consulted by developing philanthropies abroad? Some of our best people from public and family foundations, community foundations, and corporate giving programs, as well as donee groups, have not been a part of this process of consulting and technical assistance. It is important that they become involved. Indeed, the Council on Foundations, Independent Sector, and philanthropy in general have an obligation to ensure that our most stellar philanthropic performers, not only those who have the time and resources, become a part of American efforts to stimulate philanthropy internationally.

The problems and challenges facing an energized international grant-making effort provide many more questions than answers. Will giving by American foundations and corporations be strategic, aimed at the greatest public needs in other countries? Will they be able to identify and select the most appropriate groups and individuals to carry out the intended programs and activities? Given scarce resources, can American donors, many of whom appear to be operating largely as lone wolves internationally, find the wisdom and commitment to collaborate more on joint projects? Will our philanthropies be able to bend their categorical priorities to accommodate the special needs and desires of foreign nationals? Can our grant makers make substantial investments in building human capacity and strong institutions overseas, when their record at home in this respect has been less than impressive?

What is clear is that much more thought, planning and collaboration will be required if the full potential of American philanthropy is to be harnessed internationally.

∽

Turning Grief over a Princess's Death into Sound Philanthropy

From The Chronicle of Philanthropy, *October 2, 1997*

The extraordinary public response to Princess Diana's death should prompt a thorough examination of how best to honor a philanthropic superstar.

The charitable contributions made in memory of the Princess could end up doing much good for many causes. But unless strict safeguards are placed on the fund created in her name, it could fail to provide a truly lasting legacy.

A sign that such concerns are not a high priority of the royal family or the British government could be seen in their tardiness in discouraging inappropriate memorials. Their failure to provide quick direction was evident at places like the British embassy in my hometown of Washington, where for days people came with lavish bouquets and floral arrangements in memory of the Princess.

As I watched the mourners drop off their flowers, I could not help but think that Diana, a successful fund raiser for good causes, would have been horrified by the floral flow of devotion. I suspect she would have preferred that the mourners brought one flower apiece—and then donated the rest of the money they spent on the floral arrangements to charity. The tens of thousands of dollars' worth of flowers outside the embassy, she would have noted, could have provided meals and temporary accommodations for hundreds of hungry and homeless people. While the flower memorial was breathtakingly beautiful, in the long run, it only benefited the florists—not the poor and sick whom Diana worked so hard in her life to help.

The British government—through its embassies and consulates worldwide—could have set a more appropriate tone by quickly suggesting that charitable contributions would do the most lasting good. The royal family finally did encourage donations, but not until it was too late to stem the expensive floral tributes. When other governments, organizations, and families face similar tragedies in the future, they must learn to take action faster.

Diana's family has a chance to make a more solid and permanent tribute to her memory by making sure that the new philanthropy created in her name truly reflects the Princess's values and priorities. With tens of millions of dollars collected so far, and donations continuing to flow in, some experts predict that the foundation could end up with more than $1 billion in assets.

The challenge for the family is to keep the foundation focused on Diana's interests in social change and in protecting the most vulnerable members of society. It must resist the temptation to become a typically conservative British foundation that takes few risks and limits its grant making to social services and more established nonprofit organizations. And it must choose a board that includes representatives of community groups, nonestablishment charitable organizations, and people of color, instead of following the approach of most British foundations, which are governed by members of the establishment.

Those are important issues for all of British philanthropy, which has been notable for its failure to deal with many of the major socioeconomic problems of the country. Very little money has been channeled to the charitable organizations of the country's more than four million people of color, and almost nothing goes to organizations that would develop grassroots support so they could come to the bargaining table with the sufficient chips to make a difference.

What's more, Britain lacks any national civil rights organizations, largely because foundations have been unwilling to provide the money needed to sustain such institutions. Only a handful of British foundations provide money to organizations that are trying to influence public policy or institutional change. Nor is there much foundation money available for community development groups that could rebuild the economy and improve the rundown physical condition of inner cities and poor rural areas.

Those and other vital issues should be a high priority for Diana's foundation. In determining how the money will be spent, Diana's brother, who is helping to structure the trust, and his advisers would be wise to consult with such British foundations as the Cadbury Trusts, the City Parochial Foundation, and the Gulbenkian Foundation, all of which have distinguished themselves by taking risks and tackling tough social issues.

Britain doesn't need yet another run-of-the-mill foundation. What it does need is an institution that will embody the best of Princess Diana's qualities: an empathy with and passion for society's underdogs, a spirit of risk-taking, a commitment to advocacy, and a common touch. With those characteristics, Diana's foundation could become the beacon of light that might lead British philanthropy into a new age of relevance and effectiveness.

5

Nonprofit Organizations and Citizen Advocacy

Grant Makers' Aversion to Advocacy Ignores the Lessons of History

From The Chronicle of Philanthropy, August 22, 2002

The reluctance of most American foundations to support advocacy and activism flies in the face of American history. It is precisely that type of activity that distinguishes our civil society from all others and makes it the envy of all nations that are struggling to establish and strengthen their own nonprofit groups.

In other countries, nonprofit institutions in large measure have provided social and educational services, softened the edge of government and politics, and made life a little more bearable for the people. Social and institutional change has been the province of government, political parties, and labor unions. Not so in the United States.

From the very beginning, public policy work and advocacy activities, such as organizing citizens to voice their views, have been the bedrock of our democratic evolution. Nonprofit organizations, fueled by money from individual and institutional donors, have held governments accountable, helped formulate and pass public policies at the national and local levels, given voice and influence to marginal constituencies, protected our civil rights and environment, and assisted in shaping our relations with other countries.

While such groups were always a small portion of our society, they nevertheless have been responsible for most of the social and institutional changes that have occurred throughout our history. Too few foundation officials seem aware of the great legacy of policy and advocacy activities that have transformed our society, and that lack of historical background puts the nation at risk.

It is not surprising that our early colonists, fleeing religious and political persecution, developed a strong sense of individualism and suspicion of government, as well as a fondness for nonprofit organizations. Probably the first advocacy group was established by Ben Franklin in Philadelphia in 1729.

After the Revolution, Democratic-Republican societies emerged to become monitors of government activities. At the same time abolitionary societies began to agitate for an end to slavery. They were some of our earliest watchdog groups.

During the first half of the nineteenth century the growth of evangelical Protestant churches and black churches led to demands for more public services and greater activism by antislavery advocates. The seeds of women's liberation were sown by affluent white women who fought to win state charters and public money for asylums, hospitals, and orphanages that would care for the poor. A citizens' petition in 1845 in Massachusetts resulted in the first legislative inquiry about labor conditions. Nonprofit groups at that time began their campaigns for a ten-hour workday.

The end of the Civil War spawned the growth of nonprofit organizations, including some prominent antislavery organizations and the Freedmen's Bureau, which established hundred of schools in the South for children of former slaves.

During the 1880s small farmers, debtors, and other disaffected inhabitants of rural areas sought to improve their economic condition by creating granges, fraternal organizations of farmers. The public pressure exerted by more than twenty thousand granges led to important rural policy changes and the creation of the rural extension service.

At the turn of the century, urban immigrants helped form the International Institute to fight for their rights and increased economic opportunities. The settlement house movement, led by prominent personalities like Jane Addams of Hull House, surfaced to combat poverty and deteriorating health conditions in America's cities. The activities of tenant unions in the 1930s led to the Wagner Act, which legalized union organizing. And, during the Great Depression of the 1930s, the Townsend clubs, with a combined membership of more than five million people, pushed for workers' pensions, resulting in the Social Security Act of 1935.

Those victories for improved working and living conditions were won by advocacy groups that organized large constituencies and lobbied lawmakers. Their successors over the past forty years have been similarly successful. They are the thousands of activist nonprofit groups that have been the heart of the antipoverty, women's, environmental, consumer, gay rights, youth, student, and public service movements. To those one might add the many organizations that are trying to improve the quality of our health, education, low-cost housing, and criminal justice systems. They have been successful because they challenged unfair conditions and poorly functioning institutions, won new legislation and regulatory measures, fought discrimination, and preserved our First Amendment rights and civil liberties.

So why, it is fair to ask, have so many of our foundations failed to recognize the outstanding record and important role of activist groups in our history? Why do so few foundations continue to bear the burden of financing this invaluable portion of our nonprofit world? Why is it that people who live outside the United States seem to place a greater value on our advocacy, policy, and organizing activities than our own foundations? Is it foundations' ignorance, fear, values, or lack of leadership that is responsible for this situation?

The answer, I suspect, is a combination of all four factors.

Fear of risk-taking by financing activist causes is certainly a brake on most foundations' willingness to support advocacy, especially grassroots efforts. They are afraid of the publicity their grantees' activities might generate. They know that they can't control the direction and impact of such advocacy. And they fear inciting the ire of politicians or government officials.

Many raise the Tax Reform Act of 1969 as a reason they don't want to risk trying to influence policy makers and government. In too many cases, that merely is an excuse for not supporting activism. Conservative foundations have never permitted the Act to be a constraint on their strong commitment to advocacy, policy, and organizing. In their longing for neutrality, the liberal-leaning foundations have succeeded only in being neutered.

The lack of leadership from top foundation executives also accounts for the timidity of foundation grant making. University presidents, academics, a few politicians, and sundry business and nonprofit executives have rarely been risk-takers or courageous decision makers. Caution has characterized their experience and careers.

The values of foundation trustees may be the most important reason for foundations' reluctance to support advocacy activities. The boards of the major foundations are composed of wealthy and highly paid professionals who are not representative of this country's diverse population.

While they include many more women and members of minority groups than they did twenty-five years ago, most of the women as well as the blacks, Hispanics, and other minority group members are similar to their affluent white, male counterparts in class and background. In short, foundation boards lack the concerns, perspectives, and passion that could drive their support for greater activism. Comfortable and cautious, they are reluctant to underwrite social movements or social and institutional change.

In view of those roadblocks to philanthropic advocacy, can we expect our foundations to embrace a more activist posture? Much will depend on their willingness to reassess their grant making in the light of recent social, economic, and security developments in this country—the fight against terrorism, the danger to civil liberties, the failures of corporate America, the weakening of environmental standards, the poor performance of our schools, the widening gap between rich and poor, the growing destitution of our rural areas, and the loss of our prestige as an international leader, to name a few.

If poor and working-class people are to fight successfully for social and economic justice, they must receive the support they need to level the playing field. If corporations are to be held accountable and the free-enterprise system better regulated in the public interest, then nonprofit organizations—both old and new—will have to receive the necessary resources to help the federal and state governments do the job. If our political and electoral systems are to function fairly and effectively, citizen-monitoring and -action organizations will need money to assure public accountability and needed reforms. And if our rural areas are to be preserved and strengthened, it will be incumbent upon our foundations to no longer ignore advocacy efforts to revitalize rural America. And the list could go on.

Those and other major national and local problems cannot be solved by more services or by maintaining the status quo. Fundamental changes are in order. Such changes can be brought about only by activist strategies: constituency mobilization or organizing, public policy work, and advocacy activities.

They are the strategies that have made our civil society and our democracy unique and great. It would be a pity at this critical juncture in our national development if the mainstream foundations were to forget the lessons of our history.

∽

Shifting Power Requires Better Citizen Watchdogs

From The Chronicle of Philanthropy, *December 14, 1995*
The 1994 Congressional elections produced a Republican majority and led to many
changes in policies affecting the flow of money to nonprofit groups and the people
they serve. In many cases, federal funds were given directly to the states with fewer
strings attached.

As the federal government shifts responsibility for social programs to the states and localities, foundations and other donors should equip local citizens' groups to become more effective watchdogs.

In the next few years, many federal programs will be consolidated, and billions of dollars will be distributed to the states in lump sums, known as block grants. The details are still being worked out, but it is clear that states will have few limits on how they can spend their federal money. Nor will the more than three thousand local public-housing authorities face many requirements in administering aid, even though many of those organizations have not previously been very effective.

The changes are causing enormous anxiety among those who work with the poor. The first concern is that state and local governments seldom do a good job of answering to the public. Very few have effective mechanisms to monitor and evaluate their own programs. It is hard to get many details about state and local programs because not all states and very few local governments have freedom-of-information laws to guarantee public access to official documents.

Many state and local authorities have poor records in distributing public information and encouraging citizen participation. What's more, very few have done well in running the programs that exist now, so it is hard to imagine how they will handle new responsibilities.

A second worry is the changing nature of local government. As money, power, and authority have been transferred from federal agencies to local entities in the past decade and a half, strong local executive branches have been created—often at the expense of local legislative bodies. Very few local legislators have the resources or staff members they need to be effective in shaping budget policies or overseeing programs. Those weaknesses are likely to be exacerbated as states and cities get even more power. That is a problem, because we count on legislative bodies to be sensitive to the needs of the people who elected them.

A third reason for the nervousness about the shift in power comes from the fact that state governments—and many local authorities—historically have not been as sensitive to the needs of the poor and minorities as has the federal government. Will states and localities fight poverty and racism if they are not required to do so?

Because of those worries, it will be very important for private groups to track and evaluate state and local efforts. Such information will help federal policy makers decide whether states and localities can handle their new duties, and whether any changes should be made to make sure that disadvantaged people are not harmed.

There are many questions for charities and scholars to examine. Among them:

- What principles and criteria will states adopt to guide the distribution of block grant money?

- Who will be involved in making those decisions? Will the views of average citizens and grassroots community groups be taken into account?

- Will the block grant money be given to the people who need it most?

- Will states, local governments, and housing authorities create adequate procedures for citizen involvement? Will they create a system to make sure civil rights regulations will be enforced—and that people can protest unfair treatment?

- How will states actually administer the block grants?

- How will local governments distribute the money handed to them from the states?

- Can state and local governments be strengthened and reformed to handle their new responsibilities more effectively and fairly? What changes would make that happen most efficiently?

Citizens' groups could provide many of the answers to those questions, but they lack the money to do so. In the 1970s and early '80s citizens' groups— through a process that has become known as citizen monitoring—were able to raise enough money to evaluate how well government programs were working. Money is scarce because, with the exception of the Ford Foundation, few grant makers have been willing to support efforts to improve government's performance.

Through citizen monitoring, state and local groups collect information about government programs and private organizations, such as banks, and figure out how well those entities serve the public. It is ideal for local groups to base their research on a format designed by a national organization. Local groups can always add questions dealing with their particular concerns, but if they all collected the same basic information, it would be easy to aggregate their findings and develop an accurate picture of what is happening on the national scene.

To carry out such research would be cheap; groups would probably need $5,000 to $30,000 to cover computer use, travel, and other expenses involved in collecting data. Citizen monitoring is much less expensive than traditional research, especially when the very high overhead costs of universities and research institutes are taken into account.

Research produced by citizens' groups is far more useful in grassroots lobbying and influencing public policy than are most academic studies, which all too often gather dust on bookshelves. Citizens' groups rely heavily on the same kind of quantitative information that scholars use, but they also consider subjective measures. They figure out whether programs are really making any difference to their intended beneficiaries—and to the public at large. During the research process itself, civic groups learn much about how government budget and policy decisions are made—and that often turns them into more effective activists.

One of the earliest and most effective citizen monitoring projects was the General Revenue Sharing Project of the early and mid–1970s. Four national organizations joined to evaluate what happened in thirty cities and localities when the government started distributing "revenue sharing" grants with few strings attached. Community groups, affiliates of the National Urban League and the League of Women Voters, and government agencies all worked together on a research program paid for by several national foundations. In the late 1970s a similar effort was mounted to monitor use of Community Development Block Grants in some forty locales.

In both cases, local monitoring groups were given $10,000 apiece to support their data collection. They used the information they collected to influence how billions of dollars in block grants were distributed. The national organizations were able to use the aggregate data from the local groups to push successfully for major changes in the way the federal government structured its block grant system.

We need the same kind of action today. We need to find out what will happen to poor people when most decisions about Medicaid, the program that provides healthcare coverage to the poor, are made by the states. And we need to find out exactly what happens when welfare, nutrition programs, and job-training efforts are no longer operated primarily by the federal government, but by states and localities.

That is a tall order. But if citizens' groups don't hold state and local governments accountable, no one will.

~

United Way's Timid Response to a Lobbying Bill

From The Chronicle of Philanthropy, *September 21, 1995*
*This article was written in response to legislation to restrict nonprofit advocacy
that was ultimately defeated. However, in the years since the legislation was
proposed, lawmakers have continued to voice interest in restricting the nonprofits
from using federal aid to lobby.*

Once again, United Way of America and its staff leaders have managed to bring discredit and dishonor to the charity world—as if the William Aramony scandal had not caused enough damage. [William Aramony was forced to resign in 1992 after revelations that he had inappropriately spent thousands of dollars of charity money and committed numerous ethical abuses.]

The latest embarrassment is United Way's reaction to congressional legislation that would limit lobbying by nonprofit groups that receive federal grants. A month ago, Nancy Mohr Kennedy, United Way of America's senior director of government relations, sent out a memorandum urging local United Ways to "stay on the sidelines" in the fight against the lobbying measure.

The lobbying bill, which was approved by the House and will soon be considered by the Senate, would restrict federal grant recipients from using more than 5 percent of their private donations for advocacy purposes. Businesses that receive contracts from the federal government, such as defense contractors, would be excluded from the requirement.

Under the proposal, the definition of lobbying or political advocacy would be so broad that it could include virtually any activity that a nonprofit group might undertake, other than providing direct services and raising money. It would apply not only to efforts to influence pending legislation or the status of federal programs; but it would also cover any attempt to get in touch with people in the executive branches of local, state, or federal governments or efforts that involve litigation.

Moreover, all federal grantees would have to file detailed reports about how they spent private funds—which would mean additional paperwork, since charities are already required to submit similar information to the Internal Revenue Service. Nonprofit groups that violate the law would be assessed stiff financial penalties. Bounty hunters would be encouraged to report illegal activity: they would be rewarded with a percentage of any penalty fee assessed to the nonprofit groups they caught.

No one has found any evidence that charities and other groups are improperly using federal aid to lobby. By trying to fix a system that is not broken and dictating how nonprofit groups use their private money, conservative House Republicans are threatening the independence and historic role of nonprofit organizations and foundations for purely ideological reasons. If the House bill is enacted into law, it would seriously undermine the mission and self-interest of local United Ways—and the thousands of charities they support.

Why, then, has the executive leadership of United Way of America attempted to dissuade local United Ways from sponsoring or even participating in local meetings and forums to discuss the lobbying limits? Don't local United Ways—and the charities that depend on them—have the right to know about and debate the merits of the proposed new law?

The August memo from Ms. Kennedy says that the reason United Way took its position was that the Alliance for Justice, Independent Sector, OMB Watch, and other organizations that represent nonprofit groups were involved in organizing the local forums. The memo says, "These organizations have made it clear that these meetings will be highly partisan and political in nature." The memo goes on to add that "we believe that this approach to defeating [the bill] is ill-advised and might have the effect of flaming the fires . . . by engaging in partisan political meetings."

The implication is, of course, that local United Ways don't have the capacity and intelligence to sponsor nonpartisan, nonpolitical meetings without becoming captive of those "dangerous" national organizations.

United Way of America President Elaine Chao [who became Labor Secretary under President George W. Bush] and her colleagues seem to forget that the lobbying measure is not a politically partisan issue. Democrats as well as Republicans voted for it in the House. Nor are they accurate or fair in portraying national organizations such as Independent Sector as engaged in partisan politics. Those groups are concerned about the future of the nonprofit world, which is more than can be said for Ms. Chao and company. The Alliance for Justice, Independent Sector, and OMB Watch and all the groups working with them deserve an apology.

What is particularly curious about the August memo is that it takes a different approach than did another letter Ms. Kennedy sent in July. The July memo strongly urged local United Ways to oppose the lobbying measure and to write or call their members of Congress. Why did United Way of America change its tune a month later? Did someone have second thoughts?

According to my inquiries, some United Way of America staff members knew nothing about the August memo. If it was not the deliberations of staff members, was the memo the result of a decision by the United Way Board of Governors? Or were board members not consulted? Were local United Ways asked for their recommendation?

Even though excessively timid, the August memo at least implies that the United Way of America is still opposed to the lobbying curbs. Why is United

Way of America's opposition any less partisan or political than that of Independent Sector, the Council on Foundations, and many other groups?

If political partisanship is the issue, then it is the partisanship of Ms. Chao and her colleagues. They have falsely labeled groups that champion the independence of the nonprofit world as politically partisan. They have tried to discourage local United Ways from fighting a measure that threatens their self-interest and that of the charities they support.

And the strategy United Way of America proposes in the August message, to discourage the Senate from even voting on the lobbying curbs, could be a disaster when the House and Senate convene to work out a compromise. Action, not silence, is required.

The United Way network deserves better from its national leadership. Ms. Chao and her deputies should serve the interests of the United Way constituency or give way to others who could do a better and less partisan job.

~

Ducking Debate on the Repeal of the Estate Tax

From The Chronicle of Philanthropy, *July 27, 2000*
*As of this writing, the estate tax continues to be a controversial issue in Congress,
and under current law the tax is gradually being reduced and would be repealed
entirely for one year in 2010. Since the time this article was written, Independent
Sector has stated that it opposes repeal of the estate tax, but it supports
modifications to the estate tax that preserve the special treatment of charitable
bequests and strong incentives for charitable giving.
The Council on Foundations has continued its longstanding position of not
commenting on tax issues that affect far more than charitable
organizations, as does the estate tax.*

When President Clinton listed his reasons for wanting to veto legislation to eliminate the estate tax, charity was among his key concerns. Nonprofit groups, he said, stand to lose $5 billion to $6 billion a year if donors don't have any incentive to make gifts as a way to circumvent the estate tax.

While it is commendable that the president mentioned the impact on philanthropy, neither he nor members of Congress have heard all that much opposition to the estate tax legislation from nonprofit groups.

It is surprising that charitable organizations have been so silent on an issue that not only could do direct harm to their own finances but also goes so strongly against the mission of any organization whose purpose is to improve our democracy and to promote economic and social justice.

Part of the reason charities have been so silent is that the entire movement to repeal the estate tax has been a stealth initiative. The effort was carefully conceived, well organized, and above all designed to provoke little attention so that average citizens wouldn't realize the special benefits that members of Congress were trying to give to the nation's wealthiest citizens.

Even though it seems a certainty that the congressional vote to eliminate the tax won't survive a presidential veto, this issue is not going away—and the reluctance that charities have shown in taking a stand thus far is likely to weaken future efforts to preserve the tax.

The estate tax might be seen by some as a cause that primarily affects elite nonprofit institutions—the universities, museums, and philanthropic foundations that are usually the prime beneficiaries as wealthy people figure out that charity offers an excellent alternative to forcing their heirs to pay big estate taxes. Those organizations will most definitely suffer a loss in donations and bequests if the estate tax is abolished, as several studies have documented.

But that is only part of the concern. Nonprofit organizations that focus on poverty, social welfare, social services, healthcare, housing, the environment, urban problems, children, and myriad other issues will also be severely hurt. They should make preservation of the estate tax a priority.

Those organizations need to recognize that repeal of the estate tax will be costly to both federal and state governments. The U.S. Treasury will eventually lose more than $50 billion a year, while state governments also will be deprived of significant sums because they base their own taxing of estates on the federal system. The bottom line will be that nonprofit groups of many types will have a tough time obtaining more government support for their constituents and causes.

While the costs to the Treasury and the potential loss of charitable bequests are clearly the most direct reasons for nonprofit organizations to care about the estate tax, there is an important moral issue at stake. Repeal of the estate tax would seriously undermine the progressive nature of our tax code by granting additional tax relief to the wealthiest Americans.

The gap between the very rich and the poor continues to grow. Eliminating the estate tax would further widen that disparity, something that no organization dedicated to improving society should support.

The bill passed by the House and Senate this summer would provide a bonanza to the wealthiest 1 percent of American taxpayers: people whose incomes exceed $300,000 a year would receive 91 percent of the benefits.

That said, the estate tax does potentially place undue burdens on small family farms and small businesses. Such inequities could easily be cleared up without undermining the basic goal of the estate tax—that those who make great wealth in their lifetimes should pass a share of it back to the government to use for the good of the entire nation.

The president and the Democratic leadership in Congress offered a measure that would deal with the inequities, but it was rejected by Republican lawmakers who preferred to jettison the entire estate tax rather than just fix it.

Few nonprofit organizations, especially at the local and regional levels, have been aware of the estate tax debate, or even realize how close it could come to becoming law. Charities have not been particularly well served by some of the large national umbrella organizations like the Council on Foundations or Independent Sector, which have been sitting on the sidelines, slow to get out information about the estate tax issue or to take a position out of fear of alienating wealthy members who support the estate tax repeal.

Even though many of the council's foundation members have benefited from the existence of the estate tax, it is to be expected that the organization would want to avoid taking a position on the tax that would alienate wealthy foundation trustees.

Independent Sector, however, is another matter. Many of the major national charities it represents—and their constituents—have a big stake in maintaining the tax, for reasons of both principle and self-interest. Independent Sector has practiced the art of fence-sitting, not leadership. Let's hope it will, as Lady Macbeth suggested, screw its courage to the sticking post and rethink its position.

There is a disturbing irony in the congressional effort to eliminate estate taxes, one that nonprofit groups must point out whenever possible. At a time when our legislators have cut back on domestic safety-net programs and can't find the money for programs that support urgent human needs and rebuild the crumbling physical infrastructures of so many cities and towns, they have found the time and energy to fight for another welfare program for the very rich. Have they forgotten that one of every five children is growing up poor, that over 47 million Americans are not covered by any health insurance, or that there is an enormous shortage of low-cost housing?

It is time for nonprofit groups to make those issues central, and to tell our legislators to stop wasting their time worrying about tax breaks for those who need them the least. Preserving the estate tax for our wealthiest citizens is good for democracy and for the country.

6

Accountability: A Major Gap at the Nation's Nonprofit Groups

The Buck Stops with the Board of Directors

From The Chronicle of Philanthropy, *October 17, 2002*

The shadow of William Aramony still looms over the nonprofit world. The former president of United Way of America, the umbrella group for roughly fourteen hundred local United Ways, Mr. Aramony was sentenced to prison in 1995 for defrauding the charity while on the job. His actions left the public's confidence in nonprofit groups badly shaken and local United Ways struggling to overcome his legacy.

Like some corporate CEOs, Mr. Aramony lived the high life, enjoyed expensive perks, established separate project accounts that he used for private purposes, and swindled charitable dollars from his organization's coffers. His board, composed primarily of corporate CEOs, permitted him to run the United Way unchecked and unaccountably. To a great extent his do-nothing board shares the blame for what happened.

Since the Aramony scandal broke, little seems to have changed in the nonprofit world. Many boards of directors of foundations and charities, both large and small, are still failing to exercise their responsibility in ensuring the financial and programmatic health of the organizations they oversee. While the public is demanding increased accountability and transparency from nonprofit organizations, a number of them continue to operate as though they are immune from scrutiny and impervious to ethical standards of behavior.

Nonprofit boards are the first and last line of defense against poor performance, corruption, and lack of accountability. They are supposed to be the protectors of the public interest. The buck stops with them. That, at least, is the theory. In practice, it often doesn't work that way.

153

Consider, for example, the United Way of the National Capital Area, in Washington, which has been under fire for well over a year. In the summer of 2001, Ross W. Dembling, then a member of the organization's board, questioned the group's expenditures and practices. Around the same time, the head of the United Way's corporate-donation division was fired because she had complained to the CEO, Norman O. Taylor, that the organization was claiming credit for donations it had never received. Subsequently, Mr. Taylor and his top executives fired four other key staff members after they raised questions about the way the organization was run. In addition, Mr. Dembling and two other board members, who also challenged organizational practices, were forced out.

To counter allegations of executive credit card abuses and questionable accounting practices, Mr. Taylor and the board commissioned a routine audit despite a senior staff member's recommendation that a more comprehensive investigative audit be conducted. Mr. Dembling called the routine audit, which was based solely on the United Way's paperwork, a whitewash.

Further inquiries by the news media revealed serious malpractice by the United Way organization: inflating contributions by as much as $2 million, withholding money earmarked for certain local charities, and grossly overcharging for administrative costs.

In addition, the organization, with the encouragement of Mr. Taylor, had approved a $72,000-a-year consulting contract for Mr. Taylor's predecessor, Oral Suer, who, while on the job at the United Way of the National Capital Area, had taken an early pension that netted him an estimated $200,000—an action not authorized by the pension's rules, according to the *Washington Post*.

At first Mr. Taylor denied knowing about the accounting problems, improper financial practices, and Mr. Suer's contract, and he refused to listen to staff members who wanted to reform organizational procedures. A key official of the Washington United Way accused Mr. Taylor of lying about his knowledge of the arrangement with Mr. Suer. Throughout this ordeal, the board of directors—minus the critics who had been forced out—did little but support Mr. Taylor's leadership.

The board might have spared itself the trouble had it exercised due diligence in hiring Mr. Taylor in the first place. That had been done largely on the recommendation of Mr. Suer. Mr. Taylor had been terminated as president of the United Way of Central Maryland, in Baltimore, in 1995 for what its board members called "sustained unsatisfactory performance," according to the *New York Times*.

Under pressure from the news media, donors, and local leaders, the board—after almost a year and a half of turmoil—finally adopted the recommendations of an outside ethics committee to help resolve the crisis. It also accepted Mr. Taylor's resignation.

The acting president of the board, A. Neil Barkus, called Mr. Taylor's resignation a noble thing. A noble thing? After what he had done to the United Way, Mr. Taylor should have been suspended or fired long before the situation got out of hand.

Where was the board during this period? Instead of taking tough action, it preferred to drive off the few members who questioned the organization's practices and responsibly exercised their oversight duties. Board members did not investigate allegations of financial improprieties. They circled the wagons against their growing number of critics. Their inaction and irresponsibility have resulted in a national scandal, further harm to the United Way network, the loss of donors, and the erosion of public confidence.

The dissolution this month of the board of the Washington United Way and the proposed selection of a new board are promising developments, but only if the new trustees are broadly representative of the total community, and not simply corporate officials or major donors.

Circumstances at the John and Mary R. Markle Foundation, a major developer of *Sesame Street* and long known as an innovative supporter of education and communication programs, provide another example of a board that has failed in its fiduciary and oversight responsibilities.

Zoë Baird, the foundation's president, has spent only $40 million of the $100 million she promised to spend in five years. Half the $40 million has been spent on administrative costs, including salaries, consultants, and public relations help, according to the *New York Times*. She also spent a good deal of the money on projects that did not materialize. Her administration has come under attack from outside organizations, some of them Markle grant recipients, as well as from many former employees.

In fact, at least thirty employees have left the organization in the past couple of years, and some of them have openly criticized the foundation, further undermining its reputation. To make matters worse, a number of departing staff members were asked to state in writing that they would not criticize the foundation as part of their severance agreements. In addition, Ms. Baird's management policies include a rule that staff members not speak to board members without first receiving permission. Those who do so inadvertently are then required to notify Ms. Baird about such conversations.

One would have thought that the Markle board would have demonstrated some concern about the huge staff turnover and the criticism of outside groups, not to mention the high-handed administrative policies typical of autocratic regimes.

Nor has the board been disturbed by the spending practices of the foundation. High travel costs, luxurious hotels, high-priced consultants, and an expensive redesign of its offices have been marks of the foundation's activities. So were the extravagant expenditures of Ms. Baird's former chief planner, who resigned, but only after the press raised questions about her behavior. Large expenses for public relations, some of it to burnish Ms. Baird's image, also seem to have escaped the purview of the board.

Indeed, the board, chaired by Joel Fleishman, a law professor at Duke University, has defended the foundation's practices without equivocation. Had it not apparently had its head in the sand, the board might have prompted some changes that could have avoided the criticism the foundation has drawn.

Nonprofit groups such as the United Way in Washington and well-known foundations are not the only institutions that have been tainted by the brush of questionable administrative and investment practices. A few years ago, one of the pilot ships of the community development movement, Eastside Community Investments, in Indianapolis, went down in flames because of poor program investments and management, abetted by an inattentive board of directors that didn't do its job.

Many charities have been stung by the high fund-raising costs of their programs, none more so than some of the AIDS charity bike rides. The locally sponsored bikeathon in Washington, D.C., organized by the for-profit Pallotta TeamWorks, in Los Angeles, returned only 14 percent of all the money raised last year—$3.6 million—to charity. The company, which recently suspended operations, had been sued for several years by AIDS groups in California because of the enormous costs of its fund-raising operations.

The use of high-priced, for-profit fund raisers whose costly operations net only a small percentage of the funds raised for the charities they serve should be carefully monitored and investigated by prospective nonprofit clients. The latter's boards need to be heavily engaged in this process to ensure sound fund-raising practices and public accountability.

Nonprofit organizations need board members who will take the time and effort to oversee the organizations' policy and planning activities, exercise fiduciary responsibilities, and evaluate the performance of the director and staff members.

That means board members must be working board members, not names on a roster, and must be fully prepared to take responsibility for their groups' successes and failures. Being a good board member is often hard work, not fun, but it is a volunteer job that is crucial to society.

Good, tough board members are the force that can eliminate the dark cloud of William Aramony that still hovers over the nonprofit world.

~

Corporate Values Could Poison Nonprofits

From The Chronicle of Philanthropy, *March 10, 1992*

The revelations about the $463,000 compensation package, luxurious travel, and high entertainment expenses of William Aramony, the head of the United Way of America who resigned under pressure two weeks ago, are just one indication of the extent to which corporate values have permeated the nonprofit world. For years, United Way's board, made up mainly of business leaders, endorsed the lavish payments and cronyism with no questions.

The corporate way of doing business is very dangerous, not only for United Way, but for all nonprofits. Far too many charities have failed to distinguish between sound and unsound corporate policies, and a good number have conveniently forgotten the distinction between for-profit and nonprofit activities, between fulfilling a mission and survival at any cost.

Beleaguered by inadequate budgets, lackluster leadership, high staff turnover, low salaries and benefits, poorly functioning boards and little public accountability, many nonprofits have sought refuge in management techniques. Their efforts are often reinforced by grant makers who stress that the lack of money could be offset by efficient management and profit-generating activities.

With a corporate model of good management in mind, many nonprofits have adopted new organizational structures, installed new and sometimes highly complex administrative systems, introduced increasingly fancy and expensive technology, and imposed seemingly rational but all-too-often-impersonal personnel policies and practices.

Better management has clearly been a need for nonprofits, and many organizations have greatly benefited from improved management practices. But for too many, management became an end in itself, overshadowing the services to be delivered and the human factor that characterizes public service.

After all, good management boils down to people—how to care for and get the best out of employees. This is especially true for nonprofit organizations. For corporations or other large bureaucracies, large and complex administrative systems may be necessary; they do not seem in most cases appropriate for small nonprofit organizations.

The enormous emphasis on the chief executive officer is another distinctive characteristic of the corporate world that is gaining acceptance in the nonprofit sector. It is in line with this country's infatuation with stars, but it could impair the long-term health and vitality of nonprofit organizations.

A growing number of nonprofit executives are receiving salaries, benefits, and privileges that dwarf those of other staff members. Leased cars, special health benefits and insurance packages, salaries that are more than double that of the next highest-paid employee or seven to ten times as much as the lowest-salaried person, club memberships, first-class travel, and expensive hotel accommodations are no longer uncommon.

But the growing cult of the chief executive officer has involved more than perks. It includes centralizing organizational authority, being the sole spokesman for the institution, and harnessing the communications and public relations resources of the organization to highlight and celebrate the director. Instead of focusing on the strength of staff members and teamwork, many chief executives are busy building egos, not institutions. Their model is Lee A. Iacocca of Chrysler, not Robert D. Haas of Levi Strauss and Company.

Corporate America used to be the champion of long-range business planning, calculating how products and sales could be expanded many years in the future. More recently, as a result of poor management, hard economic times, and a lust for immediate gain, corporations seem to be treading water, with a planning vision that doesn't stretch beyond a few months. Like corporations, many nonprofit organizations find themselves mired in the present, unable to prepare themselves for the future. Their capacity for assessing the long-term needs of constituents, formulating long-range fund-raising strategies, and planning modified or new programs appears limited.

Nowhere is this limitation more evident than in their inability or unwillingness to recruit dynamic young people for entry- or mid-level staff positions. It is this new wave of would-be nonprofit workers who could and should be the leadership cadre of the philanthropic world in the next ten or fifteen years. Without such an infusion of talent, and the appropriate experience and training that must accompany these recruits, the nonprofit world will face a dull, uncreative, and bleak future.

Corporate boards are more often than not controlled by management. Policy and management functions are often blurred, especially when so many members of the management team also sit on the corporation board. The notions of public accountability and checks and balances on governance are not high in the corporate value system.

They are, however, essential to a nonprofit organization. While structurally and functionally different, numerous nonprofit boards have come to resemble their corporate counterparts. They have permitted themselves to become mere accessories to management. They have not held the chief executive officer and staff accountable. They have not played a significant part in setting the direction and priorities of the organization. And they have allowed, and at times encouraged, the cult of the chief executive officer.

If public accountability and, as a result, public confidence in the nonprofit sector are to be maintained, nonprofit boards of directors will have to reassert their traditional role and become important actors in the governance of their organizations.

Assertive boards are not the only instrument of public accountability. The provision of written information about a nonprofit organization to constituents, donors, and the public is equally important. It provides the basis for future financial and other support. It helps to create the integrity of the sector. This "right to know" policy stands in contrast to the refusal of many corporations to release information. The difficulty of obtaining data about much of corporate giving is the tip of the iceberg.

Yet all too many nonprofits have adopted the corporate approach, despite the fact that such a policy is against their self-interest in the long run. They don't issue financial statements, annual reports, or periodic program reviews. Curiously, some of them have the gall to criticize donors for being unaccountable and inaccessible.

We have all read or heard about the major ethical lapses, and sometimes criminal behavior, of numerous American corporations: the creation of environmental hazards, violations of Equal Employment Opportunity Commission standards, exorbitant salaries and benefits for corporate executives, unfair pricing policies, the use of cost-benefit analysis to justify the production of potentially lethal corporate products, the withholding of information from regulators, and conflict-of-interest practices. This twilight zone of corporate ethics has been increasingly criticized, largely because of growing media coverage.

The "anything goes" school of operation appears to be gaining ground within the nonprofit sector. Compared with its corporate counterpart, its twilight zone of ethics has received little attention from the media, except during the recent uproar over United Way of America. Nor have nonprofits themselves been vigilant in policing their own questionable practices.

Few of us realize—or would like to admit—how many nonprofits violate standards of ethical behavior. The pocketing of fees and honoraria—for speeches or articles and participation on boards and commissions—is one such example. So is the sacrifice of organizational mission for survival or financial benefit. Other examples include such activities as the misuse of designated funds, sophistry in raising funds, excessive staff perquisites, and hiding or distorting organizational information. And the list could go on.

In adopting the worst elements of the corporate culture, the nonprofit world may inadvertently erase the line that separates and defines the two sectors and makes charitable organizations attractive to donors. The appeal of nonprofit organizations is their commitment to public service, their work in solving society's problems, and their cost-effective way of doing business. It is not as a shadow private sector.

In a sense, nonprofits have nothing to sell but their integrity. If they undermine that, they will be in real danger of losing their soul and the public trust that sustains them.

In the United Way Case, All the Guilty May Not Pay

From The Chronicle of Philanthropy, *October 4, 1994*

The arraignment last week in federal court of William Aramony, former president of United Way of America, sends a clear signal of what can happen when an organization fails to be accountable.

Mr. Aramony and his two indicted former colleagues, Stephen J. Paulachak and Thomas J. Merlo, are charged with swindling United Way out of more than $1 million. But while the three men may eventually be punished, it is still far from clear that justice will be done and that all the guilty parties will receive their due. Nor is it obvious that the nonprofit world has learned the hard lessons of this sad chapter in the history of American philanthropy.

Unfortunately, the scandalous behavior of Mr. Aramony and a few of his cohorts, which has been the focus of the news media, has deflected our attention from other equally serious concerns about the operation and accountability of United Way of America and the large network of local United Ways. The Aramony case has overshadowed many of the accountability problems of the nonprofit world as a whole—even though the press has been publishing numerous stories about abuses at many other charities.

The United Way scandal raises many questions that have yet to be considered seriously by people who work for nonprofit organizations:

- What are the ethical implications of staff members who willingly tolerate without protest the corrupt or questionable practices of a chief executive officer and his chief lieutenants?

- How do we judge the behavior of directors of local organizations who are only too willing to endorse or overlook a national leader's disreputable habits—and who may even clone his style of high living?

- What is the responsibility of the board of directors, which has ultimate authority over the organization?

For many years a good number of high- and mid-level officials at the national United Way were familiar with the practices of their chief executive. They knew about his lavish spending habits, his love of women and good times, his drive for power and control, and his close ties to a board that exercised little or no oversight over the organization. And some of them knew that he had set up several spinoff organizations, which diverted several million dollars that rightfully belonged to United Way into the pockets of his friends and relatives. But they were well paid according to nonprofit standards and they held good positions in a prestigious national organization that provided important services to local communities. Why should they risk their jobs and careers by raising complaints internally or resigning and going public?

Some did leave quietly and went on to new jobs at other charities. Several raised some concerns internally and even consulted outside lawyers, but those efforts never went far. A few attempted subtly to alert some board members about problems in the organization, but those warnings were apparently never taken seriously.

Many of the directors of the large local United Ways had worked with Mr. Aramony for many years. Not a few owed their jobs to his patronage. Some saw him as a role model, adopting the same excessive compensation packages and perks as he had. As long as things were running smoothly, they supported the national United Way and its operations and practices. After all, they were part of a successful, highly visible, and productive national network.

They did not question Mr. Aramony's leadership, his high living, the structure of the subsidiary organizations he created, or even the local United Ways' own lack of representation on the national governing board. Nor did many of the major charities that are big beneficiaries of local United Way grant making every year. While some had problems with Mr. Aramony's policies and practices, those concerns were muted and kept in-house. It was all in the family.

If any player was the "heavy" in the conspiracy of silence that led to Bill Aramony's downfall, it was the United Way of America board. A prestigious group dominated by chief executive officers of major corporations, the board failed to detect the misappropriation of funds by staff members, the questionable structure and nature of the subsidiary organizations, and the lack of necessary financial controls. Board members placed their total trust in Mr. Aramony, who wined, dined, and golfed them in the style to which many corporate officials are accustomed.

To many United Way board members, high compensation packages, large expense accounts, and opulent entertaining and travel were natural perks conferred on chief executives. They made no distinction between practices in the business and nonprofit worlds. Their lack of oversight permitted Mr. Aramony and his colleagues to continue unchecked. Had they periodically consulted with other United Way staff members, they might have picked up some disturbing information that could have prompted an earlier intervention.

In the end, the board did what it had to do: It got involved. But it was too late. Because of the board's detachment and failure to exercise its responsibilities, the national United Way has had to pay a heavy price, as have many local United Ways. In a real sense, then, the board must share the guilt for what took place, although its members will never be punished.

What happened to United Way is similar to other nonprofit scandals in recent years. In each case, the boards of directors did not do their jobs. We must keep this in mind as we collectively try to make the nonprofit world more accountable and more respected by the public at large.

~

Will Charities Learn from the United Way Mess?

From The Chronicle of Philanthropy, *August 8, 1996*
Elaine Chao took over United Way of America after the organization's long-time
president, William Aramony, was forced to resign amid a financial scandal.
Ms. Chao was later named Secretary of Labor under President George W. Bush.

Elaine Chao's messy departure from the presidency of United Way of America raises a serious challenge for the nonprofit world. Will charity leaders pass the controversy off as just another trifle, or will they take to heart some lessons that could help strengthen both their reputation and the public's trust in them?

The problems started when Ms. Chao resigned from United Way and was offered a departure gift of $292,500, one and a half times her annual salary of $195,000. A five-year contract that Ms. Chao had signed with United Way stipulated that she would receive eighteen months' pay if she were dismissed from her job before the end of the contract. This, no doubt, prompted rumors that Ms. Chao had been forced out, but United Way's board and Ms. Chao firmly denied them. She said she had accomplished all her goals at United Way and wanted to move on. The United Way board commended her for an excellent job in restoring the organization's integrity.

Yet the circumstances surrounding the gift and the amount of the proposed contribution clouded the picture. If the $292,500 was not severance pay, why was the gift set at that amount? Why should there be any gift at all for somebody who had been with the organization less than four years?

The board added to the puzzle by announcing that the money would come from contributions by seven or eight board members. But it refused to say which board members would contribute and how much, whether those gifts would be tax-deductible, or, indeed, whether the board members expected to be reimbursed by United Way in the future. To make matters worse, the board transparently tried to circumvent the organization's code of ethics by delaying the payments until months after Ms. Chao had left.

After the scandal involving the financial and management practices of former United Way President William Aramony, it was not surprising that the press jumped all over the story, stressing both the nature of the gift and the lack of clarity about its details. Ms. Chao's decision under pressure to decline the gift—after having planned to accept it—did little to remove the blemish United Way had caused in the first place.

In the Chao matter, as in the past, United Way's board proved to be incapable of dealing with a serious matter in a candid and accountable manner. While the members may have wanted to recognize Ms. Chao's track record, they should have calculated the serious repercussions their action would have, both internally and externally.

The chair of the board, Paula Harper Bethea, cited the payment as a practice corporations often exercise when their chief executives depart. What she failed to say is that the United Way and other nonprofit organizations are not corporations and should not act as such. While the United Way board has become more diversified, in this case it still acted as a corporate and not a nonprofit board, to the detriment of the organization.

The proposed departure gift also highlighted an ethical issue for charities. Should nonprofit groups, even the large ones, give so-called golden parachutes to outgoing chief executives and senior staff members? While some nonprofit groups have done so, most do not provide goodbye gifts or benefits beyond owed vacation days and the proceeds of a retirement fund.

That is the way it should be. Tearing down the wall that separates for-profit personnel practices from those of charities is a dangerous thing to do. At stake is nothing less than the integrity and public trust that nonprofit groups must maintain in order to continue to be supported by charitable donations. The public expects executives at charities to be paid reasonably, with good benefits, but not to receive excessive perks. Termination packages violate those expectations. Those who feel that it is a sacrifice to work for an annual salary of $195,000 and not receive large termination bonuses should work in the corporate world.

What are the lessons to be gleaned from the Chao–United Way affair? I believe there are four major ones:

- The need for clarity and candor in dealing with the press.

- The importance of strong and responsible nonprofit boards.

- The inappropriateness of charitable organizations providing large gifts to departing executives.

- The need for large and prestigious charities to redouble their efforts to maintain high nonprofit operating standards and to avoid scandals.

The importance and visibility of the "heavyweight" charities mean that their lapses and failures tarnish the rest of the nonprofit world. If effective self-regulation is not a realistic goal, then tougher regulations and government oversight need to be invoked.

~

Is It Time to End the Promise?: The Failed Volunteerism Crusade

From The Chronicle of Philanthropy, *October 7, 1999*
The nonprofit group America's Promise was formed after presidents Bill Clinton,
Jimmy Carter, and George H. W. Bush joined together to push volunteerism. It was
chaired by General Colin Powell, who later was named Secretary of State by
President George W. Bush.

America's Promise, the crusade led by retired General Colin Powell to mobilize money, volunteers, and new programs to support youngsters in poor neighborhoods, has won some battles but may be losing the war. Indeed, the time may have come for the organization to fade away.

Begun in 1997 at the Presidents' Summit for America's Future, America's Promise was an immediate success because of the importance of its mission, General Powell's broad appeal, and the backing and enthusiasm of corporate leaders. It was also a resounding political success, giving President Clinton a platform from which to tout the importance of national service in the face of drastic cutbacks in social programs. Republican politicians were pleased with the opportunity to promote private efforts as an antidote to big government.

But in its two and a half years, America's Promise—a $6 million organization with fifty-one employees—has been hampered by a weak organizational structure, inexperienced staff members, the development of few real community ties, and a disregard for public accountability.

Clearly, General Powell and his organization have succeeded in raising the awareness of many Americans about the importance of investing in youth. But by stressing new resources and volunteers, the organization unwittingly has shifted the spotlight from youth work in needy neighborhoods to volunteers, corporations, and a few large providers of youth services. Despite the organization's public relations efforts, the influence that the crusade really has had on the lives of America's disadvantaged youth still is not clear.

Part of the problem lies with the organization's fondness for Hollywood-style glitz and hype. To call public attention to its successes, America's Promise early this year issued a 643-page "Report to the Nation" documenting the commitments made to the organizations and the extent to which the commitment makers have actually fulfilled their promises. Then in May, General Powell released a three-page "performance measurement" study, conducted by the accounting firm PricewaterhouseCoopers, which claimed that America's Promise had raised $285 million and had reached more than ten million young people.

The study, which was done on a pro bono basis, was not a serious assessment of performance but a puff piece based on unsubstantiated information provided by only 91 of the 441 organizations that had made a commitment to America's Promise. Susan Ellis, president of Energize, a for-profit company that works with managers of volunteers, wryly observed that since 20 percent of the commitment makers claimed to have served 20 percent of all Americans under age seventeen (about fifty million), then all 441 commitment makers must have reached the nation's entire population of adolescents.

PricewaterhouseCoopers acknowledged that it had not verified any of the data provided by the commitment makers. What's more, neither the auditing firm nor General Powell has been willing to release the full report to the public.

That is not the only information that the organization has been unwilling to release. The 1997 informational tax return the organization submitted to the Internal Revenue Service did not disclose the compensation paid to its top officers and key employees. America's Promise skirted that requirement by entering into what some observers consider to be a highly unusual arrangement—especially for so large an organization—with the billion-dollar for-profit management company Administaff, based in Kingwood, Texas. According to the terms of its contract with America's Promise, Administaff not only handles the payroll and other administrative responsibilities but also is considered to be an official co-employer of America's Promise's staff. Because of its for-profit status, Administaff does not have to disclose to the public the salaries it pays.

Partly as a result of growing news media demand for greater disclosure, America's Promise's 1998 tax forms provided the salaries of all officers and key employees, but left some unanswered questions about additional income paid to its executives. One of the reasons for the organization's initial lack of public accountability was its board of directors, which has served more as a cheerleader for General Powell than as a tough policy and oversight committee.

Several recent reports in the news media have further undermined America's Promise's credibility. In its summer issue, the magazine *Youth Today* reported that America's Promise had failed to meet many of its goals; had been slow to form local coalitions of corporate, nonprofit, and government organizations; had not involved many grassroots youth and activist organizations; and had a poor record of evaluating its performance and that of local efforts it helped to set up. And a recent Bloomberg News Services story reported, among other things, that a number of corporations listed as commitment makers by America's Promise have said that they would have started or expanded programs to help young people regardless of whether they had been urged to do so by General Powell and his organization.

The reports confirmed what many nonprofit organizations have been saying. Many feel that grassroots and small youth-service providers, as well as pol-

icy and activist organizations, have not been involved in or benefited much—
if at all—from America's Promise's national or local activities. A few of the
large youth-service organizations, such as Big Brothers Big Sisters and the Boys
& Girls Clubs, appear to have been the major beneficiaries of new money at the
local level. And a good portion of expanded business commitments have actually gone to corporate-run volunteer programs, not to youth workers in needy
neighborhoods. In other words, the initial promise of a broad coalition has not
been fulfilled.

America's Promise initially pledged to close its doors in 2000, but it has
now decided to extend its life for at least two more years. The reason, according to staff members, is that the organization is taking longer than anticipated
to reach its goals. Moreover, they say there is an urgent need to capitalize on the
enormous momentum created by General Powell.

The latter point, of course, is a problem for America's Promise. As one
board member put it, "Without Powell, there is no movement, no crusade."

Perhaps it is time for America's Promise to declare victory, close its doors
in 2000, and transfer its functions to another nonprofit organization. One possibility is the Points of Light Foundation, which was poised and wanted to take
on these responsibilities after the summit. Although the Points of Light Foundation does not focus exclusively on youth, many of its activities have revolved
around youth development and volunteering. What's more, its budget of $14
million and experienced staff could insure a smooth transition. Its network of
450 volunteer centers and more than 250 corporate members could provide a
solid base from which to expand America's Promise's work.

In Colin Powell, the country has an invaluable resource with which to raise
the level of investment in America's young people, especially its most disadvantaged youth. He is the "added value" of America's Promise. Given the
right support, the general could easily operate within the framework of the
Points of Light Foundation or another organization.

Indeed, his efforts cannot afford to be undermined by America's Promise's
weak organizational structure, poor public accountability, and diminishing
public confidence. The general and his board should not let America's Promise
become America's disappointment.

∼

General Powell's About-Face on Private Aid

From The Chronicle of Philanthropy, *August 24, 2000*

America's Promise, the national organization led by General Colin Powell, was created to mobilize private funds and other resources to help disadvantaged youths. Now the organization is doing an about-face and is eager to accept $7.5 million in federal support that Congress is expected to approve this fall—an amount greater than the organization's entire operating budget last year.

This transformation of an organization so rooted in private philanthropy to an organization that is dependent on federal funds is disturbing, especially because this poor use of scarce federal aid seems to be the result mainly of political maneuvering by the head of the Corporation for National Service, Harris Wofford.

Started with great fanfare and expectations at the Presidents' Summit for America's Future held in Philadelphia three years ago, America's Promise was supposed to be the catalytic engine that would attract new corporate and philanthropic dollars to expand youth services and programs throughout the country. An impressive list of corporations and foundations responded to the call and pledged their support.

Some of the commitments never materialized. But General Powell's enormous prestige and stature were sufficient to attract many new supporters from corporations, foundations, and individual donors.

While some of the large foundations that initially supported America's Promise—including Carnegie, Casey, Kauffman, Kellogg, and Pew—have not renewed their pledges for the current year, new donors appear to have made up for this loss, and a spokesman says the group hopes to secure additional funds that will allow it to expand. Not bad for an institution that announced at its creation that it planned to go out of business after three years.

To meet its budget of $7.3 million in 1999, America's Promise raised a little more than $9 million (counting new funds and multiple-year commitments made in 1998). Even though it took in more than it needed for last year, the organization is slated to receive an additional $2.5 million from the Defense Department's Division of Operations and Maintenance and $200,000 from the Justice Department's Office of Juvenile Justice and Delinquency Programs during the current year. And in fiscal 2001, America's Promise is likely to receive $7.5 million of the funds that Congress approves for the Corporation for National Service, which runs the AmeriCorps and VISTA national service programs.

Given the organization's popularity in corporate America, the fund-raising charisma of General Powell, and the proven ability of the charity to raise more than enough in private donations to cover its operating budget, why is it now so anxious to get a federal handout? And a more serious question: Why are the White House and Congress giving their support to the request for federal aid?

At a time when federal resources to help poor and troubled youngsters are scarce, it should be of great concern to the Clinton administration and to lawmakers that America's Promise continues to face serious questions about its performance.

The organization's persistent refusal to fully report staff salaries and benefits has raised questions of transparency and accountability. So has the organization's management contract with a billion-dollar for-profit professional employer, Administaff, based in Kingwood, Texas.

According to the terms of its contract with America's Promise, Administaff not only handles the payroll and other administrative responsibilities but also is considered to be an official co-employer of the America's Promise staff. Because of its status as a commercial organization, Administaff does not have to disclose to the public the salaries it pays.

In newspaper reports and elsewhere, critics have charged that fifty-plus staff members at America's Promise have had little experience in youth services. In addition, local youth-service organizations frequently complain that "Communities of Promise," groups created by the national organization, have failed to generate additional resources for their work, have not included grassroots groups or young people in their efforts, and have only benefited established youth organizations.

Lack of diversity has also characterized the America's Promise board, which, according to some of the organization's trustees, has been more of a rubber-stamping instrument than a true governing board that sets policy and oversees operations.

Aside from doing a poor job of helping local grassroots groups expand the services available to young people, America's Promise can also be criticized for failing to push for legislation and government programs that could substantially increase the resources available to help far more of the nation's youngsters than any private group ever will.

Nevertheless, the organization has suddenly taken an interest in Capitol Hill, lobbying for its own self-interest.

Harris Wofford, director of the Corporation for National Service, started the move to give America's Promise $7.5 million, according to sources at America's Promise.

Figuring that a Republican victory in the November elections would probably lead to a major appointment for Mr. Powell in a new administration, Mr. Wofford seems to be worried that America's Promise would be in trouble without the general.

A federal commitment to America's Promise would not only ensure the future of the organization but also make it easier to attract a prominent leader to replace Mr. Powell. As for the general, he has indicated that he would be happy to spend less time raising private funds.

Whatever the reason, the funds earmarked for America's Promise would be better used if they were spent on AmeriCorps and VISTA volunteers, who are at the heart of national service. Since the volunteers cost about $15,000 per person to maintain for a year, the $7.5 million could put another 500 volunteers to work for a full year.

For an administration that prides itself in having galvanized a sense of public service among our nation's young people, supporting more volunteers would be the right thing to do. Propping up a nonprofit organization that can and should attract substantial private resources is not doing the country a service, national or otherwise.

~

Accountability and the Weinberg Foundation

From The Chronicle of Philanthropy, *September 22, 1992*

Recent newspaper articles about the Harry and Jeanette Weinberg Foundation, in Baltimore, highlight the irresponsibility of the foundation and its trustees, the lax standards of accountability required of philanthropic institutions by both the Internal Revenue Service and the general public, and the lack of courage by nonprofit organizations and foundations in the face of outrageous behavior by one of their colleague institutions.

The five trustees of the Weinberg Foundation have apparently molded the institution in the image of its founder—secretive, arrogant, contentious, and cantankerous. The foundation's telephone number is unlisted, the location of its offices is unknown to all but a few people, and its operating style and decision making are a mystery. The phone number and address on its IRS Form 990-PF are those of the Weinberg real estate operations and not those of the foundation's offices.

The trustees have had no previous involvement with foundations and, apparently, not much with the rest of the nonprofit world. They have shown little interest in what other grant makers have done and they rarely consult with their peers. They justify their approach and style by saying "that's what Harry would have wanted or done." That may be good enough for Harry, but it's not good enough for the public, the taxpayers, and nonprofits.

The foundation does not publish grant-making guidelines or annual reports and it discourages unsolicited proposals. Darrell Friedman, president of Baltimore's Jewish Federation, argues that the trustees are accessible because they have always responded to him and the federation. But that's the problem. He and his organization are among the few that have had access to the trustees. The trustees have not responded, either in writing or by phone, to hundreds of other organizations that have tried to reach the foundation. In short, the foundation and its trustees are both inaccessible and largely unaccountable.

It is one thing for a wealthy individual to be secretive and unaccountable; it is quite another matter for one of the twenty-five largest foundations in the country to be so abusive of the public trust. Harry Weinberg could have kept or given away his money without creating a foundation, in which case he would have had to pay taxes to the federal government. But he chose not to, preferring to create a foundation, thereby avoiding substantial tax payments. In exchange for those tax benefits, he made a compact with the American people to meet urgent public needs in a publicly accountable way.

The irresponsibility of the foundation reaches the boundary of illegality in one provision of its bylaws that states that some of the foundation's second-generation trustees, and all of its third- and subsequent-generation trustees, must be Jewish. This is an outrage, especially for a philanthropic institution that claims to have as its primary purpose assistance to the poor on an ecumenical basis. What if the bylaws had stipulated that trustees could not be Jewish, Catholic, Latino, or black or could only be white Protestant males? Civil rights groups and the Baltimore Jewish community would most certainly have been up in arms.

The provision is discriminatory and should be eliminated. In view of the tax expenditures involved in the exemptions granted to Weinberg and other foundations, the IRS has a responsibility to pursue this matter. Either the bylaws should be changed or the Weinberg Foundation should lose its tax-exempt status.

To make matters worse, the bylaws also include a clause that requires its current and future Jewish trustees to have been members in good standing of a synagogue for five years prior to election to the board. Those trustees who decide after their election to resign from membership in a synagogue are automatically dismissed from the board. The foundation therefore has arrogated to itself the right to distinguish between "appropriate" and "inappropriate" Jews.

One further provision in the bylaws deserves mention. It states that any charitable organization that criticizes the foundation or "challenges, directly or indirectly, the manner in which the Trustees exercise their discretion on any subject . . . shall forever be barred from receiving any distribution from the Corporation."

Those two provisions reflect the narrowness, arrogance, and meanness of disposition that seem to infuse the very heart of the Weinberg Foundation, despite its allocation of funds to some deserving nonprofits. The foundation, unfortunately, does not embody the spirit and generosity of modern philanthropy. Not even a public relations company—which the foundation recently hired—can hide this stark fact.

Newspaper articles about the Weinberg Foundation have all stated that no one was willing to say anything critical on the record. Those who formerly reviled Harry Weinberg as a poor and mean landlord, unpleasant businessman, and surly fellow now deliver encomiums about his wisdom, generosity, and vision. Nonprofit organizations in Baltimore and elsewhere that have been denied access to the foundation, or even the courtesy of good manners, are participating in a conspiracy of silence and fear in the hope that they may someday hit the Weinberg jackpot.

With the exception of the *Baltimore Jewish Times,* no prominent Baltimore institutions and individuals have publicly expressed any concern about or criticized the foundation. Where have been the voices of other philanthropic institutions in the area that should be worried about standards in their field? Where have the leaders in the Jewish community been? Are they willing to tolerate discriminatory practices and questionable philanthropic ethics just because the foundation has given large amounts of money to some Jewish organizations? How about other community leaders and institutions? Principle seems to have given way to the demands of greed and hypocrisy.

If the Weinberg Foundation is permitted to get away with its current by-laws and practices, it will signal to other multimillion-dollar would-be philanthropists that they have total license to establish foundations, at taxpayers' expense, in whatever way they want, without respect for philanthropic standards and ethics.

The IRS has an obligation to be more thorough and careful in granting exemptions to new foundations and to investigate those institutions like Weinberg that appear to be in violation of even the minimal standards that exist. The general public and nonprofit organizations have the right to expect greater accountability from foundations, at least the large ones. Since foundations haven't managed to regulate themselves, it is time that Congress passed a requirement that all large foundations must issue an annual or biennial public report with sufficient information to permit a clear understanding of their objectives, priorities, guidelines, grant making, and investments.

The Weinberg trustees seem to be somewhat nervous about the newspaper coverage they have received so far, as indicated by their decision to hire a publicist. The pressure on the foundation should be maintained. It will be important for national organizations and associations like the Council on Foundations and Independent Sector, which are concerned about the integrity of the nonprofit world, to speak out on this issue. One can only hope that the Weinberg trustees will listen to the mounting criticism, change the foundation's by-laws and practices, and join the ranks of the large accountable and responsible philanthropies.

~

Press Coverage Sends a Message to
Nonprofits: Clean Up Your Act

From The Chronicle of Philanthropy, *July 13, 1993*

The growing press attention to the excesses and questionable activities of non-profits sends an unmistakably clear message: The nonprofit world must clean up its affairs, or Congress and the state legislatures will do the job for it. The question is, Can nonprofits do this by themselves?

The image of the nonprofit sector as full of institutions and people com-mitted to high ideals, sacrifice, ethical practices, and the public good has been shattered over the past few years by press coverage of organizations like Covenant House [whose founder resigned amid charges he was a child moles-ter], United Way of America and some of its local members, and the Blue Cross/ Blue Shield companies [which were trying to convert to for-profit status]. Nonprofits' reputations have also been damaged by reports about the misuse of federal aid by some universities, about nonprofit hospitals that don't serve the needy, about lavish spending on administration at the Freedom Forum [a foundation created by the founders of the Gannett news company], and about excessive salaries and perks awarded to nonprofit chief executives.

The seamier side of many nonprofits was further exposed in April in a re-markable seven-part series in the *Philadelphia Inquirer.* The series revealed the excessive fees, benefits, and perks awarded to executives of many nonprofit groups; the huge growth in charities' money-making operations; the lack of public accountability by tax-exempt groups; and the lax oversight and en-forcement of such organizations by the Internal Revenue Service.

In a demonstration that the topic had not been exhausted, even in Penn-sylvania, the *Harrisburg Sunday Patriot-News* carried a well-researched, three-part series in June by Adam Bell on the Milton Hershey School, a huge and largely unaccountable institution controlling a financial empire larger than the budgets of some developing countries.

And there is probably much more to come.

What is one to make of this development? Defensiveness has characterized a good deal of the reaction by charities and foundations to the *Philadelphia In-quirer* series in particular.

Some called the series unfair and biased, and said it was an exercise in non-profit bashing. Others viewed it as an attempt to condemn the barrel because of a few bad apples. Representatives of smaller charities have smugly com-plained that the stories focused only on large institutions, implying that their organizations do not have similar difficulties. More than a few nonprofit offi-cials responded by saying that a major part of the problem was that the charity world needed better working relations with the press and more effective public relations.

It is easy to criticize parts of a substantial and detailed story about a segment of our society that has such a wide-ranging impact. A few facts may have been wrong, the number of nonprofit groups examined may have been inadequate, and some interpretations could be challenged. By and large, however, the *Philadelphia Inquirer*'s series is a sterling piece of journalism that documents accurately and in detail the malpractice and excesses of many nonprofits and the major problems we face in improving the charitable world. We cannot blame the messenger for the bad news he has brought us.

The *Inquirer* has performed a notable public service. One of the reasons that its expose and other recent stories seem so harsh today is that the press, historically, has treated the nonprofit sector with kid gloves. Try to find more than a relative handful of critical pieces about nonprofit groups over the past decade in the *New York Times* and other major newspapers. If there has been any imbalance in reporting, the tilt has been heavily on the side of uncritical analysis and praise. The role of the press is to examine and report as objectively as possible on the institutions of our society. We should be pleased, not disappointed, that it is finally beginning to pay adequate attention to nonprofit groups.

The most disturbing aspect of the *Inquirer* articles is that they touched on so many of our major, large nonprofit organizations. They are not an insignificant portion of the nonprofit sector. And I suspect they may be only the visible section of a larger iceberg. While only a relatively small minority of all nonprofits in this country, the big institutions nevertheless have the visibility and influence to paint the entire sector with their negative brush, unless they remedy—or are forced to remedy—their questionable practices.

Nor should we take comfort in the fact that the *Inquirer* and other recent stories concentrated only on large and wealthy nonprofit institutions. A surprisingly large number of small nonprofits have exhibited the same types of malpractices and ethical lapses as their more powerful and prestigious counterparts.

While their executive directors may not have received exorbitant salaries, many of them have pocketed fees and honoraria on company time, given themselves benefits and perks not available to other staff members, and run their organizations as though they were personal fiefdoms. A huge number of small nonprofit groups do not publish annual reports or conduct financial audits. Some have been plagued by corruption and political cronyism. Many of their boards do little to insure the fiscal and programmatic health of the institutions they oversee. Some, in seeking business ventures to assure survival, have lost sight of the mission for which they were originally created.

The problems of nonprofits are not limited to one type: they affect local groups as well as national organizations, establishment institutions and grassroots organizations, small and large institutions. They are the cumulative result of deep cutbacks in federal funds and tough economic conditions, the benign neglect of press coverage (until recently), the absence of serious federal regulation and oversight, the corporatization of the nonprofit sector with its high salaries and perks, questionable ethics, a value system that gives much weight to growth and bigness, and, finally, the unwillingness of charities to police their own activities.

Many of those problems are so deeply rooted that they will take years to solve. Yet nonprofits cannot afford to waste any time in starting a serious effort to reform. Public confidence in charities—the very basis for donor support—seems already to be declining. This erosion can be seen in the decrease in giving to many United Ways at a time when the demands on charities have become more serious than ever. Better press relations and communications hype are not the answer. The issue is not a question of external perception but of internal change.

Is the nonprofit world capable of reforming and regulating itself? The history of nonprofits—both grant makers and charities—is not very encouraging. The excessive collegiality, especially among foundations, precludes serious collective efforts to set and enforce higher standards and practices. The field's trade associations usually cater to the lowest common denominator among their members and are therefore immobilized from taking tough positions and action.

Only the federal government has the capability, authority, and power to bring about needed changes in the nonprofit sector, changes that could assure public trust and support. While some risks are always involved in government regulation, the danger of doing little or nothing about the current crisis far outweighs the possibility of federal excesses. Moreover, the cooperation of nonprofits in helping the federal government establish fair and reasonable standards would go a long way toward making certain that government policies are balanced and practical.

What could the federal government do, with the help of nonprofit organizations? Here are some ideas:

- Require public accountability. All foundations and other nonprofit organizations are required each year to submit an informational tax return, Form 990, to the Internal Revenue Service. This form, which provides details about an organization's finances and programs, should be revamped so it provides additional essential information and should be made much more user-friendly. The forms should be made readily available to the public, either from state attorneys general offices or from nonprofit organizations themselves.

All foundations wealthy enough to merit listing in the *Foundation Directory* (those with assets of at least $2 million or an annual grants budgets of at least $200,000) should be required to issue a public report at least every two years describing their activities, finances, grant-making criteria, and personnel. Such reports should be made readily available to the public, press, and charities at no charge.

All other nonprofit organizations with budgets of more than $150,000 should be required to issue a public report at least every two years, describing their missions, programs, and donors. Those reports should include a statement of their expenditures and financial status. They should be readily available to the public on demand at a reasonable charge that covers the cost of printing and postage.

- Improve the ability of the Internal Revenue Service to oversee nonprofit activity. Congress should force the agency to step up its review of the 990 reports, allow the service to impose new kinds of penalties to enforce appropriate standards and practices, and encourage it to withdraw nonprofit tax exemptions more frequently where necessary. Currently the IRS has neither the staff nor resources to review 990's adequately or to conduct more than a minimal number of audits. The agency's staff should be enlarged significantly to be able to police nonprofit groups.

- Eliminate the automatic granting of tax-exempt status. The IRS approves nearly 30,000 applications for tax-exempt status every year without any careful review. Few organizations or would-be organizations are turned down. The service should be given the resources to conduct serious reviews of groups seeking tax exemptions to screen out inappropriate organizations.

- Redefine what types of revenue are subject to the unrelated-business income tax. The line has blurred between what kinds of income are related to a charity's mission—and therefore not subject to taxation—and what are unrelated, and therefore taxable. Too many organizations are escaping their tax obligations by declaring what are really nonessential business activities as related business income. The *Inquirer* and other newspapers have cited a number of such cases. A much tighter definition of related business income would discourage nonprofits from starting unrelated-business ventures and would raise additional tax money to pay for social programs.

- Tighten the eligibility standards for a tax exemption. Too many organizations are allowed to qualify as tax-exempt groups. Those organizations that don't serve society, such as trade and professional associations, should not get special tax benefits.

Nonprofits can take some steps on their own. Private organizations that give out money—including foundations, United Ways, and churches—could stop supporting groups that provide unreasonable salaries or benefits to their executives.

But the solution does not lie in self-regulation and self-reform. It never has and never will. Once charities understand this and begin to work with the federal government on a more effective system of regulations and oversight, the possibility of real progress will be at hand. This is the type of public and private collaboration that can restore the health and prestige of the nonprofit world.

~

The Nonprofit World Must Improve Its Ties to the Press

From The Chronicle of Philanthropy, May 7, 1998

Charitable organizations have long been ambivalent about the news media. At times, they have viewed the press as a somewhat hostile force, either uninterested in nonprofit activities or looking for scandals and inappropriate behavior. On other occasions, charities have considered the press to be an essential instrument for influencing policy and for selling the country on the importance of the nonprofit world.

As nonprofit organizations grow in number, size, wealth, and influence—and, correspondingly, as attention to the nonprofit world increases—charities will need to focus on clarifying and improving their relationships with the press. In a world where self-regulation and self-reform are abysmally absent, charities must understand the crucial role the news media can play in keeping nonprofit organizations accountable, ethical, and effective. Consequently, they will have to formulate a more creative approach to dealing with journalists and broadcasters, with whom they have never been very comfortable.

The anxieties and paranoia of nonprofit organizations were reflected several years ago in their reaction to an extraordinary seven-part series of articles by the *Philadelphia Inquirer* on the problems and excesses of thousands of medium- to large-sized charitable groups. The reporters, who had already won Pulitzer Prizes, criticized the nonprofit world for a lack of accountability, conflicts of interest, nonfunctioning boards of directors, questionable practices, and excessively high compensation of executives.

Instead of taking those revelations seriously, many nonprofit groups and spokesmen, especially the large umbrella organizations, cried "foul" and tried to kill the messenger. Citing the authors' examples as a few rotten apples in the barrel, they conveniently forgot that the barrel held many rotten apples.

Under some pressure to do more than "nay-say," Independent Sector, a coalition of more than seven hundred nonprofit groups, established a committee to study charities' accountability. After circulating an initial and exceedingly tepid draft report, the committee quietly went out of business. No final report was ever issued. Although Independent Sector recently decided to re-establish a task force on accountability, the organization is devoting much more energy and money to educating and selling the public about the merits of the charitable sector.

The same is true for the foundation world. The Council on Foundations, the largest of philanthropy's trade associations, has begun a $3 million campaign to educate the American people about the wonderful efforts and accomplishments of the country's foundations. That appears to be the council's major mission and program. The council has done little or nothing about raising the standards of accountability, performance, innovation, access, leadership, and governance in its own community.

That role has been left to outside critics and the press, which, increasingly, are starting to focus on the problems as well as the good works of foundations. Yet those criticisms are often met with a thin-skinned defensiveness and petulance by grant makers, who don't understand the fact that the news media is a double-edged sword.

If the charitable sector wants greater access and closer ties to the media, it will have to risk greater scrutiny of its own poor practices and shortcomings. In other words, to receive positive exposure, it will have to clean up its own act.

For its part, the press has not been adequately responsive to the increasingly important role that nonprofit organizations play in our society. Journalists and broadcasters devote little time to the coverage of charitable groups, thereby giving short shrift to the views of the tens of millions of people represented by these organizations, many of whom have no access to the established institutions in our country. When journalists do focus on such groups, they tend to stress the scandals and problems, not the solid day-in-and-day-out accomplishments that provide the bedrock of vital neighborhoods and communities.

The changing nature of journalism is partly responsible for this state of affairs. Not too long ago, newspapers had journalists on their staffs who specialized in issues of particular importance to nonprofit organizations. Those writers had Rolodexes filled with names of nonprofit staff members whom they could call for information or quotes on specific stories they were covering.

Today, there are few journalists in the mainstream press with expertise on issues of concern to the nonprofit world. When given two or three days to get a story, most writers tend to call somebody at the White House, a contact in a federal department, a congressional aide, and, if there is time, perhaps one well-known nonprofit representative.

Often the constituencies that are most affected by a particular regulation, piece of legislation, or policy have no opportunity to air their views in the newspapers or broadcast news. One example last year was the inability of public housing residents and advocates to get any attention or coverage by newspapers throughout the country during the congressional debates on housing legislation.

What's more, the opinion pages of major newspapers are not open—except on rare occasions—to nonprofit representatives. The proliferation of syndicated columnists, all fighting for space no matter what the quality of their essays, has all but squeezed out outside observers, except those with political clout or recognition. Op-ed pages that had been open forums for a diversity of opinion are now closed discussion groups for a narrow range of commentators.

The growth of alternative journalism—for example, small radio stations, the new American News Service (which distributes stories to about seventy-five newspapers) and community newspapers—has begun to produce expanded coverage of nonprofit organizations and their activities. And a few mainstream newspapers and television programs are experimenting with what is called "solution-oriented journalism," news that offers solutions to social or community problems. Yet despite those promising developments, it is not likely that mainstream journalism will change its practices much over the next few years, unless there is substantial outside pressure to do so.

How, then, can charitable organizations get greater press coverage?

First, they will have to overcome their nervousness about dealing with journalists and broadcasters and accept the latter's role as an instrument of public accountability.

Second, they will need to spend greater staff and board resources to cultivate individual journalists over time and to provide them with a steady flow of information that can be useful to their jobs. Coalitions, in particular, should focus more attention on the news media, not only to advance their agendas but also to introduce their members to key writers and broadcasters.

Third, special efforts should be made to relate to the press in smaller cities and towns, where newspapers and local stations are always looking for material.

Fourth, nonprofit groups will need to become far more aggressive in seeking meetings with editorial boards of newspapers.

Finally, foundations should begin to provide "media development" grants that supplement funds they already give to nonprofit groups. Many organizations that are struggling for survival just do not have the money to devote to press relations and associated activities.

Nonprofit groups have slowly come to realize that the success of their programs and efforts to influence policy will depend more and more on the exposure they can get in the press. They will need, either individually or collectively, to apply much greater pressure on journalists for adequate coverage—and on foundations for additional money to build their capacities for effective cultivation of the press.

Both efforts will have to be pursued simultaneously. It is not clear, however, whether charities, foundations, and the news media will be willing to embrace a new partnership. If such a partnership doesn't emerge, nonprofit organizations will continue to find the voices of their constituents muted and their policy efforts severely limited.

$\sim$

How to Help the IRS Improve Charity Oversight

From The Chronicle of Philanthropy, *October 18, 2001*

The Internal Revenue Service and most states do a poor job of policing tax-exempt groups, and much of the reason can be traced to a lack of adequate funds. But the money to fix the problem is readily available. It should come from the federal excise tax that is levied annually on the net investment income of private foundations.

Currently, the excise tax is imposed under a two-tiered system that neither provides an adequate incentive for increased grant making nor makes much economic sense. About two-thirds of foundations pay a tax of 2 percent. The rest pay only 1 percent because they spend more than the minimum legal requirement of 5 percent of their net assets each year.

The formula for determining which foundations receive this reward is complex, based on a grant maker's average distribution of assets over five years. But because the payout includes not only grants but all costs associated with running the foundation, including employees' salaries and real estate payments, it is unlikely that groups that receive a 1-percentage-point reduction in the excise tax have much of an incentive to increase their grant making.

The excise tax should be cut from 2 percent to 1 percent for all private foundations, and the income from the tax should be used to support a greatly expanded effort by the Internal Revenue Service and state attorneys general to oversee nonprofit organizations. What's more, foundations should be required to use the savings solely for additional grant making.

Right now, foundations that pay only 1 percent in excise taxes use much of the savings for administrative and operational costs. Even with a lower excise tax, many large foundations still pay out only 3.8 percent to 4 percent of their net assets in grants to nonprofit organizations. The only way that foundations will substantially increase the amount of money they spend on grants is if the minimum-distribution requirement is raised.

When Congress levied the excise tax on foundations in 1969 as part of the Tax Reform Act, it wanted the federal government to use the income to regulate tax-exempt organizations and handle the myriad administrative tasks associated with them. But things didn't work out that way. That income has gone into the general treasury.

The tax generates far more money than is being spent now on oversight of the nonprofit world.

In 1999 the excise tax raised $499 million, approximately eight times the amount that the IRS spent on supervising nonprofit groups. Were the excise tax reduced to 1 percent for all private foundations, the annual revenue from the tax would still generate nearly $300 million in 2003. It is difficult to justify the enormous disparity between revenue from the tax and the paltry resources allocated to the oversight of philanthropy.

Because of the federal government's lackluster support of the IRS division that oversees nonprofit groups, the service has been roundly, and justifiably, criticized by both charities and foundations for poorly regulating and policing charities and foundations. As the number of financial scandals and episodes of mismanagement of nonprofit groups has grown in recent years, that criticism has intensified.

Moreover, the IRS's authority to punish nonprofit groups that pay overly generous salaries to their executives has, unfortunately, not been accompanied by added enforcement capacity. Nor is the service equipped to evaluate the tens of thousands of applications for tax-exempt status that come its way each year. The IRS simply does not have the employees and money to do its job effectively.

Changing the excise tax would provide Congress with an excellent opportunity to remedy the situation. It should earmark most, if not all, of the excise-tax revenue for the regulation and supervision of nonprofit organizations. Doing so would entail a vast expansion of the tax-exempt organization division of the IRS, including substantial growth in the number of auditors, investigators, researchers, and other personnel.

As part of this expanded role, the IRS should finance efforts to make the data it collects from Form 990 annual reports of charities and foundations more readily available to the public Philanthropic Research, a nonprofit group in Williamsburg, Virginia, that operates the Guidestar Web site, and the Urban Institute, a Washington think-tank, have worked together to digitize and put information from Forms 990 online. Yet they have struggled each year to raise money from foundations to do it. Money for this activity, which is so essential to public accountability, should come from the government, not foundations.

To ensure even more oversight of nonprofit groups, a portion of the excise tax revenue should be allocated, either directly or through the IRS, to the state attorneys general, possibly with the states required to match new federal grants. State attorneys general have responsibility within their respective jurisdictions to oversee charities and foundations, but in almost all states, the divisions that regulate tax-exempt groups are small and understaffed, when they exist at all.

Legislation to reduce and redirect the excise tax could be an important mechanism to increase the public accountability of nonprofit groups, greatly expand the capacity of the IRS and states to oversee nonprofit organizations, and channel additional foundation money to needy charities.

If charities and foundations truly want to serve the public, they should support such a measure. And if Congress fails to act, lawmakers will have lost a golden opportunity to make both economic and regulatory sense out of the current haphazard system of managing the nonprofit world.

~

IRS Must Slam the Door on High Salaries

From The Chronicle of Philanthropy, *August 13, 1998*

In recent years, the nonprofit world has been shaken by a series of scandals and news media exposés that have undermined the public's trust in the integrity of charitable organizations. One of the major reasons for that shaken trust has been the high salaries and benefits received by some officials of large charities and foundations.

Public doubts were stirred once again by a recent front-page article in the *Washington Post* that reported that the chief executive officers of the country's seven richest foundations last year received salary increases of five times the rate of inflation. The average salary of those officials was $363,000 a year, with some receiving annual total compensation packages exceeding $500,000.

When the large majority of charities are struggling not only to make their modest budgets but also to give their executive directors a reasonable salary and benefits, such increases are clearly inappropriate. The time has come for the government to help establish limits on the compensation packages earned by nonprofit leaders.

Congress passed the so-called intermediate-sanctions law in 1996, in part to crack down on excessive salaries and other instances of unfair financial benefits that have accrued to officials at nonprofit organizations. Last week the Internal Revenue Service issued its proposed rules on how it will enforce the law.

Yet the law and the proposed rules don't set any dollar limits on salaries or benefits. They simply ask charities to insure that their salaries are in line with the salaries paid at comparable for-profit and nonprofit organizations. Such a requirement does little to deal with the fact that salaries are now out of line— and it misses the critical distinction between the for-profit and nonprofit job markets.

Foundation officials and board members usually cite two reasons as justifications for high salaries and benefits. The first is that, like leaders of large businesses, the leaders of major foundations are responsible for managing hundreds of millions or billions of dollars. Therefore, they argue, it is reasonable to pay foundation leaders what their counterparts in the business world earn.

That argument is based on the belief that there must be a strong correlation between the size of assets and the size of managers' salaries. But the strength of the nonprofit world—indeed, of civil society as a whole—is that it is based on more than financial considerations. The notions of caring, social commitment, public service, community improvement, and satisfaction in making society better are the pulse that drives the work of nonprofit organizations and earns the respect of the general public. Focusing on "market factors" that can dictate exorbitant salaries erodes that trust.

Foundation officials also claim that high salaries and benefits are necessary to attract the very best talent available. Colburn S. Wilbur, executive director of the David and Lucile Packard Foundation, was quoted in the *Washington Post* as saying, "We have to compete to get qualified people. . . . We want people who will make a big difference, alleviate problems, change things, make the world a better place. This is much more important than asking individuals to sacrifice to save a few dollars."

That claim is nonsense. The truth is that you don't need salaries of $300,000 to $600,000 to recruit top talent to jobs at major foundations. Plenty of talent is available for charitable organizations—at much lower compensation packages than those currently in vogue. Foundations need leaders with vision, courage, connections with communities, and a willingness to take risks. Such admirable qualities don't carry a price tag.

It is not the pool of talent that is lacking. Rather, the problem is that foundation boards and their executive-search firms appear to be seeking only a particular type of candidate—current or former university and college presidents, high-profile people with name recognition, or safe, predictable establishment insiders.

Using the standards set by some foundations and corporations, many charities also award excessive salaries to top executives chosen from a limited pool of candidates. This growing cult of the CEO among nonprofit groups— charities and foundations alike—is neither beneficial to the morale and effectiveness of the organizations nor helpful in maintaining the public trust in the nonprofit world.

Since not all charities and foundations seem to understand why it is wrong to try to match the salaries paid by big business, government regulation is essential. Federal or state legislation could put a firm ceiling on nonprofit salaries and benefits, but such an approach would be politically impossible to implement.

More feasible would be a federal incentive—written into the tax law and overseen by the Internal Revenue Service—for nonprofit groups to give their top employees more reasonable salaries and benefits. For example, IRS regulations could be modified to require that all nonprofit organizations, including foundations, pay a 25- to 40-percent tax on that portion of a staff member's salary and benefits that exceed, say, $250,000 or $300,000.

A federal mandate to put a brake on the growth of excessive compensation packages would be a clear signal to charitable organizations and their boards. It would help restore public confidence in the work and integrity of the nonprofit world. Because it would be in their long-term self-interest, it is a measure that charitable organizations themselves should champion.

～

Why Charities Think They Can Regulate Themselves

From The Chronicle of Philanthropy, *May 4, 2000*

The decline in the popularity and prestige of government has had an unexpected result: It seems to have emboldened nonprofit organizations to assert their right to regulate themselves—a trend with potentially ominous implications.

It is not surprising that charities and foundations are feeling their oats. After all, the nonprofit world is larger, richer, more diverse, and more influential than ever. Its role has been championed by conservatives intent on diminishing the size and reach of government and by liberals concerned about providing social services and an advocacy voice to the poor. Foundation assets have far surpassed the $300 billion mark and promise even more astounding growth during the next twenty years. Employing more than ten million people and producing more than 7 percent of the gross national product, nonprofit organizations have become a major economic force.

Unfortunately, this new status has not had the effect one would have hoped. More and more, nonprofit organizations self-righteously argue that because they provide good works, they need not be accountable to anybody—including the donors who support their work. Confidence has given way to cockiness. That arrogant attitude has been allowed to thrive largely because the federal government has lost its ability to keep charities in line. The Internal Revenue Service is too weak to enforce nonprofit laws. And even if it could do a better job of oversight, it is charged with enforcing laws that Congress has failed to update and clarify to keep in step with the times.

In this atmosphere, nonprofit groups feel there is no risk in arguing that they need only be accountable to one another. A reflection of that attitude can be found in the position recently taken by Independent Sector—an umbrella organization with more than 700 member groups—in its recent comments on a Congressional proposal to require nonprofit organizations to disclose much more financial information than they do now.

The Congressional Joint Committee on Taxation, which has been pushing for more stringent requirements, argues that because charities receive substantial tax benefits, they should be forced to make public much information that is now private. Independent Sector, while agreeing with some of the recommendations and disagreeing with others, rejected the conceptual basis for the committee's position. It said that the obligation of charities to disclose information is derived solely from their unique social role and their responsibility for maintaining the public trust. It is not tied to any favorable tax treatment or to the federal government's duty to assure the public that charitable funds are accountable and spent for lawful purposes.

The implication of such an argument is that nonprofit organizations have the right to set their own disclosure standards and are not accountable to a higher authority. That is something of a stretch in a democracy with representative government.

No doubt Independent Sector's position has been influenced by its understandable fear of right-wing efforts to undermine the advocacy voice and integrity of nonprofit organizations. It is therefore convenient for Independent Sector to argue that neither the tax exemptions that nonprofit groups receive nor the charitable-tax deductions available to their donors are subsidies that involve federal strings or obligations. That would mean that nonprofit groups cannot be considered quasi-government organizations and, in theory at least, should be out of the reach of legislators who want to take away the right of charities to speak out on any issue.

But the anxiety over restrictions on advocacy should not be allowed to obfuscate a fundamental matter. Whatever we want to call the tax benefits enjoyed by nonprofit groups, they are dollars that the federal government makes available for charities to carry out their missions. To pretend they are not may be a fine legal point, but that position cannot gainsay the fact that donors to charities escape paying taxes on those gifts. As such, the federal government has a fiduciary responsibility to the public to make certain that charities and foundations disclose information about their operations and finances to the public.

As Independent Sector points out, such requirements for disclosure should be reasonable and not overly intrusive. But that doesn't negate the fact that government must take a primary role in ensuring accountability. As nonprofit groups grow larger and become more involved in for-profit activities, the need for government regulation and oversight will become even more important. Independent Sector would have stood on more reasonable ground if it had been willing to acknowledge the roles of both government and nonprofit organizations in assuring that charities and foundations remain accountable.

Another example of the growing presumptuousness of nonprofit groups can be seen in the courtroom, where the New York Community Trust is battling the Community Service Society. The society sued the trust, claiming that many years before the trust—the nation's largest community foundation—had capriciously and unfairly denied the social services group money that had been earmarked for it in bequests.

New York's Surrogate Court ruled in the society's favor, declaring that the trust had overstepped its authority in unfairly withholding the society's funds. The trust is appealing the case, supported by a friend-of-the-court brief filed by the Council on Foundations and by seven major community foundations. In its appeal, the trust and its supporters argue that the trust's decision should

be subject only to narrowly circumscribed judicial review. To be sure, community foundations need to have the discretion to redirect bequests when circumstances change well beyond what a donor anticipated, but the New York
Community Trust and its supporters have overstepped those boundaries. They
seem to think that they should be largely accountable only to themselves. Such
arrogance is stunning.

It is just such arrogance—plus the lack of strict disclosure laws—that has
led to many of the major scandals that have harmed nonprofit groups, most
notably the United Way of America debacle, where William Aramony [who
was forced to resign as president in 1992] was embezzling millions of dollars.

The need for disclosure and for charities to be accountable to the public is
particularly acute in the rapidly growing commercial activities of charitable
organizations. Many universities, for instance, are not divulging financial information about corporate sponsors of scientific research, including potential
conflicts of interest and confidentiality agreements between professors and
corporations.

The public should have a much clearer idea of the transfers of funds to and
from charitable groups and their for-profit subsidiaries. But many charities are
reluctant to divulge such information, believing it to be in the private domain.
Minnesota Public Radio, for instance, argued that it did not have to disclose
the salaries of the officers who ran its for-profit subsidiary because that would
place the unit at a disadvantage with its competitors. In response, the Minnesota Legislature said that was going too far and required the radio station to
make the information public. That is the kind of action citizens need to demand of government.

The public has a right to know about charitable behavior and to demand
a high degree of accountability. Only the federal government, aided by state
and local governments, has the authority and power to enforce such accountability. All the nonprofit bluster about self-regulation and the need for privacy
cannot wipe away this fundamental obligation of government to ensure that
the public's interest is protected.

What many nonprofit groups really need is a heavy dose of humility.

Filer Redux: Philanthropy at a Crossroads

From The Chronicle of Philanthropy, *February 10, 2000*

Twenty-five years ago, the Commission on Private Philanthropy and Public Needs issued its historic report—which, among many other positive things, firmly established the importance of nonprofit organizations in helping to sustain America's democracy.

The panel—known as the Filer Commission, after its chairman, the insurance company executive John Filer—was created at a time when serious questions about the appropriate role of charities, and their relationship to government and businesses, were being raised by lawmakers and the public. Many of the distinguished panel's recommendations—based on two years of research and extensive consultations with charity, business, and government leaders—had a lasting influence. But much has changed in American society and the nonprofit world since 1975. Indeed, the time has come to establish another such commission.

Today, institutions of higher education and hospitals have become so large that it is difficult to find similarities between them and smaller social-service and community organizations—yet both are governed by the same set of regulations. The growing commercialization of nonprofit activities—and the blurring of the boundaries between nonprofit, government, and commercial activities—raises serious questions about the appropriateness of certain tax-exempt practices.

What's more, the financial scandals and incidents of poor management in recent years call out for more effective standards of accountability and public transparency. The inability of the financially and politically beleaguered Internal Revenue Service to oversee and police the charitable world adds to the problem. The nonprofit world clearly needs to study how it can strengthen itself, adapt to the many changes that have taken place in the social and economic landscape, and meet the new demands for its services and products.

In many ways the enormous changes over the past decade are far greater—and, perhaps, more threatening to the health of nonprofit organizations—than those that led to the creation of the Filer Commission. The financial scandals, far broader than many defenders of the nonprofit world will admit, seriously undermine the integrity of charities and, therefore, their ability to attract tax-exempt contributions. Excessive compensation packages pose a similar problem.

Yet the IRS can't even muster the resources it needs to adequately review the informational tax returns that charities are required to submit each year. Indeed, so complex and incongruous has the nonprofit world become that there is an urgent need to rethink and redefine its parameters, structure, functions, and rules.

The new panel, like the Filer Commission, should be composed of outstanding people from various parts of our society, including government, business, the news media, and nonprofit organizations. It should operate for two to three years with sufficient funds, staff, and logistical support to carry out a thorough inquiry. And its members should be representative of the great diversity that characterizes both charities and philanthropy today.

The cost of such an undertaking might amount to about $10 million—a small price to pay in view of what is at stake, and compared with the trillions of dollars in assets held by foundations and charities. Such an effort should be financed by foundations and could be sponsored by leading nonprofit organizations like the National Council of Nonprofit Associations, Independent Sector, the National Committee for Responsive Philanthropy, the Council on Foundations, and a few others.

Among other things, the new panel should study and make recommendations on the following issues:

Accountability. Is the current charity-reporting system adequate? How can the IRS be strengthened? Would additional staff members, for example, resolve the current problem? If not, should we replace the organization with another institution—something akin to the Securities and Exchange Commission or the quasi-governmental British Charities Commission?

Tax exemptions. As charities increasingly walk a tightrope between two worlds, which of their enterprises should be considered business-related and which should not? At what point should a charity lose its tax-exempt status because of a surfeit of commercial activity?

Foundation size. With the huge wealth amassed in recent years, we can now foresee the formation of foundations worth $50 billion or $100 billion—larger than the budgets of a good many countries in the world. How big is too big? Should government invoke antitrust measures and break them up into smaller institutions? And what, if anything, should be done to broaden representation on the boards of these mega-entities?

Advocacy. The continuing attempts by some lawmakers to curtail the advocacy voice of charities, while repugnant, have shown that our lobbying laws are complex, involve a lot of paperwork, are poorly understood, and should be updated. The commission should explore whether the laws on lobbying should just be tinkered with, or whether most of the restrictions against lobbying should be eliminated to create a much simpler system.

Those and many other issues deserve serious and immediate attention. To be sure, a few researchers and some umbrella charity organizations have already done some thinking about these concerns, and a few conferences and strategy groups have commissioned papers, held meetings, and issued reports. But there has been no broadly organized attempt to study and tackle these issues as a whole—or in any significant depth.

A commission along the lines of the Filer Commission would fill that need. By recommending appropriate action, it could ensure that problems are dealt with before they spin out of control. The nonprofit sector may not be broke, but it is increasingly in a state of disarray and ambiguity. Like all evolving systems, it requires periodic inspection and renewal.

We need a clearer definition of the values, nature, and structure of the nonprofit world; updated regulations to govern nonprofit activity; and accountability mechanisms that will preserve the integrity of the sector. Those will enable charities and foundations to meet the demanding challenges of the coming century. A new commission should be created soon—or it may be too late.

7

Leadership

OVERVIEW

Separate, We Lose: Fragmentation Weakens the Nonprofit World

From the Nonprofit Quarterly, December 2000

The problem of fragmentation has characterized the nonprofit world from its very beginning. As the sector has grown at a dizzying pace in recent years, the virus of separateness has become more deadly, dividing ostensibly related fields of activity from one another, narrowing the vision of old and new organizations alike, and paralyzing the potential of unified action on major public issues of the day. In simpler times, when our economy was much less complicated, our population much smaller and less diverse, and our nonprofits comparatively few in number, single organizations or initiatives could and did have an enormous impact on American society. The grange movement, with some twenty thousand local chapters, played a major role in developing rural policy, leading to the creation of the rural extension service. The Townsend Clubs, which at one point numbered as many as five million members, were largely responsible for the 1936 passage of the Social Security Act. During the aftermath of World War II, the American Legion successfully lobbied the Congress to launch the GI Bill offering education benefits to returning veterans.

Today, only a handful of nonprofits exercise such a disproportionate influence on politics (the National Rifle Association, AARP, and the Christian Coalition come to mind).

The paradox of our current nonprofit sector's huge growth is that its very size has rendered it weaker, not stronger. The larger it has grown, the more splintered and divided it has become. Its leadership, responding to the pressures of one-issue constituencies and narrowly targeted financial support, has abandoned broad organizational vision for organizational mission. Except in rare cases, nonprofits have demonstrated their inability to win on major issues in the public interest such as strong gun-control measures, national health insurance for all Americans, campaign-finance reform, increased payout requirements for foundations, and affordable housing for low-income residents.

Our many organizations, large and small, find it difficult, if not impossible, to join in a common cause beyond the immediate self-interest of their individual nonprofits. Why should this be the case? During the past forty years, a vast number of new nonprofits have come into being, reflecting new social issues, subject areas, populist movements, ethnic and gender concerns, and political developments. The very large majority of these have been focused on one or two issues, not on broad-based problems of our society. Whether their priorities were health, education, gay rights, the environment, or consumerism, such organizations have attracted boards of directors with interest in and passion for their particular issue. The leaders chosen by these boards to run their organizations have tended to reflect their own predilections. It is not surprising that the organizations' missions, for the most part, have been narrow. Staff leadership has been rewarded for its adherence to limited organizational goals, not to broader objectives.

Philanthropic practices have reinforced this narrowness, helping to keep nonprofit organizations in their program and policy silos. Categorical or special project grants are the mainstay of foundation funding. In 1997, only a little more than 13 percent of all the money distributed by foundations went to general operating support. Education groups are encouraged to run strictly education projects, community development organizations to operate exclusively housing and commercial deals, and social service groups to focus only on their assistance programs. All these financial incentives drive nonprofits to constrict their activities and vision. There is little money available for coalition efforts that can bring different constituencies and organizations together for joint action on major issues of common concern. For all their talk about the importance of crosscutting issues, foundations prefer the safety and comfort of limited projects and initiatives that carry few risks.

America's growing culture of celebrity and the star system has also undermined the nonprofit sector's capacity for co-operation and collaboration. Too many nonprofit leaders behave like prima donnas, unwilling to share either the spotlight or credit for their organizations' success. These leaders serve as their organizations' sole spokesperson; they are the ones who testify before the legislatures and they build their communication units around themselves. While such ego-building destroys organizational team spirit, these leaders nevertheless are rewarded for their behavior by their boards and donors and by the publicity they generate. Is it any wonder that they are reluctant to participate in coalitions and collaborations that depend on partnership and shared credit? Some of them actually come to believe that they and their organizations can win major policy battles by themselves. Recent nonprofit history is the story of battlefields littered with the bodies of these lone wolves.

Obstacles

Despite the many obstacles we face in overcoming fragmentation, there have been a number of successful coalitions in recent years. Yet it is much more difficult today to form a powerful coalition than it was twenty years ago. Back then, it was possible to convene forty organizations—thirty-five of which would be regularly represented at meetings by their executive directors. The other five representatives would be high-level executives with the authority to speak for their organizations. Today, in a similar situation, one could expect only eight or ten of the organizations to be represented by their CEO and the remainder would consist of mid-level staff and interns with no authority to make an organizational decision. For a number of reasons, coalitions appear to be less of a priority to nonprofit leadership than was the case two decades ago. While many nonprofit leaders stress the significance of "coalitioning," few are either serious about or adept at creating and maintaining coalitions.

Nonprofit organizations focused on poverty know that affordable housing, poor health conditions, crime and drugs, underperforming schools and the lack of social services are all interconnected and inseparable. Yet, their activities don't reflect this understanding. If, for example, the organizations are health groups, they tend to spend little or no time on affordable housing or educational problems. The same is true for other organizations. When affordable housing issues were being legislated in the Congress, few non-housing nonprofits lent their active lobbying support. Similarly, housing organizations were not active supporters of health or children's organizations when the former's legislative measures were being considered. The inability or unwillingness of some nonprofits to lend a hand to colleague institutions is a major reason why antipoverty efforts in recent years have not been sterling.

Continued violence in our urban and suburban areas and an irresponsible electoral system are two of the most serious obstacles to the development of a democratic civil society. The former stunts the healthy growth of our cities, casts a pall on our schools and creates a sense of insecurity everywhere. The latter has produced political leaders indebted to big money and special interests, unresponsive to the public interest.

Most nonprofits have a vested interest in the resolution of both problems. Why, then, have we not yet passed serious gun-control measures or campaign-finance reform? Many nonprofits would be prepared to devote a part of their agendas, maybe a substantial part, to a campaign focused on tackling both challenges. When I was executive director of the Center for Community Change, a national organization providing technical and advocacy assistance to low-income grassroots organizations, the Center either took the lead or participated significantly in a number of coalitions tackling important social issues. Yet, the Center was never asked by gun-control groups or by electoral-reform organizations to lend support to their causes, or join a coalition under their leadership. Knowing how crucial these two issues were to our mission, we would have been happy to spend some of our resources in helping resolve these problems. Numerous other nonprofits would have been similarly inclined. They were never asked.

As long as this state of affairs permeates the sector and fragmentation continues to increase, nonprofits will harvest their own little gardens, score some notable victories here and there, but remain incapable of resolving the big issues that impede our march toward greater economic and social justice. Can we do something abut this? What steps can our nonprofit organizations, philanthropic institutions and universities and colleges take to remedy the situation?

Funders' Opportunities

First, foundations must begin to alter the way they do business in order to meet our civil society's most urgent public needs. There is no reason that foundations cannot give more of their money for general operating support—what all nonprofits need and want. Flexible funds would permit charities to join and financially support coalitions and policy campaigns from their own budgets, something that many groups currently find impossible to do.

Foundations, including those that are reluctant to depart from their emphasis on special-project funding, could set aside a special pot of money reserved for crosscutting policy efforts and building coalitions. Not only would this development signal to donees the importance of a broad vision and unified action, but it would also provide a financial incentive to organizations concerned that coalitions will take funds away from potential member groups. Unfortunately, the avoidance of risk-taking, policy and advocacy efforts and coalitions has been the hallmark of mainstream foundations. Is it not time that the heads of these foundations begin to exercise their leadership on behalf of a more effective, less fragmented nonprofit sector?

The leadership of nonprofit groups, including their boards, also has a responsibility for engaging in the big issues that transcend organizational missions and self-interest. So-called "umbrella" organizations, management support, and technical assistance groups and associations of nonprofit professionals need to shift the focus of their concerns and conversations. Discussions of management techniques, improved technology, increased professionalization, methods of technical assistance and better personnel policies are important, but they are only a part of nonprofit life. The dialogue needs to be enlarged to embrace the policy and advocacy issues that are at the heart of our democracy and civil society. We require better administrators and technicians, but we need nonprofit leaders and visionaries even more. We should develop excellent program specialists, but there is an even greater need for coalition builders. When honors and awards are conferred to outstanding nonprofit leaders, the criteria for this recognition should be not what they have done for their organizations, but what they have contributed to the sector and our society.

Devolution is transferring much of government and nonprofit action to the states and localities, yet many national and regional nonprofit groups do not reflect this new configuration. Instead of building their local membership bases, they continue to operate as centralized, professionally run lobby groups, with membership involvement limited primarily to financial contributions. Left to themselves, many nonprofit professionals tend to become specialized, comfortable in routine, limited in vision. Strong, active nonprofit membership bases, such as those of Common Cause, Handgun Control, Inc., or the NAACP, provide the best chance for broader approaches to our social problems. If wars are too important to leave to the generals, then our social problems are too crucial to leave to our nonprofit professionals.

For our universities and colleges, there is a special challenge: the education of broad-gauged, visionary leadership. The institutions have not yet met that challenge. Too few of our academic centers of philanthropy, nonprofit management, and public-policy studies are conducting programs that lift their students' sights, enhance their coalition-building skills and nurture their courage and integrity. These centers need to develop leaders, not just program analysts, managers, and technicians.

The nonprofit world cannot afford to sit back and passively accept the growing fragmentation of the sector. Foundations, nonprofits, and institutions of higher education must unite to overcome this debilitating condition. Let this effort begin now.

∼

Nonprofit Leaders
for the Twenty-first Century

From Neighborhood Funders Group Reports, Fall 1999

Our nation's values, priorities, direction, and commitment to democracy are being tested as never before. The twenty-first century will require a new national vision and the leaders to realize it.

The problems and opportunities we will encounter are challenging and daunting: providing social and economic justice for all Americans; protecting the global environment; rebuilding the public's trust in the fairness and effectiveness of our political system and government; eliminating poverty and creating livable wage jobs for all who can work; ensuring health protection for all Americans; limiting the excesses of corporate power; strengthening the network of nonprofit organizations that constitute our civil society; and exercising responsible leadership in world affairs.

It is a tall order. But our country can afford nothing less.

Much of the responsibility for reinvigorating our society and its democratic institutions will fall on our nonprofit sector, as in the past. One hallmark that has distinguished our society is a strong, dynamic, and unique network of nonprofit organizations, fueled by private and institutional philanthropy. These civil society institutions have been an essential feature of our system of checks and balances, serving as the bulwark against the potential tyranny of both government and the majority. They have been a major spawning ground for political, business, and public service leadership and a significant instrument for social and economic change. These nonprofits have kept the American tradition of public service and volunteering alive.

Today, the nonprofit sector faces unprecedented challenges. Some are external pressures, but many are internal. The latter are more insidious and very difficult to meet. The growing absence of leadership is perhaps the most worrisome and threatening. In my view, many of the most competent and dedicated executives have left the nonprofit field. For many, one reason has been their frustration with the increasingly difficult and time-consuming task of fund raising. In general, these leaders have not been replaced with commensurate quality leadership.

I am struck by the narrow agendas and lack of vision and courage of many national nonprofit organizations. The same can be said for many local, regional, and state charitable organizations. Today, the talent pool for top executive jobs is limited. Search firms constantly complain about the shortage of outstanding candidates for executive positions in nonprofit institutions. While money is sometimes an important factor, it is not the major reason recruiting first-class people is proving more difficult.

What is most surprising is that charitable organizations are doing little or nothing to develop new leadership. Funders removed from the day-to-day operations of nonprofits are also not engaged in this process. Some organizations are not even aware of the looming crisis. Dulling their sensitivity are such factors as the "survival" posture of many organizations, especially at the local level; battle fatigue; limited opportunities for intellectual stimulation and organizational reflection; the lack of young, energetic staff; ineffectual boards of directors; the so-called "founders syndrome," a reluctance to face future transitions; and a lack of funds to invest for the future.

These are not the only reasons charities have so much trouble keeping and attracting capable top people. Many nonprofit groups have suffered so many cuts in government or private support that they have lost their flexibility and ability to continue to be exciting, cutting-edge places to work. Some nonprofit leaders are discouraged by the growing fragmentation of the sector. More and more organizations focus only on special interests and issues. Fueled by the categorical funding of foundations, charities and their executives have found it difficult to tackle the broader, generic issues and problems our society faces. For many, a narrow organizational mission has replaced a broader vision. Not being able to work for the common good is a turnoff for many talented and idealistic people.

The phenomenal growth of the sector has also played a part in driving away promising people. Its big-business qualities—employing over nine million people and amounting to 7 percent of the gross national product—is a cause of some major problems. For many employees, working in nonprofits has become just another job, an employment option that job seekers must explore, regardless of principles and commitments. The increasing use of specialists and technicians not grounded in an organizational mission is symptomatic of the problem. The result has been a loss of people with passion, idealism, and some anger, committed to making a difference in the world.

Perhaps more damaging than anything else, many nonprofits have adopted the worst practices of corporate America, especially its fixation on the cult of the CEO. While this emphasis reflects our national infatuation with stars and celebrities, it is dangerous to the long-term health of nonprofit groups. It attracts egotistical leaders, not the kind of people who care about building collegiality—the organizational environment many young people are attracted to. In an August 1998 Peter Hart and Associates survey conducted for Public Allies, young people strongly rejected the traditional top-down notion of leadership, preferring collegial, consensus-building leadership. Many young people cite leaders' building of egos—not institutions—and the lack of teamwork as a major reason they do not want to enter the nonprofit world.

Identifying the causes of the impending leadership crisis is easy, but providing effective remedies is extraordinarily difficult. How do we transform our civil society institutions into visionary organizations that can work for the public interest? Where do we begin, knowing that there are no simple solutions and that the process will take time?

The qualities of vision, courage, dynamism, accountability, ethics, and competence are all associated with leadership. This, then, is where we must begin. We must begin to recruit young people in their twenties with idealism, vigor, and a commitment to public service. They will become the leaders of our civil society in the year 2015. We need to introduce them to the positive features of nonprofit work and use their energy to spark a rededication to public service among all of us who work at the nation's charitable institutions.

Many young people have tasted nonprofit life through internships, national service, the Peace Corps, and volunteering. All too often their internships are short and focus on minor menial tasks. It doesn't do much to persuade young people to consider careers in nonprofit work. Lengthier internships, such as the Mickey Leland Congressional Hunger Fellows Program, provide a more substantial experience. Unfortunately, these tend to be underfunded and in perpetual risk of losing financial support.

Interns who want to stay in the nonprofit world—the vast majority—often can't find a job. Few nonprofits can afford to hire their departing interns, let alone those leaving other organizations. Other nonprofits that do have the money are either unwilling to make recruiting young staff an organizational priority or have no interest in their future leadership.

The failure to use internships, whatever their nature or duration, as a bridge to full-time positions is probably the greatest weakness in the nonprofit world's recruiting system. It is a natural point of intervention. Foundations, in consultation with nonprofits seriously interested in leadership development, should establish a "Twenty-first Century Nonprofit Fellowship Program." It would provide two-year fellowships for full-time nonprofit jobs in a supportive, collegial environment. Fellows would earn $24,000 to $35,000 a year (depending on living costs in the areas where they worked) and receive full fringe benefits paid by the charities where they worked. Young recruits could try out real jobs with real responsibilities and develop some roots in the nonprofit community. During their tenure, fellows could establish their reputations and learn about long-term nonprofit career opportunities.

Assuming an average annual salary of $30,000 per person, 100 fellows would cost only $3 million a year or $6 million for two years. An increase to

200 two-year fellowships would cost $12 million. A crucial element of the program would be matching fellows with appropriate, nurturing organizations at the local, regional, and national levels. This matching function, job placement assistance during the second year of the internship, and other administrative costs would be included in the program. The last feature would be periodic meetings—once or twice a year—of all the fellows for sharing and exchanging ideas and training by skilled nonprofit practitioners and academics.

Other forms of leadership training, from short internships to mid-career programs, have an important place in an overall effort to strengthen the sector's leadership. They should continue to be supported. So should ongoing efforts to strengthen nonprofits' middle-management capacity. A few foundations and corporations have started and support leadership development initiatives that are more recognition programs than development efforts. These have focused primarily on celebrating the accomplishments of mid-career nonprofit executives. They have paid little attention to the development of young leaders, where the return on such investment can be much greater. Unless capable and dedicated young people can find full-time opening level jobs and, thereby a meaningful entree into the nonprofit community, we will not succeed in developing that new generation of leaders we so desperately need.

Given the huge amount of money foundations and other donors spend each year on capital campaigns—many of them for strictly bricks and mortar projects—shouldn't we be thinking about investing more in human capital? For far less than the price of a building, a hospital wing, or a campus research laboratory, a few foundations could help shape the future leadership of the nonprofit sector. The billions of dollars that Americans and their philanthropic institutions give each year won't make much of a difference unless we do something now to produce the leaders of the twenty-first century.

~

A Lack of Civic Commitment: Will
Today's Young People Become Leaders?

From Youth Today, *February 1999*

A recent study on youth leadership and community service, conducted by Peter D. Hart Associates for Public Allies (a Washington, D.C., nonprofit that promotes youth leadership), found that today's young Americans are committed to community service and direct, personal assistance to others. But the survey of 728 people age 18 to 30 also raised disturbing questions about the young generation's commitment to civic engagement and social change.

The focus of these young Americans seems primarily personal, revolving around the satisfaction they draw from direct services and personal relationships. Their vision doesn't appear to encompass the broader community or the commonweal. They manifest little concern for collective action to change public policies or abusive institutions. Only 18 percent said they had volunteered for social or political causes.

When young people cited the need to work together (27 percent did so), they indicated that such activities should be in small groups at the local level. Reared in cynical times, they expressed little or no confidence in governments, political leaders, or traditional nonprofit institutions. They seem unconcerned about the interconnection between local, state, and national policies and public administration. They fail to grasp (or are uninterested in) the notion that in a representative democracy, citizens have to engage in the process of reforming the system and strengthening its leadership. They display the attitude of bystanders, not active citizens.

This lack of interest in civic engagement is perhaps the most troubling finding of the study. There is no vision among the youth about what this country should be or what direction it should take. There is little sense of what policies or mechanisms will be needed (other than vaguely defined local groups) to create a better society. Only 52 percent viewed voting in elections as important. Apolitical in nature, the group seemingly has adopted a personal rather than civic agenda.

Much of this personal agenda, the study found, is based (commendably) on the young adults' strong sense of value, principles, and standards. They expressed a deep respect for individual differences and working with people from different racial, ethnic, and cultural backgrounds. In contrast to their parents' generation, they see racial and ethnic diversity as the norm.

They also reject the traditional leadership model: top-down, autocratic, and noncollegial. They consider seeing differing points of view, sharing leadership roles, getting along with others, and bringing diverse people together as the most admirable leadership qualities. But they did not mention courage, decisiveness, and making tough decisions, which are often at the heart of timely and effective decision making. They seem oblivious that popular and consensual decisions frequently lead to poor choices and paralysis.

The good news is the heavy involvement of young Americans in community service and volunteering. Nearly 70 percent said they had been involved in community activities during the past three years. Fifty-four percent said they had done so at least once a month. The study leaves us ambivalent about the capacity and willingness of young Americans to provide the leadership our country needs to become a more vital and equitable society. Do they have the desire and toughness to get us from here to there? Will they be willing to complement their voluntary service with collective action to bring about social change? Will they help to strengthen and reform government at all levels? Will they muster the zeal to become effective citizens in the political process? Will they participate in efforts to identify and support new political leadership? Will they be willing to enter the political arena?

If the answer to these questions is "yes," we can have some assurances that many of the changes this nation requires will be implemented. If the answer is "no," we may find that we have produced a generation more rooted in self than community, more concerned about personal feelings than the common good; a generation ironically ill-prepared to provide the leadership to put into practice its values and idealism.

Why Nonprofit Workers Should Get Sabbaticals

From The Chronicle of Philanthropy, *May 4, 1995*

The nonprofit world needs to start taking sabbaticals seriously.

Academics have profited from sabbaticals for many years. A small number of people at charities, foundations, and religious organizations have also benefited from sabbaticals. Most people who have taken such leaves—including me—cannot say enough good things about them; so why is it that so few nonprofit groups offer their employees sabbaticals?

One reason is the alleged cost of sabbaticals. Leaders of organizations with tight budgets often feel sabbaticals are a luxury their organizations cannot afford. Surprisingly, the same attitude is often taken by officials at organizations that have no serious budget constraints. The idea that an important staff member will be away for two to four months raises the specter that program activities will be suspended and that the money used for the sabbatical will not be well spent.

Sabbaticals are greeted somewhat more warmly when a charity manages to get a donor to support a staff member's leave—and the organization is then able to count the money in its fund-raising total for the year. Unfortunately, grants are rarely available for this purpose.

With the exception of very small nonprofit groups, which can manage the loss of one of their staff members only with great difficulty, the cost of sabbaticals is minimal. Nor is it very expensive to help an employee travel during the leave to learn new skills from others.

Some organizations that do offer sabbaticals try to save money by making them available only to the chief executive. That can be more damaging to an organization than not offering sabbaticals at all, since it leads to resentment among staff members, low morale, and declining collegiality. All professional staff members can benefit from sabbaticals without putting an undue burden on an organization's budget.

Many nonprofit boards seem eager to expand the number of programs operated by their organizations, but they are reluctant to invest in the long-term development of their employees. That is one of the major reasons that so many nonprofit groups have such high turnover on their staffs. Refusing to offer sabbaticals is penny-wise and pound-foolish. It is not a question of money but of vision.

The Center for Community Change [the nonprofit organization Mr. Eisenberg headed] has provided sabbaticals for the past seven years. All professional staff members who have worked for the center for at least seven years are allowed to take up to four months of paid leave. We provide up to $2,000 to help cover travel and other costs for people who want to use their leaves to do work or research related to the center's mission. Thus far, ten of us have enjoyed sabbaticals and two are about to start them. Three of us received travel stipends of $2,000 to go overseas. In seven years, the net cost of sabbaticals, other than staff time, has been $6,000.

The return on the center's investment has been enormous: staff members return to their jobs with new energy, enthusiasm, and ideas, as well as a renewed commitment to the institution.

The large majority of nonprofit organizations cannot provide financial compensation nearly as substantial as those offered by the professions, or even local government. Low pay, long hours, poor benefits, persistent crises, struggles for institutional survival, personal strain, and "burnout" are common ingredients of life in much of the nonprofit world.

Sabbaticals are benefits that offer opportunities for rest and relief, a time to think, a chance to pursue other interests. They make our jobs more attractive and bearable, and bind us more closely to the institutions for which we work.

Sabbaticals could also do much to stimulate intellectual ferment in and research on the nonprofit world.

Few of the people who work for nonprofit organizations have had the time to document their experiences and insights, the problems they have had, and the prescriptions for change and innovation that they would like to introduce. While the work of academic scholars has been important, it has not proved an adequate substitute for the experience and perspectives of people who know from firsthand experience how nonprofit groups really operate.

If more nonprofit workers were offered the time and encouragement to conduct research, write articles, or begin a book, that could provide benefits to many charities and foundations. Either by collaborating with academics or working on their own, charity officials could add new luster to the field of nonprofit research. Their availability for such work might stimulate more donors to pay for travel and accommodations to facilitate their research and writing.

Sabbaticals need not be limited to charities. Foundations could make good use of them, too. A few months of work at a charity might be an eye-opener for many grant makers. Who knows how much philanthropic performance might be improved after such an experience?

∼

Philanthropy Misses a Chance to
Show a Commitment to Diversity

From The Chronicle of Philanthropy, *May 18, 1993*

A recent action by a California community foundation has raised a serious question about philanthropy: how truly committed are foundations to the notions of diversity and equal opportunity?

The East Bay Community Foundation in Oakland, California, decided last month to hire a white male as its executive director instead of one of the two other finalists for the job—both highly qualified African Americans.

The fact that this occurred at a community foundation—which, as a public charity with preferential tax benefits, has a special obligation to serve and reflect the community in which it works—underscores the severity of the problem.

Board members of the East Bay Community Foundation defended their decision by saying that fund-raising ability was the key criterion in their selection process and that Michael Howe, the white candidate, was the person most qualified to help enlarge the foundation's assets. There appears to be little evidence, however, that Mr. Howe, who had no responsibility for bringing in contributions at the Marin Community Foundation, has any serious credentials as a fund-raiser.

On the other hand, Constance Walker, one of the finalists, has had considerable fund-raising experience: she has been executive director of the Greater Richmond Community Development Corporation in California and manager of the San Francisco office of the Local Initiatives Support Corporation. She is now a program officer at the James Irvine Foundation in San Francisco.

And who can doubt that Hugh Burroughs, a vice president of the Henry J. Kaiser Foundation and one of the senior, most respected people in the foundation world, could be an excellent fund-raiser if given the opportunity to do so?

The decision underscores a false view that members of minority groups cannot be as effective as whites in raising money. It also calls attention to the questionable obsession many community foundations have with fund raising—often at the expense of solid programming, grant making, and the kind of community involvement that goes beyond the giving away of money. Too many community foundations judge their success by the amount of money they raise, not by what they do in the community, and their choice of staff and board members is often determined by that perspective.

In making its selection, the board of the East Bay Community Foundation neglected to consider the foundation's history, staff composition, and the community it serves. In its sixty-five-year existence, the foundation has not had a minority staff member, despite the heavy concentration of diverse racial and ethnic groups in the East Bay area. Seventy-two percent of the population of Oakland, for example, is nonwhite.

Here, then, was an exciting opportunity to appoint a black or other minority-group member as executive director. The foundation missed it.

Board members—two of whom are black and one a Latina—say their decision was not racist in nature. That may well be true, but it is nevertheless hard to understand the basis for their selection. At best, it appears to reflect gross insensitivity and stupidity.

Foundation and nonprofit officials across the country have expressed concern, anxiety, and anger, but very few have been willing to be quoted by name in news stories. Some foundation people have dismissed the issue by saying it is a Bay Area or California problem. But the reason many foundation officials who are uncomfortable about the decision just won't say so is that they don't want to call attention to the track records of their own foundations.

What occurred in Oakland is not an isolated or one-time event. It is part of a much larger national pattern in which minorities have had little access to the top jobs in foundations.

Of the four hundred community foundations in the country, only a handful have a minority person as executive director. Very few people of color head major or moderately sized private foundations. If you expand that list to include the second and third highest-ranking positions at foundations, the numbers will not increase significantly.

Given the large number of foundations that operate in cities and areas with large concentrations of minority populations, the equal-opportunity-employment track record of philanthropic institutions is dismal and discouraging. It represents a missed opportunity for philanthropy to open its doors to a greater talent pool and to improve the quality of its grant making by having diverse staff members who are highly sensitive to community problems.

It is unfortunate that many progressive foundations that support diversity in the community think that they don't have to worry about getting a better racial and ethnic mix among their own staff members. Good grant making does not exempt an institution from its obligation to improve its own hiring record.

The lack of diversity in foundations is not limited to their staffs. It is an issue that plagues boards, too, although some real progress has been made in recent years.

While the number of women and minority representatives on foundation boards has increased, they tend to come from the same elite class as their white counterparts—corporate executives, prominent educators, and well-established lawyers and other professionals. There is little or no diversity on the basis of occupation or class. The absence of grassroots leaders, union officials, nonprofit representatives, teachers, social workers, members of the clergy, small-business owners, and young adults deprives foundations of a wealth of perspectives, experience, and understanding that would enrich the process of grant making.

Nor does there seem to be much diversity in temperament on foundation boards. Trustees tend to be appointed on the basis of their prominence, establishment credentials, ability to work smoothly among peers, and capacity to maintain the bona fides of the institution. They are not often selected because of their creativity, candor, community activism, willingness to challenge and debate old traditions or new ideas, and commitment to innovation and risk-taking. The latter, in fact, are often viewed as elements of possible disloyalty to the institution. In stressing loyalty, getting along, and not rocking the boat, boards of many foundations have failed to tap the enormous potential of collective community intelligence and intellectual energy.

In light of the Oakland experience, what can be done to forestall similar occurrences and bring greater diversity to philanthropy? After debating the issue, the Northern California Grantmakers Association, one of the most progressive regional associations in the country, decided to form a committee on diversity to help its members grapple more effectively with the problem.

That was hardly a tough stand, but it is unrealistic to expect harsher stands or measures by philanthropic institutions individually or collectively in a world so driven by collegiality and the lack of standards and regulations.

The path to greater diversity and equal opportunity is likely to be long and arduous. Efforts by regional associations of grant makers and the Council on Foundations to keep the issue on the front burner, to set criteria for promoting and evaluating diversity, and to help their member organizations move in this direction could be an important first step. The hiring of executive-search firms with respectable records on issues of diversity would also be valuable. While legislative incentives might be effective in enhancing greater diversity, such measures seem politically improbable.

Perhaps the most effective prod would be increased oversight by the community and the press. The recent spotlight on executive salaries, conflicts of interest, and corruption among nonprofit groups has demonstrated the influence the press can have on philanthropy. Increased pressure on the press to extend its coverage of nonprofits could have an enormous payoff.

So would community organizing and pressure. Grassroots and civic groups, which rarely, if ever, focus their attention on philanthropic institutions, could have a demonstrable impact if they choose to do so. The fear of retaliation by donors would be mitigated if those activities were undertaken by broad coalitions.

The East Bay Community Foundation made a grave mistake. But it did what many other foundations have done. We can only hope that the lessons learned from this experience will be taken seriously by philanthropy and all of us who have a stake in its health and performance.

~

How to Improve Nonprofit Research

*From a speech delivered at the annual conference of the Association for Research on
Nonprofit Organizations and Voluntary Action, in November 2003.*

Nonprofit studies and research seem to be the Rodney Dangerfield of the academic world. They don't get the respect they deserve.

They tend to be scorned by the disciplines for being multidisciplinary. They are often undervalued for being too imprecise and fuzzy, lacking the gravitas of basic research. And they are criticized by many nonprofits and practitioners for not reflecting the reality of practice, an accusation that not infrequently has some merit. It's enough to make us lose our sense of self-respect.

The fact that nonprofit studies, whether they are policy- or management-focused, are not a single discipline is the essence of their strength, because they accurately reflect the nature of the nonprofit sector with all its disciplines and varieties of experience. We who teach, research, and practice nonprofit work shouldn't worry about either creating a discipline or trying to legitimize our activities within the academic community. We should be proud, not defensive, about what we do. We need to turn a deaf ear to those "disciplinarians" who would like us to incorporate our efforts into their particular discipline. What our real concern should be is how to teach better, how to strengthen our research and, most important of all, how to build a strong nonprofit sector, something we haven't always done very well in the past.

Here are some ways that researchers can improve the nonprofit world: The first is helping to build nonprofit leadership. There is a growing consensus among observers of nonprofits, even within the sector, that nonprofit organizations and foundations are in an acute crisis of leadership. The reasons are many: the loss over the past fifteen years of excellent visionary executives, many of whom have not been replaced by commensurate quality; the loss of passion and zeal for public service; our loss of confidence in the public sector and public service; the growth of one-issue groups with their narrow concerns; the growing corporatization of the sector with its borderline ethics and the cult of the CEO; the increasing fragmentation of our nonprofit world and resulting narrow vision; and the decline of advocacy. Whatever the reason, our current leadership is slim and unimpressive.

To date, our graduate academic centers have put much more stress on developing nonprofit technicians, budget analysts, and narrow-visioned managers than on creating nonprofit and public sector leaders of the future. This needs to change.

The curricula of our centers have focused overwhelmingly on quantitative analysis and the details of management such as finance, budgets, personnel policies, planning, and evaluation. They have paid too little attention to leadership development, to those qualities of vision, ethics, integrity, and courage that are the soul of leadership. They need to emphasize such subjects as public policy advocacy, lobbying, coalition building, the importance of politics, the role of the media, the relationship of nonprofits to both government and corporate America, as well as the exposure of students to outstanding practitioners.

Regression analysis is an important analytical tool, but it contributed little to the victories of the major social movements from the 1960s through the 1990s. Community organizing, advocacy, and lobbying did. It didn't do much for the efforts of Common Cause and other national nonprofits in passing campaign-finance reform legislation. Coalition building and lobbying did. Nor did it have any role in the successful global campaign to ban landmines. Mass mobilization and the Internet did.

In short, there must be a better balance in what we teach and stress to our students. Parenthetically, we might want to take a hard look at improving the writing skills of our graduate students, many of whom find it difficult to write a simple declarative sentence or punctuate correctly.

The second way toward improvement is to make better use of our practitioners, to involve them in the life of our centers and in our teaching. They could enhance the curricula and courses we offer to our students, lending that element of reality and practice that is often missing from our work. There are too few practitioners in our academic centers. We need many more, both as permanent and adjunct faculty members.

Many teachers teach well, but it is the practitioners who inspire. Our students need to be inspired, to hear and learn from those among us who have made a difference in the front lines of public service. They can move and influence students in a way traditional professors cannot.

The third way is to do a better job in linking academic studies to the world of work. Given the shortage of opening-level jobs with decent pay and benefits among nonprofits, our centers must become far more knowledgeable and aggressive about opening the doors of the nonprofit world to their students. Practitioners on staff could be instrumental in accomplishing this task, one for which most academics are unsuited, owing to their lack of experience in either nonprofit organizations or government agencies.

Invigorating the intellectual foundations of the nonprofit sector is the fourth recommendation. Excluding academic institutions, the sector lacks the intellectual depth and vitality it needs to meet the challenges of the future.

It seems incapable of doing much introspection, reflection, and analysis, and rarely documents what it has achieved or where it has failed. For many reasons, few practitioners write much, if anything; even fewer foundation officials do so. The result? We are losing the experience, wisdom, and lessons of our best people as they retire or otherwise leave the field. Academics could play an important role in capturing this information by partnering with practitioners to help them reflect and write about the field. Today such partnerships are rare.

The fifth and final means toward improvement is for researchers to begin focusing on the toughest and most provocative issues facing the sector.

There has been a great deal of research on volunteers and voluntary action, the history of nonprofits, especially foundations, management practices, and, that latest of trendy topics, capacity building. Researchers seem to have paid little attention to such issues as the governance of nonprofit institutions, including relatively unaccountable universities and foundations, excessive executive and trustee compensation, self-dealing problems, conflicts of interest, government oversight and enforcement questions, issues of nonprofit advocacy, ties between corporate America and universities, and corporate excesses. We've tended to shy away from the burning questions that are among the most important and controversial.

During the past few years, we've witnessed the eruption of nonprofit scandals, the revelations in the media of excessive compensation, corruption, other questionable practices and the lack of government oversight. All of these, in some sense, are a sad reflection of the state of nonprofit research. It has been the media that unearthed and analyzed the data that has exposed the excesses of the sector. Where were our nonprofit researchers? They should have been there first.

~

ROLE MODELS

Paul Ylvisaker: A Master of the Art of Inducing Epiphanies

From The Chronicle of Philanthropy, *April 7, 1992*

The death last month of Paul Ylvisaker, after a lifetime of extraordinary accomplishments and dedicated public service, leaves a void that cannot be filled. It is hard to imagine the nonprofit world without him. He was, as Sherwood Anderson might have written, "a unique."

In a world increasingly populated with specialists and technicians, Paul was a generalist and visionary, unafraid to delve into a large number of fields, always looking for relationships between issues and people. He was one of the last of the Renaissance men in our sector: inspiring teacher, brilliant lecturer, academic administrator, government official and adviser, ethicist, foundation executive, and personal counselor to countless nonprofit, philanthropic, government, and for-profit institutions.

During his tenure as director of the public-affairs program at the Ford Foundation, he helped start the Gray Areas program, which created multi-purpose organizations to encourage people to get involved in efforts to fight poverty and other problems affecting cities. The organizations became the models for the Community Action Program and the Office of Economic Opportunity under President Lyndon B. Johnson.

As the first Commissioner of Community Affairs for the State of New Jersey, Paul planned and began the implementation of a radical transformation of the Meadowlands from a swampy region of garbage dumps and illicit trade to a redeveloped area of sports complexes, shops, and housing. In pursuing this goal, he braved the skepticism and indifference of colleagues and the threats of organized crime. His efforts earned him the sobriquet "Father of the Meadowlands."

Paul brought luster to Harvard's School of Education as its dean for a decade and as a teacher until his death. He expanded the school's vision of what education should be by relating it to other disciplines and through a more effective fusion of theory and practice. He stressed the relationship between education and urban problems. He enriched the student body and faculty by opening both to a greater number of minority-group members and women. And his encouragement of visits by outside academics, nonprofit leaders, and government officials gave an added dimension to the school's teaching and influence.

Even more impressive than those significant achievements was the enormous personal influence he exercised during the course of his life over hundreds, if not thousands, of students, colleagues, clients, and others in a wide variety of settings. A member of numerous foundation boards, an adviser to the Council on Foundations and consultant to many philanthropists and grant-making institutions, he was responsible for improving the vision, quality, and integrity of many philanthropic programs.

Although Paul was a fighter—until the end he overcame most of the major illnesses known to the human species with a toughness that astounded his friends and doctors—his weapons were not sharp-edged but, rather, those of reason, illuminating experience, and gentle persuasion. He had an enviable way of making people understand their problems and identify an appropriate course of action. He could press a point and be persistent without alienating the subject of his attention. He could do this, I think, because all of us felt his warmth and love of people.

Several years ago, I was privileged to visit several foundations with him to discuss philanthropic problems and ethics. At one, which had serious internal difficulties, he attacked the problems of the institution through a brilliant analysis of philanthropic history, ethics, and current tensions. He pointed the finger without the finger. At the end of the long meeting, a foundation officer said, "Thank you, Mr. Ylvisaker. I see what I did not see before." Few have better mastered the art of inducing epiphanies than Paul Ylvisaker.

Although his writings were lucid and insightful, he preferred to spend his time with people rather than with research and the word processor. After his recent retirement, he gave increasing thought to writing about his experiences and the lessons learned from forty years in the nonprofit world. His untimely death deprived us of this rich source of material.

It is as a teacher, motivator, and mentor that his legacy will shine the brightest. In an age in which academics carefully husband their time, propelled by the demands of research and professional ambition, Paul's doors were always open to students, colleagues, friends, and others in search of advice and assistance. His intelligence, enthusiasm, and boundless energy sparked and illuminated many lives and careers. Through his love and encouragement, he brought out the best in many of us. His reach encompassed thousands of people, many of whom consider him their special mentor.

Unlike his literary counterpart, Mr. Chips, his influence extended beyond a single institution, beyond the nonprofit world, to politicians, business executives, government administrators, and foreign institutions and officials.

His epitaph should read: "He shaped several generations of dedicated public servants like himself." Paul Ylvisaker enjoyed a rich and diverse life, and we all benefited from his celebration of excellence. What a record to leave behind.

∽

Remembering David Hunter: Risk-Taker, Visionary, Activist

From The Chronicle of Philanthropy, *February 8, 2001*

When David Hunter, former executive director of the Stern Fund and the Ot-tinger Foundation, died at age 84 two months ago, he left both an impressive legacy and a vacuum that none of today's foundation leaders seem willing or able to fill. Mr. Hunter was the embodiment of a social progressive, visionary, intellectual, risk-taker, mentor, and activist, all rolled into one. An influential leader in his field, he displayed a humility and quiet forcefulness that only added to his luster.

The power of Mr. Hunter's voice was in its courage and conviction. Twenty-six years ago, in a speech to the Council on Foundations—a speech that re-mains relevant today—Mr. Hunter challenged his colleagues "to be more yeasty, to make more ferment, to produce more action for social change, not to be so far above the battle, to get into the fray more."

He wanted foundations to pay more attention to civil rights and demo-cratic ideals, and to do more to help improve economic opportunities for all Americans. Likewise, he had a vision of philanthropy as more thoughtful, en-ergetic, concerned about its performance, full of ideas, innovative, and inclined to action more than study. His was a lonely voice then, and his message is still a lonely one today.

While many in the foundation establishment regrettably turned a deaf ear to Mr. Hunter, that was not the case with the long trail of wealthy young phi-lanthropists who were inspired by his idealism and sense of social and eco-nomic justice. He cultivated a network of promising young givers as a gardener carefully nurtures his flowers.

Trustee of the French American Charitable Trust, Diane Feeney recalls his influence as she began her philanthropic career. "His guidance and friendship during my first couple of years was an indispensable education, enabling me to see possibilities I otherwise would never have considered and avoid many of the pitfalls that face inexperienced grant makers," said Ms. Feeney, who is thirty-two. "And he stayed with me until the end."

Indeed, Mr. Hunter's mentorship was not a one-time gift. He continually kept in touch with his charges, sending them memos, news items, and impor-tant reports and articles. He made certain they met other key philanthropists and innovative nonprofit executives. He relished opportunities to meet with them, and over time they became part of his extended family. But most impor-tant of all, he challenged his youthful colleagues to keep open minds, question existing assumptions, and take risks.

His legions grew as the years passed. It was not surprising that more than two hundred donors and leaders of nonprofit organizations came to New York from all over the country in 1996 for a daylong celebration of his eightieth birthday.

Mr. Hunter had an inimitable style that made him a fine teacher, one who could lead by both his example and his intellect. He dressed in a suit and tie, maintaining a dignity and demeanor that, despite his unorthodox ideas, gave him an entrée into the rarefied world of conventional philanthropy. And unlike so many of the current crop of foundation leaders, he would never impose an idea or program on any of his grantees or followers.

"He would listen to you, analyze the problem, and suggest some options, but he felt that it was totally inappropriate for a foundation to be preaching or pushing," recalled David Stern, forty-one, chair of the Stern Family Fund and another young protégé of Mr. Hunter. "He really respected the integrity of his donees as well as other people's views. He taught me to take risks, betting on hot people with powerful ideas."

Mr. Hunter served his apprenticeship by working in Europe with refugees for the United Nations Relief and Rehabilitation Administration, and then with UNICEF in Mexico for nine years. He began his philanthropic career at the Ford Foundation, where, from 1959 to 1963, he helped to shape some inner-city antipoverty programs that became an important part of President Lyndon Johnson's War on Poverty.

For the next twenty-two years he was the executive director of the Stern Fund, a progressive foundation that supported many outstanding organizations, coalitions, and program initiatives. His grants and support were instrumental in seeding voter-registration programs that led to motor-voter legislation. In addition, Mr. Hunter's support helped the Center for Law and Social Policy, the South Shore Bank (a neighborhood bank in Chicago), the Woman's Action Alliance—forerunner of the Ms. Foundation for Women—Fairness and Accuracy in Reporting, several progressive regional foundations and self-help programs in Appalachia and elsewhere, plus the Funding Exchange.

He stretched a little money a long way. His calm and reassuring manner convinced many mainstream foundations to join his efforts.

Just as important as Mr. Hunter's grant making was his moral fervor and outspoken views about the obligations and responsibilities of foundations. He believed that they hold a public trust and thus should deal with the most critical public needs.

In his 1975 speech to the Council on Foundations' annual meeting, he asserted that "not enough foundations are close enough to critical and fundamental issues of our society, not aggressively active enough on them, too distant from the controversies that pervade our public discourse, not political enough, if you will." He added that "too many foundations support only people and projects that unquestioningly accept orthodox assumptions about the nature and consequences of the institutions that mold our society."

He went on to chide his colleagues for failing to actively support the constitutional right of citizens to organize to protect their rights. "Foundations ought to be interested in helping to keep this tradition alive and healthy," he said. "Words speak louder than actions in this arena. Where minority people have organized to move closer to equality, they have had precious little help."

Foundations, he added, had to do a better job in dealing with such issues as the distributions of wealth and power, the role of government, the effects of poverty and poor housing, matters of privacy, and the empowerment of women. They should do so with a critical eye, he said, and where they found problems that produced inequality, privilege, and injustice, they should support corrective public-policy efforts. It is a speech that, if given at the next Council on Foundations meeting, would probably annoy as many people as it did in 1975.

In promoting more activism, greater public-policy and advocacy support, additional focus on crosscutting issues and coalitions, and long-term financing of efforts to improve foundation management, Mr. Hunter was an outsider to the mainstream philanthropic world. And the problems he strove to correct continue today: grant makers persist in their reluctance to pay for programs that organize poor people and mobilize effective coalitions. They still avoid taking risks. And they still sidestep many of the critical public needs of this new century.

Still, David Hunter's voice was a hopeful one. He was always an optimist, believing that the world of philanthropy could change, that others would develop a vision, and that a golden age of more responsive philanthropy was just ahead. We don't know whether the latter is around the corner, but we can be comforted by the fact that a number of his young protégés share his broad vision.

Mr. Hunter was fond of citing a quotation from George Bernard Shaw: "Life is no 'brief candle' for me. It is a sort of splendid torch which I have got hold of for the moment, and I want to make it burn as brightly as possible before handing it on to future generations."

Mr. Hunter's torch illuminated the world of philanthropy for many years. Its memory still glows, but there is a need to rekindle the fire. Are there any who are ready and willing to pick up and carry his torch for the next twenty years?

∼

John Filer: The Standard-Setter
for Corporate Philanthropy

From The Chronicle of Philanthropy, November 1, 1994*
This article was written with William A. Whiteside, former executive director of the
Neighborhood Reinvestment Corporation.

The death last month of John H. Filer deprives the nonprofit world of one of its brightest stars.

As chairman and CEO of the Aetna Life and Casualty Insurance Company, Mr. Filer was instrumental in establishing what was probably the most enlightened, farsighted, and innovative philanthropic program in corporate history. He set the standard for all others in the field.

Mr. Filer led Aetna at a time when the insurance industry had numerous troubles. Working with the national Neighborhood Housing Services Network, he became personally involved in an effort to understand the impact of "insurance redlining" on communities. His leadership prompted both Aetna and other insurers to change their ways of doing business and to design new kinds of insurance policies that were more responsive to the needs of low-income and minority homeowners.

He also came to understand the economic troubles of local neighborhood groups and encouraged Aetna and other companies to provide grant money and loans to nonprofit groups that serve disadvantaged neighborhoods. He also served as chairman of the Commission on Private Philanthropy and Public Needs, the most important group ever assembled to assess the state of the nonprofit world. His openness to new ideas and issues, his sense of fairness, and his willingness to take risks marked his tenure both at the commission and at Aetna.

Under his strong leadership, the commission developed guidelines to make philanthropy more accountable. The guidelines emphasized that foundation assets were not exclusively private money but, because donors got a tax break for giving, a form of public money with public obligations. What's more, they stressed that the primary goal for foundations was to meet today's most urgent societal needs—not those of yesterday.

When a group of charities challenged the first year's work of the commission, Mr. Filer invited them to get involved in the deliberations and provided the organizations with the money they needed to conduct research and be active participants. He publicly gave the charity coalition credit for improving the quality of the commission's recommendations. And after the coalition decided to form a permanent watchdog organization to hold philanthropy accountable, John Filer and Aetna were the first to give the National Committee for Responsive Philanthropy an operating grant.

Unlike many of his peers, he respected the nonprofit organizations his company supported and those that it did not, treating them as equals. He was not touched by the arrogance that often accompanies the philanthropic process.

After his retirement from Aetna, he sought to raise the standards of performance and integrity throughout the nonprofit world. He did so with a sharp sense of humor that kept us smiling as we worked hard to meet his demanding challenges. He became chairman of Independent Sector, providing the organization with the same energy, wisdom, and leadership that had characterized his previous commitments.

We will miss his strong voice of reason and advocacy within corporate and philanthropic America. The corporate world has yet to find his successor. He remains our philanthropic model for all seasons, an example to all of us who care about the accountability, integrity, and performance of nonprofit institutions.

∼

Philanthropy's Loss: Remembering
James Patrick Shannon

From The Chronicle of Philanthropy, *October 2, 2003*

Philanthropy lost a towering figure when James Patrick Shannon died in August at age 82.

After a distinguished career as a priest in the Catholic Church, which named him auxiliary bishop of St. Paul [Minnesota] at age forty-four, he left the priesthood and became a grant maker, first as the executive director of the Minneapolis Foundation and later as executive director of the General Mills Foundation and vice president of the corporation. Minneapolis and St. Paul have been enriched because of his record of philanthropic achievement, but the impact of his work was felt nationwide.

As an educator, journalist, academic, philosopher, outstanding speaker, spiritual counselor, mentor to aspiring public servants, supporter of social- and economic-justice efforts, and superb grant maker, Jim Shannon was one of the last of our dwindling number of renaissance people who combine a visionary view of the world with a pragmatic sense of the possible. He was both an idealist and a down-to-earth negotiator.

His work as a priest served as the crucible from which he developed his work as a grant maker. After being ordained in 1946, he received a doctorate in American studies from Yale University in 1955. At age thirty-five, he was appointed president of the University of Saint Thomas, in St. Paul, becoming one of the youngest leaders of a higher-education institution.

His tenure as bishop was marked by frequent criticism from his conservative colleagues in the church. He was attacked for being one of the first bishops to oppose publicly U.S. policy in Vietnam. His strong support for the civil rights movement raised some anxieties and concerns. And his belief that such contentious issues as birth control, the ordination of women, and marriage for clergymen should be openly discussed within the church infuriated many of his peers, so much so that he was reprimanded by an official body of the church.

Under those circumstances, Jim Shannon felt he had no option but to resign from his position. While he married and became a lawyer, he remained a practicing Catholic. Despite his profound differences with some papal teachings and his shabby treatment by many bishops, he was never angry with either the church or his critics; he understood, tolerated, and even respected their position.

The conscience, compassion, and humility that he demonstrated throughout his ecclesiastical life characterized his philanthropic career. When he came to the Minneapolis Foundation, the institution had relatively little money and low standing within the Twin Cities. Under his leadership, the community foundation expanded its assets and, more significantly, gained stature as an important player in community affairs. His integrity, concern for needy citizens, and courage in tackling the toughest issues were widely admired, even by those who disagreed with him.

Jim Shannon built an institutional culture that has been carried on by his successors. Emmett Carson, the foundation's chief executive officer, says that the Minneapolis Foundation "continues to look to Jim's legacy in speaking out on difficult issues of social and economic justice in our community."

Mr. Shannon's vision transcended the interests of his own foundation. He became a major force in trying to raise the standards of other foundations in the state through the creation of a state association of grant makers. He was named that organization's first chair. His views, priorities, and moral authority continued to influence grant makers in Minnesota and elsewhere until his death.

He left the foundation to write a book and do a little consulting. But after several years, he was persuaded to refocus his attention on philanthropy, this time on corporate-giving practices. His tenure at General Mills from 1980 to 1988 marked a high spot in corporate philanthropy, a time when corporations like Aetna, Arco, General Mills, Dayton Hudson (now Target), Levi Strauss, and Prudential balanced their self-interests with the real needs of the regions where they operated and the nonprofit organizations that served local residents. It was a day when their corporate giving was truly philanthropy and not just bottom-line business expenditures, as is so often the case today.

While Jim's loyalties to the company were strong, his commitment to community progress, especially to constituencies and groups at the margin, was equally stalwart. He supported policy and advocacy groups that others shunned. He was the first to give money to the Philanthropy Project, an effort to monitor and evaluate the performance of foundations in Minnesota. He took risks unusual for a corporate donor, but then, he was Jim Shannon, and General Mills profited from his leadership.

After leaving General Mills, he remained involved in community life, serving on boards, speaking out on key issues, being the wise adviser behind the scenes. He even became the president of the Minneapolis Club, an elite membership organization of socially and economically powerful people in the Twin Cities. When I asked him whether serving in this capacity didn't go against his notions of social equity, he said, "There is goodness and compassion among rich and powerful people just as there is among those who are not so privileged. I can serve as a bridge between the two." And, indeed, he did.

Jim Shannon was a good, great man. He left an indelible mark on both the spiritual and temporal worlds. Those of us who knew him have lost a great friend and mentor. The many people who did not know him but were nevertheless touched by his work have lost a superb teacher and catalyst for progress.

Unfortunately, Jim Shannon is irreplaceable. As one friend of his said some time ago, "They just don't make them like that anymore."

$\sim$

The Unsung Heroes of Philanthropy

From The Chronicle of Philanthropy, May 1, 2003

Douglas McCandlish Lawson, associate director of national programs at the Catholic Campaign for Human Development, the foundation inspired by Monsignor Geno Baroni and sponsored by the U.S. Conference of Catholic Bishops, died on March 30 at the age of fifty-eight. His legacy of achievement stands out among foundation program officers and their efforts to make the world a better place.

He did not enjoy celebrity status. Unlike the icons of philanthropy, such as John Gardner and Paul Ylvisaker, Doug Lawson was never considered a member of the nonprofit hall of fame. Yet, in his quiet, unassuming way, he left a mark on philanthropy that will be as profound and lasting as those of his more illustrious counterparts. His work was the heartbeat of the best of philanthropic practice.

For twenty-eight years he worked diligently and with passion to carry out the Campaign for Human Development's commitment to empower poor people and their grassroots organizations and to bring about social justice. He did his job exceptionally well because he cared deeply about people and listened to their agenda for social change.

Like many creative, yet sensitive, program officers, he did not impose his own ideas or solutions upon those he served, preferring instead to draw on the experience and desires of his grantees. For him, "strategic philanthropy" was a concept that emphasized the needs and satisfaction of nonprofit groups and the public, not those of the donors.

With such a passion for his work, Doug nevertheless had an extraordinarily rich personal life. He traveled extensively in the United States and around the world. He loved water, becoming an accomplished swimmer, snorkeler, and white-water rafter. His drawings reflected both an artistic talent and a deep appreciation of nature. His family and friends were the foundation of his full life. His keen sense of humor served to keep his perspective in balance.

It was this balance that made him such a fine program officer. Philanthropy, while important to him, was not all consuming. His circles and contacts were broad enough for him to know that people liked him for reasons other than the money he could dispense. He was confident enough to know that he could make mistakes. And, perhaps most significant of all, he was a good listener who actually heard what people told him.

It is a pity that Doug Lawson, like many other excellent program officers, never had the opportunity to become the director of an important foundation. He would have been a good one.

Unfortunately, America's nonprofit groups often fail to reward those who have earned the right of leadership. Foundations—as well as many charities—seem to prefer to go outside their institutions for new leadership, even when such leadership is to be found inside, or to choose college presidents and celebrity figures instead of seasoned program officers and other qualified nonprofit executives.

The current ranks of leadership in the foundation and nonprofit world, unfortunately, are exceedingly thin. If we are to develop the leadership that the public expects and deserves, then boards of directors will have to change their practices to select only those who have the vision, experience, integrity, and courage to be effective nonprofit directors.

Doug Lawson, who epitomized the best of his profession, was among the bright, hardworking, committed, and creative program officers who encourage and enable good nonprofit organizations to do their jobs well. They are the unsung heroes of philanthropy. We often take them for granted, rarely give them sufficient credit, and too infrequently express our appreciation for their work and assistance. Many of our achievements are their success stories.

~

Remembering John Gardner, an Idealist Who Knew How to Lead

From The Chronicle of Philanthropy, *March 7, 2002*

The death last month of John Gardner, the founder of Common Cause and Independent Sector, has cast a shadow over the nonprofit world, leaving it with no leaders of comparable vision, integrity, and moral stature.

A mentor to thousands, a hero to many, Mr. Gardner, who was eighty-nine, set the standard for all who work at nonprofit organizations. He taught the meaning of public service, citizen activism, and leadership.

When he left his job as Secretary of the Department of Health, Education and Welfare in the Johnson administration to head the newly formed National Urban Coalition, a nonprofit organization created to tackle urban problems, observers wondered whether he would stay the nonprofit course for more than a few years before going back to government or switching to university life. He turned out to be a long-distance runner in a field dotted with sprinters.

A man gifted with great intelligence, understanding of human nature, enormous prestige and stature among the nation's leaders, and an extraordinary ability to write clearly and persuasively, Mr. Gardner could have accepted any number of positions at the center of American power and influence. Yet he turned down the opportunity to become a senator from New York after the death of Robert Kennedy, head a major university or large corporation, or run for president or vice-president. Instead, he chose the career of being a devoted and crusading private citizen.

His accomplishments reflected the spirit and soul of a Renaissance man: president of the Carnegie Corporation of New York, college professor, presidential cabinet member, adviser to several presidents, author of seven books, member of numerous corporate and foundation boards, and catalyst for the White House Fellows program and efforts that led to public broadcasting and various measures to improve education.

Mr. Gardner's passion was democracy. He understood that secrecy, big money, and the lack of citizen involvement were threats to democratic institutions. With this in mind, he created Common Cause as a people's pressure group to hold governments accountable. At its height, the organization had more than 300,000 members.

One of Mr. Gardner's greatest contributions was his persistent effort to change the nation's campaign-finance laws—an effort that helped push both houses of Congress this year to pass measures aimed at overhauling the campaign system.

Under his watch Common Cause also effectively lobbied for measures to open government meetings, require the disclosure of lobbyists' payments and gifts, and make state and local governments more accountable.

He did not shy away from causes in which he believed, however unpopular. He and Common Cause advocated an end to the Vietnam War effort in 1971 and, shortly thereafter, he mobilized more than one hundred corporate CEOs in support of President Nixon's efforts to improve benefits for welfare recipients.

Though an accepted member of the American establishment and reserved in bearing, he championed the average citizen's right to be an active part of the democratic process. In his writings, speeches, and personal interactions he insisted that broad citizen participation, especially at the grassroots level, was the key to effective government and a just society. Unlike so many members of today's political elite who care more for money than the public good, Mr. Gardner was one of the rare "wise" men who always placed the national interest above his own.

In the late 1970s, when it appeared that the nonprofit world was dangerously fragmented and uncertain about its future, Mr. Gardner helped establish an umbrella organization of national charities and foundations to protect and enhance the role of what he called the independent sector.

Under his guidance, with the assistance of co-founder Brian O'Connell, Independent Sector, as the organization was called, became one of the most influential forces in the nonprofit world. Both principled and pragmatic, Mr. Gardner and Mr. O'Connell worked to forge more effective ties with government, pushed for increasing the accountability of nonprofit groups, started an effort to increase research on nonprofit activities, and spoke out for greater social justice. It was the organization's golden age.

As Mr. Gardner grew older, he turned increasingly to the issue that he felt was at the heart of society's problems and future: leadership. His promotion of effective leadership was, perhaps, his greatest contribution.

His concept of leadership did not square with more traditional notions that viewed leadership as top-down, noncollegial, and charismatic. He argued persuasively that effective leadership is institution-building, not ego-building, based on sharing leadership tasks with other colleagues and followers. As he wrote in his book, *On Leadership,* "Team leadership enhances the possibility that different styles of leadership—and different skills—can be brought to bear simultaneously. . . . The best leader is one who ensures that the appropriate talent and skill are built into the team." It is a lesson that many current nonprofit leaders need to learn.

His views resonate with today's young people who reject old-fashioned leadership styles in favor of shared and more collegial approaches. In John Gardner, venerable sage of nonprofit organizations, they have, ironically, found their champion, a man who was as young in mind as they are in age.

The leadership he exerted within the nonprofit world was quiet and unassuming. He did not bask in the glow of celebrities, as do so many politicians. He always lavished credit on others for jobs well done. He was not glitzy; his charisma came from a deeper moral presence and integrity. He led by example. Although his was not a household name, Americans have benefited from his work and teachings.

In a world grasping for visionary and intelligent leadership, we shall miss him. But we should be grateful that he was here when we needed him.

8

Looking Ahead: What Is the Future
for the Nonprofit World?

January 2004

The nonprofit sector has experienced rapid changes in its composition, size, values, nature, and finances over the past few years. This transformation can be expected to accelerate in the next two or three decades. Yet its practitioners and researchers have done little or nothing to anticipate and prepare for these developments. Instead of looking hard at the future, they have chosen to bury their heads in the sand, avoiding some of the tough analyses and choices they invariably will have to make to keep the sector healthy and worthy of the public trust.

Not since the Commission on Private Philanthropy and Public Needs issued its report in 1976 has the sector collectively attempted to assess its current status—including both its achievements and problems—and to recommend changes in policies and practices. Organizations like Independent Sector, a coalition of some six hundred national nonprofit groups and donor institutions, and the Council on Foundations, which represents two thousand grant makers, were established to serve and protect the interests of their members, but they have failed to exercise their responsibility to look at the future.

Academics and researchers in the nonprofit field have reinforced this tendency by avoiding the toughest and most controversial issues—the ones whose implications and consequences will be most important to nonprofits in the future. They have paid a great deal of attention, for example, to such issues as voluntary action and volunteers, the history of foundations and nonprofit organizations, management practices, and, most recently, they have been studying efforts to build the management capacity of nonprofit groups. They are paying very little attention to such matters as the governance of major institutions, excessive compensation of nonprofit officers and executives, sweetheart deals that provide financial benefits to nonprofit officials, and conflict of interest problems. Nor are they doing much to deal with the lack of public accountability by nonprofit organizations, government oversight, nonprofit advocacy, ties between universities and corporate America, the effect on nonprofits of the sector's rapidly growing commercialization, and the impact of privatization on government-financed programs.

While it may be difficult to attract money to conduct research on these issues because of the reluctance of donors to sponsor "risky" topics, they are, nevertheless, the burning issues that are key to the nonprofit sector's future. Our research community will be doing an enormous disservice to all of us if it continues to avoid these issues by seeking shelter in safe projects. Through a more germane and gutsy research agenda, it could provide us with a useful road map for productive change.

Public Accountability

What are the major areas of concern with which the nonprofit community must begin to grapple? The most important by far is the pressing need for transparency and public accountability. Foundations, which to date have been relatively unaccountable, depend on enormous tax benefits for their donors and for their operations. Ultimately, they answer to the elected politicians who represent American taxpayers. Nonprofit organizations depend entirely on charitable contributions, which, in turn, are based on one and only one factor: the public trust. Without it, nonprofit organizations cannot raise money and, therefore, cannot exist. Both sets of institutions ultimately depend on public esteem and support for their existence.

During the past couple of years the public trust in the nation's nonprofit groups has been shaken by a series of scandals, excessive compensation, shoddy practices, corruption, ethical lapses, and poor board oversight. While our nonprofit apologists argue that the problem lies with a just a few bad apples in the barrel, the prevalence of such behavior is far more widespread than we believed several years ago. There are many bad apples in the nonprofit barrel.

A Georgetown Public Policy Institute study of foundation trustee fees issued in September 2003—of which I was an author—revealed that a high percentage of the foundations in its sample gave their individual trustees compensation, many well in excess of $25,000. In 1998 the 238 foundations in the study actually paid its trustees $33 million for their charitable activities, money that might otherwise have gone to financially strapped nonprofits. These payments contrast sharply with the policies of nonprofit organizations that do not pay any fees to their board members. The study also found that neither the Internal Revenue Service nor the state attorneys general had the resources, staff, or political will to oversee and police the foundation community.

These findings have been echoed by the growing revelations of foundation abuses in newspapers across the country. Not only have the media detailed the huge amounts paid in trustee fees at many foundations, but they have also spotlighted self-dealing activities, conflicts of interest, falsification of information on IRS reporting forms, a lack of transparency, and the absence of any federal and state oversight.

Such problems are not confined to foundations. They are prevalent among nonprofit organizations as well. There are many nonprofits that pay excessive compensation to staff members; do not pay taxes on their earnings from businesses unrelated to their missions, as required by law; do not provide information about their operations or boards; engage in board activities that are self-dealing; and conduct questionable fund-raising practices.

What's more, embezzlement is not infrequent. The most publicized cases are merely the tip of a much larger mass of charities. Harvard University's Hauser Center for Nonprofit Organizations reported, in November 2003, that top charity executives in a selected 152 nonprofit organizations stole or misused at least $1.28 billion from 1995 to 2002. The report was careful to point out that its findings were not a comprehensive assessment of charities' fraudulent activities.

As the news media pay increasing attention to the nonprofit sector, the list of suspect organizations is likely to grow and, with it, a decline in public confidence in our charitable organizations.

The abuses in the sector are compounded by the lack of oversight and enforcement on the part of federal and state regulators, as well as by the absence of tougher regulations that could assure greater public accountability.

Congress must bear a great deal of responsibility for this abysmal situation. It has largely ignored the operations of the nonprofit sector, content to let its problems slide as long as public scandals are minimal. Lawmakers focused little attention on the needs of the IRS's tax-exempt division and never imparted to the regulators a sense that oversight was an important public matter. Until Congress, the IRS, and state attorneys general get their act together, the news media will remain the only reliable accountability mechanism we have.

The substantial federal excise tax paid by private foundations on their net investment income has never been used for its intended purpose—the oversight and policing of the nonprofit sector. While some organizations like Independent Sector, the National Council of Nonprofit Associations (representing statewide coalitions of nonprofit groups) and the Council on Foundations have gone on record supporting congressional action to target at least a portion of the excise tax for oversight, they have spent little or no time, energy, and resources to lobby for legislation that would give the IRS and state regulators the resources they urgently need. Had the large foundations and the Council on Foundations spent one-fifth of the time and money for this purpose that they expended in their recent efforts to kill the congressional measure to eliminate administrative costs from the calculation of foundations' minimal payout requirements, at least a portion of the excise tax might have been channeled to oversight activities.

If the nonprofit world is to prosper and better serve civil society, it will have to deal with the problems of transparency and public accountability. Jealous of their independence and fearful of government intrusion, nonprofit executives for years have claimed that self-reform is the path to sectoral sanctity. Their rhetoric is strong and, sometimes, convincing, but their efforts have been minimal and unproductive. The truth is that self-reform rarely works, not at the New York Stock Exchange, nor among other nonprofits.

The reports filed annually to IRS by both nonprofits and foundations currently are not an adequate mechanism for assuring transparency and public accountability. These reports need to be strengthened by requiring more data about self-dealing, conflicts of interest, excessive compensation, and trustee activities.

For example, the 990-PF forms that foundations are required to submit annually to the IRS do not ask specifically for the amount of time spent on foundation work by trustees, for a breakdown of allowances, and other expenses, including travel, received by trustees, or for the relationship of trustees to contractors and service providers. The anti–self-dealing provisions in the regulations provide a huge loophole that has been exploited by foundations. They permit trustees and foundation managers to receive payment for services to their foundations that are "reasonable and necessary to carrying out the exempt purpose of the trust . . . and is not excessive." As the Georgetown Public Institute study observed, "Because the standards are so unclear, the judgment of what is reasonable, necessary, and not excessive has essentially been left to the foundations themselves."

Requiring nonprofit groups of a certain size to provide annual or biennial program and financial reports could provide additional information, so that the public can better evaluate nonprofit performance of at least the larger organizations. Small organizations often can't afford to spend the time and money on extra paperwork, nor can government regulators keep up with all the nonprofit groups that exist—so focusing on the largest ones makes most sense.

Federal regulations governing self-dealing, compensation, and ethical behavior need tightening. While more effective regulations and clearer criteria for evaluating nonprofit abuses are urgently needed, a major defect of the oversight system now in place continues to be the lackadaisical enforcement measures by both federal and state regulators. The number of audits of nonprofits conducted by the IRS remains minimal. Slightly more than 1 percent of groups are audited, as the IRS has done little to increase the number of staff members who monitor charities, even though the number of charities more than doubled in the past decade.

The criteria by which the IRS assesses excessive compensation often appear to be driven by corporate standards. And only a minuscule number of nonprofits have been fined or punished by the agency for excessive-benefits transactions. Several states don't even have a tax-exempt unit in the attorney general's office; with few exceptions the offices of the attorneys general have neither the resources nor the interest to pursue charity abuses.

Whether the IRS is the proper agency to oversee the nonprofit sector or should be replaced by a new quasi-public entity like Britain's Charity Commission for England and Wales, which acts as application clearinghouse, adviser, and investigator, has been a subject of discussion among researchers. Such an agency could oversee charity officials, in much the way securities dealers here are regulated by quasi-governmental agencies under the supervision of the Securities and Exchange Commission. While the IRS needs restructuring, I think it would be unwise to delegate responsibility for oversight to anything but a government entity that has a vested interest in ensuring that tax-subsidized nonprofit groups are working in the public interest.

Public or Private?

Recent congressional efforts to increase the amount of money private foundations are required to distribute each year triggered an energetic public debate over the past year, the first time in decades that such a discussion extended beyond closed-door conversations between foundations and legislators.

Gone are the days when matters concerning philanthropy or nonprofits could easily be hidden in the shadows. That is one of the major reasons foundations were so disturbed by the efforts of some nonprofits and lawmakers to bring the payout issue into the open. It also explains the anxieties of some nonprofits about divulging the names of their supporters. Transparency is the cornerstone of accountability; it is a trait that Congress must require of all tax-exempt organizations.

Foundation assets are not the only endowments that require further inspection. Donor-advised funds, which operate like charity checking accounts, should be subject to a minimum payout requirement. Now donors can keep putting money away in donor-advised funds year after year, claim their tax deduction, and never give away a cent until they die.

Nor are universities or other nonprofit groups that have endowments required to distribute any of their assets. Should these institutions be permitted to accumulate vast sums of money at taxpayer expense without distributing an adequate amount of money for charitable purposes, such as scholarships and programs to serve society? If not, what minimum percentage of their endowments should they distribute each year?

Are Too Many Organizations Given Tax-Exempt Status?

To many observers the composition of the nonprofit sector doesn't make much sense. It includes such disparate institutions as hospitals and universities, social service agencies, grassroots activist groups, cemeteries, trade associations, a few insurance companies, co-operatives and fraternal organizations.

Should they all continue to be lumped into the category of tax-exempt groups governed by some of the same rules, or should the sector be more narrowly defined? Hospitals and higher-education institutions account for roughly two-thirds of the operating revenue of all organizations categorized as charities under the tax-exempt section of the Internal Revenue Code. Should such organizations be placed into a separate category of nonprofits? Why should the New York Stock Exchange have any type of tax-exempt status, since it serves profitmaking entities on Wall Street and provides compensation to its executives that can only be described as excessive by nonprofit standards? Why are professional sports associations and corporate trade associations that lobby for profitmaking corporate interests allowed to have tax-exempt status?

One of the distinguishing characteristics of nonprofit organizations is their mission of serving the public interest. Many would argue that some of the groups that have tax-exempt status do not meet that test.

Far more attention needs to be given to what types of organizations the IRS approves as charities. Under the current system, applications for tax-exempt status are almost automatically approved. The IRS simply doesn't now have the resources to do a more thorough job of examination.

As one might suspect, a number of questionable organizations have slipped through this screening, including a number of charities that are as much, if not more, political than charitable. One example is an organization called Celebrations for Children established by the House of Representative's majority leader, Tom DeLay. Its purpose was to help throw parties and trips for legislators attending the 2004 Republican National Convention in New York. Though Mr. DeLay claims some of the money the charity raises will be spent for needy children, the primary purpose of the organization is political. In short, it is a sham nonprofit that doesn't deserve charity status. Other highly political organizations have been approved as charities in the past. The sector needs to assess this practice and take measures to stop it.

Growing Commerciality

Under pressure from declining public revenues and increased competition for scarce philanthropic dollars, a large number of charities are charging fees for services and starting profitmaking enterprises. The growing privatization of publicly financed social programs, formerly the almost exclusive dominion of nonprofits, has pushed charities to become more corporate in nature to remain competitive. The line between what is nonprofit and for-profit has become even more fuzzy than it was.

The corporatization of a large number of nonprofit organizations has opened institutions to questionable practices: an undermining of standards and ethical practices; an increasing focus on the bottom line; the weakening of organizational mission; special attention to the CEOs with their high salaries and special perks; and an aversion to policy activism and risk-taking. Many nonprofits are in danger of losing what Paul Light of the Brookings Institution has called their "nonprofitness."

For many years the IRS has required nonprofit organizations to pay taxes on their for-profit enterprises that are deemed to be not "business related" — that is, not intrinsic or connected to their charitable missions. But the criteria by which the agency decides what is or is not related remain vague and uncertain, an imprecise guideline for nonprofits to follow. Many nonprofit-run businesses can be called "related" only by the stretch of one's imagination. The Metropolitan Museum, for example, sells items found in its museum shop in New York in a number of shopping centers outside the city and it does not pay taxes on a share of the money made in those stores. That ruse enables many charities to avoid paying taxes that they should have to pay as part of their responsibility to be good citizens. As public funds diminish and charities desperately seek new sources of support, they will increasingly turn to the creation of new business ventures as a way out of their financial crises. All the more reason that the IRS, with assistance from the nonprofit sector, must more clearly define the line between what is and is not "business related."

Neither the regulators nor the nonprofit community can afford to postpone facing and resolving this issue. It has festered for too long a time. Until clarity is provided, many individual and institutional donors will hesitate to give their money to nonprofit organizations that look as though they have become more of a business than a charity.

Charities increasingly seem to be lowering their ethical standards as part of their fund-raising strategies. Local Boys and Girls Clubs, for instance, put soda machines in their buildings in exchange for a huge donation to the Boys & Girls Clubs of America by Coca-Cola. Money appears to have trumped a concern for the health of the children who attend the clubs. Similarly, the selling of billboards at university stadiums to companies willing to pony up large contributions or deals between sports equipment firms and university basketball or football officials send a message that institutions of higher learning can be bought by whoever is willing to pay the price.

The selling of nonprofit America is a trend that endangers the sector's "nonprofitness." Can we prevent the further erosion of nonprofit values? How? It is a matter that doesn't lend itself easily, or at all, to government regulation and oversight.

But here, surely, is an issue that can test the sector's desire for self-reform. Will the chancellors and presidents of our universities and colleges be willing collectively to stop the selling of their institutions to corporate and other financial interests? Will nonprofit organizations voluntarily adopt a code of ethics and conduct that will give top priority to organizational mission instead of fund raising at any cost? Will the major nonprofit associations be willing to organize a mass effort to promote and enforce among their members higher standards of conduct and ethical behavior? And will foundations, much in need of reform themselves, support such efforts financially?

And what about the problems of unethical behavior and conflicts of interest in the nonprofit world? For example: board members who have close ties, financial and family, to companies that provide services to their organizations; highly paid staff members of nonprofits who moonlight for other organizations; and the selling of mailing lists to commercial enterprises. Can we do something about these disturbing practices?

Clearly, some large nonprofit organizations like AARP can have an inherent conflict of interest between the services they sell to their members and the public-policy decisions they take and the profitmaking enterprises they operate. A growing number of universities are accepting substantial corporate donations in exchange for corporate influence on their faculties and research efforts, including, in some instances, the right to review research findings before publication. Where do you draw the line? What is an acceptable balance between an organization's mission and its business interests?

The answers to these questions will determine the extent to which the nonprofit sector is capable, in John Gardner's words, of renewing itself.

Promoting Democracy

An even greater challenge to our nonprofit institutions will be their collective ability to promote and strengthen democratic institutions and practices.

From its earliest days, a primary mission of the nonprofit sector has been the preservation and strengthening of American democracy. This role has taken many forms: protecting civil liberties and individual rights; leveling the playing field for all its citizens; building strong democratic institutions; providing a social safety net for the neediest members of society; and assuring a competitive free-enterprise system. Writing in the 1830s, the astute French observer of American society, Alexis de Tocqueville, noted that voluntary associations were at the heart of American democracy. Were he writing today, would he give such high marks to our voluntary sector as an effective promoter of American democracy?

The inequities in wealth and income have grown exponentially over the past two decades. The rich are richer and the poor are poorer than ever before in our history. The differential in pay between top executives of American corporations and the average worker in these corporations rose from a ratio of 72:1 in 1989 to 310:1 in 2000. The social safety net has been shredded, if not entirely destroyed by our lawmakers. The minimum wage adjusted for inflation is lower today than it was twenty-five years ago. For many Americans—the poor, people of color, the disabled, and other disadvantaged populations—the playing field is not level.

The enormous expansion of foundation assets in recent years has added to the inequities in American life. As public support for social programs, job training, affordable housing, and projects to feed the poor and temporarily house the homeless have been reduced, the burden for such responsibilities has increasingly fallen on private individual and institutional philanthropy. Public responsibilities are becoming a matter of private charity. An elite, growing, and unrepresentative group of private foundations are now making decisions about the allocation of funds for social welfare. In a sense, "noblesse oblige" is slowly taking over what should be public decision making.

Far from leveling the playing field, civil society appears to have acquiesced or, at worst, abetted a national policy that has slowly made it more difficult for many citizens to enjoy equal opportunities and, at the same time, made it easier for wealthy citizens to assert greater control over society. Nowhere is this more evident than in the enormous abuse of power and influence that corporate America has exercised in recent years, both in the public and private sectors. Few checks and balances are in place to stem this corporate force. This was a role nonprofits were supposed to play, assisted by government and our political elites. What happened? Were nonprofits bought off, too weak and fragmented or without the leadership and financing to counter this development? Whatever the reason, it is imperative for the nonprofit sector to resume this role, to serve as a watchdog against further corporate abuse, as well as government excesses.

Research, monitoring, and advocacy by citizen groups are the weapons that can provide the institutional balance between government, corporations, and civil society that is essential for democracy. Whether nonprofits will have the vision, resources, and courage to wage this important struggle will depend on two major factors: their acceptance—a departure for the large majority— of this role and a willingness to broaden their program agenda; and the willingness of foundations to end their reluctance to support the type of monitoring and advocacy that is needed to do the job.

Nonprofits have another major responsibility in assuring the vitality of our democracy: strengthening a political system that has become corrupted by big money, and rebuilding the credibility of government, especially the federal government, from which many citizens have become alienated. That is a tall order, but one for which the nonprofit sector is well suited.

Its hundreds of thousands of organizations have the capacity to support and sustain campaign-finance reform measures; to promote greater civic engagement, especially by our young people; to encourage greater voter turnout through voter registration and education initiatives; to persuade young people to become more involved in politics; to make certain that our schools teach American history and citizenship; and to make certain that their own organizations remain democratic, reaching out to those they represent so that their members may become more involved in organizational governance and programs.

Making Nonprofit Groups More Democratic

That task, what may be called the democratic renewal of nonprofit organizations, probably poses the most difficult challenge. During the past twenty-five years, the large national nonprofit organizations have lost much of their former membership. In a number of cases, their chapters have lost influence; new large organizations have emerged without chapters.

Professional staff members and lobbyists have assumed many of the responsibilities once exercised by members. Many people have become less engaged in community affairs. For so many, civic engagement now means writing a membership check. Many nonprofits have thus lost their real base in the community. Do they continue to speak for the people, for the community? If they want to be a greater force for influence and change, nonprofits will need to re-engage with their members, their constituents, and their communities. In a real sense, they will have to become more democratic.

Who speaks for nonprofits? Large organizations, some actually trade associations, have been established to be a voice for their nonprofit members. Independent Sector purports to represent the views of nonprofits on sectorwide issues. Similarly, the Council on Foundations attempts to reflect the interests and opinions of the foundation world. And the National Council of Nonprofit

Associations is a voice for the forty or so state associations of nonprofits. But do they and the other significant associations really reflect the views of their members or the sector as a whole?

Independent Sector, for example, does not have any local or state members. A substantial portion of its membership comes from foundations that represent only a tiny sliver of the nonprofit world. Their nonprofit organizational members represent the most established, large nonprofits in the country; this membership doesn't include many organizations that reflect the interests of activists, women, union members, youths, or low-income people. It is, in short, not a diverse group. While it has been a force for good on several national issues, its influence will be limited until it reaches out to encompass more diverse organizations and listens more carefully to what the field is saying. As long as such a large number of its members are foundations, the organization will find it difficult, if not impossible, to steer an independent course on philanthropic issues. Its missteps have come from too great a dependence on a small coterie of board members.

In protecting and promoting our democracy, civil society must be careful to assure that its own nonprofit institutions govern and act democratically. Many nonprofits and their umbrella organizations have not had the time or inclination to join together in an effort to study their sector, analyze its problems, and suggest ways to strengthen and improve its work.

It is time for a national commission—like the Commission on Private Philanthropy and Public Needs headed by John Filer—to undertake this task and look seriously at the future. Composed of representatives from a cross-section of society, supported by an outstanding staff of researchers, policy analysts, and practitioners, this commission could not only provide useful data but also suggest a blueprint for civil society's renewal and change. For several million dollars a year over a two- or three-year period, it could be one of the best investments ever made by our foundation community. There is nothing to lose and much to gain by such an effort.

A Sense of Perspective

In building for the future, nonprofit practitioners must try to regain their sense of humor. Not too long ago, it was impossible to attend a conference of nonprofits or philanthropists without hearing jokes and funny stories from featured speakers and other presenters. Laughter was an important ingredient of our work then, balancing our hard, sometimes frustrating efforts with a light touch that reminded us not to take ourselves too seriously.

Today, there is little humor in our conferences, nor among our personal interactions. We seem often to be driven by a puritanical streak that seals off our lighter side. Aren't we, after all, doing good in the public interest, the Lord's work as it were, plugging the dikes that protect our society? Is it such serious business that there is no place for laughter? Is it surprising, therefore, that some view us as self-righteous prigs, cocooned in our little solipsistic world? There is, unfortunately, a good deal of truth in this observation.

For sometimes we tend to forget that fun is part of our job. We need to enjoy our organizational responsibilities, our colleagues, our competitors, our opponents, and our benefits as nonprofit workers. We need to take our challenges, successes, and mistakes in stride. We have to understand the tensions and ironies that undergird our activities with a willingness to laugh at ourselves, not only at others. Joy and laughter—those are the elements that can provide a wholesome balance to dedication, zeal, hard work, and perseverance. A healthy sense of humor is the link that connects both sets of ingredients. It is what the nonprofit world desperately needs as it struggles to meet the challenges of the future.

Acknowledgments

The publisher gratefully acknowledges the following:

Articles from *The Chronicle of Philanthropy* reprinted with permission of *The Chronicle of Philanthropy*, http:philanthropy.com.

"The Filer Commission: A Critical Perspective" reprinted with permission of The Grantsmanship Center.

"Desperately Seeking . . . Leadership" and "The Problems and Challenges of International Philanthropy" reprinted with permission from *Foundation News and Commentary*, 1-800-771-8187.

"The Case for General Support." Copyright 1999 All rights reserved by Third Sector New England, Boston, MA (Volume 6, Issue 4). The *Nonprofit Quarterly* features innovative thinking and management practices in the nonprofit sector. For reprint permission or subscription information please call 1-800-281-7770, www.nonprofitquarterly.org.

"Capacity Building: Beware the Easy Fix." Copyright 2001. All rights reserved by Third Sector New England, Boston, MA (Volume 8, Issue 2). The *Nonprofit Quarterly* features innovative thinking and management practices in the nonprofit sector. For reprint permission or subscription information please call 1-800-281-7770, www.nonprofitquarterly.org.

"Separate, We Lose." Copyright 2000. All rights reserved by Third Sector New England, Boston, MA (Volume 7, Issue 2). The *Nonprofit Quarterly* features innovative thinking and management practices in the nonprofit sector. For reprint permission or subscription information please call 1-800-281-7770, www.nonprofitquarterly.org.

"Penetrating the Mystique of Philanthropy." Copyright 1999. All rights reserved by Third Sector New England, Boston, MA (Volume 6, Issue 2). The *Nonprofit Quarterly* features innovative thinking and management practices in the nonprofit sector. For reprint permission or subscription information please call 1-800-281-7770, www.nonprofitquarterly.org.

"Time to Remove the Rose-Colored Glasses" reprinted from *Shelterforce Magazine* with the permission of the National Housing Institute, www.nhi.org.

"Philanthropy and Community Building," by Pablo Eisenberg, reprinted